AN INTRODUCTION TO MEDIEVAL ROMANCE

AN INTRODUCTION TO
MEDIEVAL ROMANCE

By A. B. TAYLOR, M.A.

*Professor of English Language and Literature in the
University of Tasmania*

BARNES & NOBLE, Inc.
NEW YORK
PUBLISHERS & BOOKSELLERS SINCE 1873

First published, 1930
Reprinted, 1969
by Barnes & Noble, Inc.

Printed in the United States of America

PREFACE

THE AIM OF THIS WORK IS MERELY TO offer a general survey of the chief themes and features of medieval romance to readers who have made no deep study of the subject but are sufficiently interested to desire a systematic survey. No attempt has been made to cover the whole field of European romance, which could be satisfactorily done only in a very large work and by the combined efforts of many scholars. The present discussion is largely confined to those themes of romance ˙represented in English versions, with occasional reference to French romances unrepresented in English, but of outstanding fame. But since almost all English romances are mere translations more or less close from French versions, it has been necessary to pay close attention to the French originals, because in them originated the form and spirit of all medieval romance. The method adopted has been to classify the chief themes, using the French versions as basis and alluding to the English versions; to group in one chapter the main differences between English and French romance; and finally to discuss the prominent features of romance, again illustrating any important differences between the English and the French. In these final chapters the aim has been to stress differences between English and French romance where they reflect real differences in sentiment between the two nations; since many English romances were composed only for the uneducated classes, while the French originals were composed for the educated, their variations often only represent differences between educated and uneducated people, and these differences are noted in Chapter IX; racial differences may clearly be seen only by comparing the English romances written for the educated classes after English had once again become the national language.

To give a synopsis of each theme is rendered almost impossible by the numerous variations in different versions, and to give a synopsis of each romance cited would make the work unreasonably large. It has been assumed, therefore, that every reader will have some knowledge of the stories relating to the chief heroes of romance— Charlemagne and Roland, Arthur and his knights—even if only from modern versions; of the lesser-known themes brief mention is sometimes made of the plot, sufficient to show what the story illustrates, and its significance as a reflection of aspects of medieval life and ideals of conduct. In this way it is hoped that the work will be of help both to students just entering on a systematic study of Middle English literature and to general readers who are interested in the growth and development of early romance but who have made no definite study of the subject. As a further aid to general readers, quotations and the titles of romances have been modernised wherever such modernisation would not disguise the original form. Where modernisation would so disguise the original form as to make possible any distortion of meaning or to make reference to bibliographies difficult, no change has been made, but explanations have been given in footnotes.

Occasional attempts have been made to draw comparisons between features of medieval life and romance and those of modern life and literature, even though they may seem out of place or even incongruous in such a work. It is so common to accept everything contemporary as sane and rational, and to use this as the basis for judging past variations, that the absurdity of things medieval may be easily over-estimated. For this reason comparisons may serve to show that many opinions, ideals, and aspirations of the Middle Ages, though seemingly ridiculous, are little if any more absurd than ours of to-day, although the personal prejudices of the author have no doubt led to distortions, perhaps even serious distortions. But in this respect the reader may judge for himself, and so should not be led astray.

Modern research has given rise to so many conflicting hypotheses in nearly every theme of romance that no systematic account of them is possible. Before any definite hypothesis could be supported or disclaimed, all the evidence on both sides would have to be adduced, and that is clearly impossible here. Where any conclusion has been definitely accepted by scholars it is stated as definite certainty; where a hypothesis is generally accepted it is included but stated as a hypothesis; where there is serious disagreement, the various opinions are briefly mentioned where they are of interest or importance, and omitted where omission entails no disadvantage. It will be obvious, therefore, that this work contains little that is original, and nothing probably that adds anything of value to already existing knowledge. My sole object has been to read the romances and the works of all the well-known scholars on this subject, and to compile a brief and systematic survey, which, as far as I know, has not yet been done, but which is just as necessary as a survey of any other period or group of literary works.

To state my indebtedness to other scholars in every section of the work would seriously clog the narrative, so I must here acknowledge my great obligations to many works, particularly those of W. P. Ker, J. L. Weston, A. Nutt, and J. Rhys, of England, J. Bédier and Gaston Paris, of France, and J. D. Bruce and J. E. Wells, of America.

A. B. TAYLOR.

The University of Tasmania,
February 1930.

CONTENTS

MEDIEVAL ROMANCE

CHAPTER I

INTRODUCTION

THE WORD "ROMANCE" IS A VARIANT OF the Old French word "romans" which was used both for the French language and for those poems written in the French language which purported to relate historical facts. It is still used to denote the languages of all those countries which were originally Roman provinces and whose speech is derived from Latin. The basis of the French language was Latin, but several centuries of unchecked change in spelling, pronunciation, and meaning, together with continual incorporations of Celtic and particularly Germanic elements had resulted in very wide divergence from the Latin language employed by the Church, which had changed but little from the classical form. The word "romans" was therefore employed to differentiate this changed and ever-changing language of the people from that of the Church.

Until the twelfth century, literature in France was almost entirely written in Latin, and when the language of the people came to be used as a medium of literature, first of all in poems which claimed to relate history, these works were called "romans." This term is still used in France for what we call the novel, and its other form, "romance," we employ to designate the whole field of imaginative fiction.

Romance, therefore, was originally only a term differentiating history written in the vernacular language from that written in Latin. The "Roman de Troie," for example, was designed, and accepted, as the history of the Siege of Troy written for people who could not understand

B

Latin. But authentic history is very rare in the Middle Ages, and is almost invariably confined to Chronicles written in Latin. From the beginning the authors who used the vernacular realised that they must please as well as edify, that history would not be acceptable to their patrons unless made entertaining. They therefore added to the historical matter legends, folk-lore, and popular superstitions, so freely that historical truth became almost entirely lost. It is impossible to estimate how much credence was given by the audience, but it is quite evident that, as early as the twelfth century, the authors claimed historical truth merely as a matter of convention. The audience wished for entertaining history. The writer provided entertainment and called it history, and both parties were satisfied. The term "Medieval Romance" is therefore used to cover all these pretended historical accounts of famous men, Charlemagne, Arthur, and a host of lesser names, but does not include any French writings which were serious attempts at historical writing, nor any of the writings definitely designed for religious purposes, whether historical or fictional, such as the Lives of the Saints.

Though written and accepted as history, most medieval romance is pure fiction, and must be regarded as such in all discussion of its origins and characteristics. The period of medieval romance extends from the twelfth to the fifteenth century. How much, or what types of, oral literature existed earlier we have little means of knowing By the twelfth century the French nation no longer was a race simply of Romanised Gauls, but through repeated invasions of Germanic tribes had become more a Germanic than a Celtic race. The very name, France, derives from a Germanic race, the Franks, who for centuries had ruled over nearly the whole of Gaul. But although the Franks easily subjugated the Gauls, and greatly modified the Celtic strain, they were unable to overcome or to resist the influence of that Latin spirit which has been so dominant in those races formerly under Roman rule that we now call them neither Celtic nor Germanic, but Latin races.

By the twelfth century the French nation, though Celtic in origin, though further inundated by Germanic elements, was neither Celtic nor Germanic in spirit, but essentially Latin. From the Latin race it has taken not only its language and its laws, but even its customs and its mental character. Medieval romance originated in France, and from there spread to other countries. It is therefore necessary, in studying this subject, to remember that, whatever the origin of the various themes of romance may be, the romances reflect the Latin spirit as it existed in France in the twelfth and thirteenth centuries.

From the break-up of the Roman Empire until the tenth century the French were, to all intents and purposes, a Germanic race, ruled for the most part by Frankish kings. Any oral literature existing before the eleventh century would, therefore, be Germanic, not Celtic. We know from Tacitus that from an early period the Germanic tribes celebrated famous men and events in epic songs. Much of the written Germanic literature of the later Middle Ages— the Icelandic Sagas, the German "Kudrun" and "Nibelungenlied"—derives from early oral literature, and one race, the Anglo-Saxons, had a highly developed written literature long before the Norman Conquest. Although the Germanic race, as a whole, was composed of many distinct elements, continually warring against each other, there seems to have existed a communal literature, probably originating in a period where there had been a fairly strong sense of racial unity. The Anglo-Saxon epic poem, "Beowulf," celebrates, not an Anglo-Saxon champion, but a North German of the tribe called Geats.[1] The "Nibelungenlied" likewise can hardly be regarded as the product of any single tribe, but as a network woven of many strands from varied sources.

It is fairly safe to assume, therefore, that the Franks also had an oral literature, some of it probably based on

[1] Professor Moorman suggested that some Geats may have taken part in the invasion of Britain, and been the originators of the "Beowulf" story in England. See "Essays and Studies of the English Association," Vol. V.

traditions common to the whole Germanic race, and some based on their own traditions. The greatest of all Frankish kings was Charlemagne, and after his death oral stories relating his exploits must have been widely circulated. But whether such oral traditions continued after the downfall of the Carolingian dynasty in the tenth century we do not know. The French nation almost certainly would receive its literary stimulus from the Franks, but whether the written romances of the twelfth and later centuries are based on oral traditions which extend back to the reign of Charlemagne, or on traditions which arose only in the tenth and eleventh centuries is by no means certain.

The nations of medieval Europe offer a striking contrast to the Greek and Roman nations, because, in addition to the natural divisions of rank common to both groups, they were sharply divided into two distinct classes, the clergy and the laity. The ablest Greek and Roman scholars did not belong to an exclusive religious body, and so wrote literature which reflected the spirit and character of their race, and which was adapted to the tastes of all the educated classes. The scholars of the Middle Ages were almost all ecclesiastics; they wrote exclusively for their own body, and in a language, Latin, which was intelligible to very few of the laity. The literature written for the educated laity and in the vernacular was written, not by uneducated men, but by men whose scholarship and ability were certainly inferior to those of the ablest ecclesiastics. It therefore remained distinctly inferior to that of Greece and Rome until the various new forces which arose in the fifteen and sixteenth centuries paved the way for a good secular literature, written by the ablest scholars in the vernaculars, and capable of attaining the heights reached by classical literature. During the Middle Ages learning and scholarship were regarded as necessary only as a preparation for the Church, to be restricted to what was essential only for religious purposes, and to be used only for those purposes. The laity had not sufficient learning to write literature of enduring value, and when ecclesiastics wrote secular literature in the vernacular, neither did they seriously apply all their learning to the task, nor was their knowledge as a rule of the right type.

The Carolingian dynasty ended in 987, and under the Capetian kings the French people made rapid progress towards unity. The Frankish custom of dividing the realm amongst all the sons after the monarch's death effectually prevented national unity and also was productive of incessant turmoil. The Capetian custom of hereditary succession minimised internal warfare and fostered both unity and progress. This led to more extended social intercourse and to increased luxury and refinement. Men's efforts were now directed to social activities, and various types of recreation were invented to relieve the dullness of castle life. The urgent need for occupation during winter evenings or at any times when outdoor sports were impossible would stimulate the production of oral literature designed less for instruction than for entertainment, and that literature would reflect contemporary events and sentiment rather than those of an earlier period. By the twelfth century Frankish traditions could not possibly have made a strong appeal to the French people, and so epic poems of the old Germanic type were almost impossible. Literary activity was further stimulated by the Crusades, which, by opening up to Western Europe the learning of Alexandria, Arabia, and Byzantium, broke down the long tyranny of an effete and distorted Latin learning which, carefully fostered by the Church, had reigned supreme throughout the Dark Ages. The introduction of new ideas from the East stirred the imagination of writers and led to a temporary Renascence, which was, however, not based on sufficiently firm and solid grounds to resist the domination of the Church, and so again decayed. Continual incorporation of new elements leads to activity in all periods, and the new sources of knowledge opened up during the twelfth century not only encouraged writers to discard traditional forms and themes, but also led to an increased desire for education among the leisured classes, and especially among women. The south of France had produced a great volume of lyric poetry, which probably had drawn inspiration from Arabian or Moorish sources, and during the twelfth century this also came to influence Northern French writers. The period of most intense activity was the first half of the twelfth century, and by about 1150 this temporary Renascence was in full swing. Writers were exploring every possible avenue for new subjects and new methods. In place of the old Germanic epic arose romance, and romance which celebrated nearly all the historical and legendary heroes in European history, from Hector of Troy to Charlemagne, from Alexander the Great to King Arthur. The two most momentous results of this renewed activity were the incorporation of Arthurian legends into romance and the re-fashioning of literature to please a female audience; the first has provided a source of inspiration to numberless authors throughout the ages, the second produced romance of chivalry in place of heroic poems celebrating warfare.

But in spite of this temporary decline in the domination of ecclesiastical scholarship, men did not lose their traditional respect for Latin learning. Since Latin was the universal medium of scholarship, all new learning—even that introduced from Eastern countries—was first written up in Latin treatises, which would be the only sources of knowledge for most romancers. All writers of romance, therefore, knew that the surest way of gaining credence for their stories was to claim a Latin original. It is known that many romances—e.g. most of the Charlemagne romances —were based on monkish chronicles, because the chronicles still remain; how many of those for which no originals have been found were based on a Latin source now lost can never be estimated. The author of "Guillaume de Palerne" states that he translated it from a Latin work at the request of the Countess Yolande, Chrétien de Troyes claims that his "Perceval" is but a French version of a Latin book; but how many of these and similar claims are genuine it is impossible to say. It is to be suspected that sometimes no Latin original ever existed, and when Latin chronicles were used as a basis the romancers often altered so drastically as to make what is to all intents and purposes a new story.

The most active period of romance was 1150–1250, and romances composed later were frequently mere remodellings of earlier versions at greater length, generally also of inferior merit. Even the earliest English romances seem to have been composed later than this active period of French romance, and most of them long after the original inspiration had spent its force. The best romances—those composed by educated poets for the higher classes—arose only during the fourteenth century, for it was not until then that English replaced French as the national language of England; by this time the spirit of romance was fast decaying, not to be revived again, except for sporadic outbursts, until the Elizabethan period, when it arose again, strengthened by classical influence, in the hands of Spenser and the dramatists.

The great difference in spirit between the earlier heroic poetry and medieval romance is due to a deeply significant change in the national character. Heroic poetry is the name given to that poetry which voices the feelings and aspirations of a nation animated by some one strong national sentiment against the menace of an external foe. The greatest examples are Homer's "Iliad" and Virgil's "Æneid," and the best known examples of later times are the Anglo-Saxon "Beowulf," and the French "La Chanson de Roland." Such poems celebrate the deeds of famous heroes who had come to be regarded as national champions symbolising the spirit and aspirations of their race— Achilles, Ulysses, and Æneas, Beowulf and Roland. They voice the opinions not of the author as an individual, but of the nation as a whole; the virtues, vices, crimes portrayed represent the ethical code of the nation, and the character of the hero represents the ideals of the nation. In later periods authors have sometimes reflected national sentiment in general, but their judgments on character, morality or ethics are individual, not national judgments. At each succeeding stage authors have tended more and more to analyse human nature and to state or imply what they consider fundamentally good or bad. Medieval romance arose too early to reflect strongly individualistic views, but instead represented the views of limited classes or families. Any reflection of universal national sentiment is largely incidental.

A strong and united sentiment can exist only under rare circumstances, usually the banding together of a whole race under some great and universally respected leader against a common foe. In modern times England has passed through a heroic period in the reign of Queen Elizabeth, when the whole nation was welded together under the Queen against Catholic domination in general and Spain in particular. No strict epic poetry arose to voice the national spirit, but Spenser's "Faerie Queene" and the chronicle plays of Shakespeare and other dramatists were inspired by and reflect this national sentiment. A similar but very temporary national unity arose during the Great War of 1914–1918. But when the crisis which has banded the nation together has passed, unity of sentiment will also cease, and there will be neither any stimulus for further heroic poetry nor any deep respect for that composed earlier. The heroic age of France was the period of the Carolingian dynasty, and especially the reign of Charlemagne. No other great national hero succeeded him, and so he remained the central figure of French epic poetry as long as it endured. But conditions changed, themes which once had symbolised the spirit of the whole nation had lost their significance because divested of their original stimulus, and so were gradually distorted until the old heroic and national spirit was lost. With the passing of the Carolingian dynasty in the tenth century Charlemagne could but faintly represent French national ideals, oral poetry composed during the late tenth and eleventh centuries to extol his prowess would almost certainly be devoid of all real heroic character, and the written poetry of the twelfth and later centuries, whether it originated in such oral poems or whether independent of them, is naturally lacking in true national spirit.

The basis of heroic poetry has always been an aristocratic society, but a society firmly united and devoid of rigid caste distinctions. Both features are essential to the rise of national unity, and existed in the heroic periods of Greece, of Anglo-Saxon England, and of Iceland in the period when its Sagas were composed. But the period of French romance was a feudal period, and feudalism accentuated not only a rigid caste distinction, but also jealousy and civil warfare. The barons of France owed allegiance to the king, but strove jealously to maintain their independence. The lack of discipline and of unity during such a great national undertaking as the First Crusade clearly shows the unwillingness of the barons to accept any leader and the absence of any strong national sentiment. Without this unity heroic poetry cannot flourish.

In heroic poetry the theme and characters alone are sufficient to stir the imagination of an audience; the poet need not rely on sensational episodes to win attention. In the absence of strong national feeling the theme and characters are not sufficiently impressive in themselves, especially if the exploits recorded are already known. Just as a child will eagerly listen to the recital of some favourite fairy tale or the deeds of some famous national hero like Lord Nelson, so the people of heroic ages never tired of hearing their national heroes celebrated in song. When the heroes themselves have ceased to inspire, the poet must rely on novelty to hold his audience. The writers of romance, therefore, even when extolling the deeds of a Charlemagne or a Roland, were obliged to add extraneous matter for the sake of variety, to depend on the sensational and the mysterious to stimulate a waning interest. Heroic poetry is characterised by simplicity and naturalness, romance by fantasy and exaggeration. The warfare of heroic periods is such as imperils, and therefore involves, the whole State, and is therefore most impressive when most realistically portrayed. The warfare of the later Middle Ages, especially the Crusades, was in itself romantic, regarded as an exciting pastime rather than a national service. Defensive armour made feudal warfare an adventurous sport rather than a deadly conflict, because the castles were almost impregnable and open fighting rarely led to a large death-rate amongst the barons and knights; defeat usually entailed only capture and the payment of a ransom. The Crusades were fought on foreign soil and in an emotional atmosphere. The Crusaders and feudal barons were as brutal, rough and vigorous as were the Vikings, but devoid of their sobriety, and their fanatical and undisciplined warfare offers a strong contrast to the well-organised raids of the Vikings, or the cool strategic fighting of the Icelanders. Heroic literature reflects real life and, as a result, the hero's combats are regarded seriously. If opposed by two or more foes simultaneously, his chances of success are small, and the poet holds his audience in breathless suspense by narrating how he manœuvred for position, and with what skill he prevented all his assailants from attacking him together. The hero is rarely portrayed as successfully facing great odds unless from a strategic position like a doorway or a high rock. But where he is no longer a vivid personality, the audience soon tires of hearing accounts of deeds that any courageous man might perform, and so each succeeding romancer strove to make his hero greater than all previous ones by accrediting him with greater exploits, until the killing of a hundred or even a thousand foes single-handed became a commonplace. When this stage is reached, not only the heroic spirit, but even the spirit of true romance is dead, because an invincible hero is too unhuman to stir the imagination. But from romance generally, in the twentieth as well as the twelfth century, the audience demands the uncommon and the sensational. If the hero rescues from drowning the maiden whom Fate, in the person of the author, has destined for his bride, it must be during a storm, or close to a weir, or in a shark-infested bay. If the heroine is ensnared by a villain, a miscellaneous assortment of satellite villains must be introduced, so that the hero will not be faced by the disgraceful position of having only one assailant. The personages of heroic literature are humanised also by being portrayed against a background of familiar life. The hero of an Icelandic Saga is not always fighting; there are other necessary duties to perform—chopping wood, cutting hay and gathering in the harvest. Romance usually avoids these familiar details, and so ceases to be dramatic, because devoid of strong contrasts. Heroic literature concentrates on character, making the incidents such as to impress us with the hero's courage, manliness, and loyalty to race or clan. Romance usually presents us with a theory of character, and frequently too exalted and fantastic to be human. Finally the fighting of heroic literature has always a good reason behind it: the hero fights not for the sake of adventure, not because he loves warfare, but for his country, as in the "Iliad," or to help a friendly tribe, as in "Beowulf"; or in defence of his life or the rights of his clan, as in the Icelandic Sagas. In romance there may be a theoretically good reason for fighting, but the stress is upon the adventures; the hero takes the same keen delight in combat as the modern athlete does in a cricket or a football match. Any real urging motive, such as duty to king or country, is never stressed throughout as the primary basis of the story. The primary motive is the recital of adventures, and this is well exemplified in the English prose romance "Merlin," where it is stated that four clerks were appointed to record the future deeds of Sir Gawain and his knights. In heroic literature it would not be assumed that recording clerks would be necessary, or even that the hero was destined to undergo further adventures at all. The epic hero fought when he had to, but wisely avoided unnecessary dangers; the hero of romance was never happy unless some dangerous enterprise awaited him. And the keynote of all romance is contained in two statements made by the hero in "Huon of Bordeaux": "Any adventure that I might hear of, though it were never so perilous, that I should never eschew it for fear of death," and "I departed out of France for no other thing but to seek strange adventures." This drastic change in the spirit of literature arose not from one single cause. The chief reason was the change in national life—from national unity to feudalism, and from national warfare to civil strife and fantastic Crusades—but other elements assisted: continual incorporation of Celtic folk-lore, classical legends, and Eastern influences. Whether epic poems were composed by the Franks we do not know, but the most famous of all French medieval poems, "La Chanson de Roland," is one solitary relic of the epic type. Apart from its literary merits, it is important as illustrating the transition from epic to romance. In its general conception it is of the heroic type, in its details it is romance. It presents vividly the spirit of heroic warfare, and Roland is an epic warrior, fighting and dying for his country and his Faith. But the exaggeration of his prowess, the magic and the miracles incorporated to enhance the interest, both mar the heroic spirit and show how impossible it was to maintain the strictly heroic type once the original stimulus had decayed. The later poems celebrating the exploits of Charlemagne and his twelve peers, even where based on historical events, are pure romance, because lacking that inspiration which can only come from strong national sentiment. These romances and, even more so, those written to extol the fame of Arthur and his knights were not designed to enhance the glory of the French nation, but, under the pretence of historical instruction, to provide an audience with sensational stories of adventure and of love. The best of them were inspired by lofty ideals—of loyalty, service, chastity, self-sacrifice—but not by national ideals. And, at a later stage, continual pandering to a desire for novelty and sensationalism brought romance into a well-deserved disrepute, and led to the necessary satire of Cervantes in

"Don Quixote" and of Beaumont and Fletcher in "The Knight of the Burning Pestle." This degradation and the consequential satire did not kill the spirit of romance, which was revived and carried to even greater heights by Malory, Ariosto, and Spenser. Nor could the satire exercise an enduring influence, or permanently check the craving for sensationalism, which still remains as strong as ever.

In a period when few can read, and when an author can reach the public only through oral recitation, verse is the natural medium of literature, whether its object be to instruct or to entertain. The regular rhythm of verse assists the reciter to appeal directly to the emotions of his audience, and only by appealing to their emotions can he hope to hold their attention, because an illiterate audience cannot be swayed by any appeal to their reasoning faculties. The imagination is still further stirred if the verse be chanted to the accompaniment of a harp or other musical instrument. For this reason the Creed, the Psalms, and even sometimes the whole Communion Service are still chanted in church instead of being read. That the early romances were read or recited to an audience is not based on supposition, but is clearly evidenced by passages in which the reader or reciter addresses his audience personally. That some poems were chanted to the accompaniment of a musical instrument is evidenced by the statement of Marie de France that the Breton Lays were sung to the accompaniment of a harp.[1] And the most famous of all French romances, "Aucassin et Nicolette," mingles prose narrative with lyrical verses obviously intended to be sung.[2] But although the English romances, composed for the entertainment of the lower classes, may have been chanted frequently and for a long time, practically all of the French romances, even the earliest, seem to have been read, not chanted. As education spread during the twelfth and thirteenth centuries, reading aloud by a minstrel or professional reader became no longer essential. Many of the higher classes, parti-

[1] See p. 48.   [2] See p. 48.

cularly the women, were able to read for themselves, but as copies were necessarily scarce before the days of printing, and reading from manuscript was rather irksome, the ordinary custom seems to have been that maids of honour and perhaps pages read aloud to their mistresses, and probably at times to groups of ladies and knights. In the romance of "Yvain," the hero, on entering a castle, sees a maiden reading a romance to the lord and lady of the castle. Intelligible and impressive reading aloud from a manuscript written by someone else was regarded as a much-prized gift, and in "Guy of Warwick," the daughter of the King of Africa is described as being expert in romance-reading.

In the days of oral literature, when poems had to be committed to memory, and recited or chanted from memory, they were probably short, consisting of not more than a few hundred lines. As soon as minstrels or professional story-tellers were able to read from manuscript, it became possible to increase the length of romances indefinitely, but an audience would probably prefer those which could be read at one sitting, and therefore not exceeding three or four thousand lines at most, although some of even the earliest romances of the twelfth century were considerably longer. But when people ceased to depend upon professional readers the length of a romance would matter very little, because it could be continued at any time. Also, as people learned to read for themselves, it became no longer necessary to compose in verse, and early in the thirteenth century prose romances were written in French, but not until the fifteenth century in English, because not until then had English become definitely established as the literary language of England. Until the end of the fourteenth century the higher classes in England—the only class of the laity who could read— read French, not English literature. For the lower classes reading aloud by a professional reader or minstrel was necessary, and therefore verse was the only satisfactory medium.

The prose romances carried to further extremes the elements of exaggeration and sensationalism which had been a marked feature even of the earliest verse romances. Even Caxton, in his preface to Malory's "Morte d'Arthur," states his absolute faith in the historical accuracy of the work, and expresses great indignation against those who had called it fiction. The Spanish romances of the fifteenth and sixteenth centuries, which turned the brain of poor Don Quixote, were similarly accepted as truth, although founded neither on history, as were those of Charlemagne, nor on popular tradition, as were those of King Arthur, but on pure inventions of the authors.

One of the earliest French romancers, Jean Bodel, classified French romance into three main categories, which he called "The Matter of France," "The Matter of Britain," and "The Matter of Rome the Great." The first includes all those which deal, directly or indirectly, with Charlemagne; the second, those relating stories of Arthur and his knights; the third, those based on subjects derived from classical Greek and Latin sources—the stories of Troy, Thebes, Æneas, and Alexander the Great. This classification does not include all French, and even less all European romance. There are, in addition, a large number of miscellaneous themes which can be grouped into more or less artificial categories, but in this work are simply grouped together in one chapter, called "Miscellaneous Themes of Romance." One group of romances, based on purely English traditions, which arose during the period of Norse invasion and rule of England, did not originate in France, and therefore did not come under the notice of Bodel, but, following his classification, it has been called, in recent years, "The Matter of England." These five classes of romances will be discussed in the seven following chapters.

CHAPTER II

THE CHARLEMAGNE ROMANCES

THE ROMANCES BASED ON THE TRADITIONS which had gathered round the name of Charlemagne, the greatest of the Carolingian monarchs, form a connecting link between the earlier heroic type of poetry and the later romance of chivalry which, from the twelfth century on, became the predominating type of literature in Western Europe. Their chief theme is national warfare, and they mirror the national unity of an heroic age, but they reflect the heroic spirit far too faintly to be called epics, and only one, "La Chanson de Roland," shows the stimulus of that fervent national sentiment of which Charlemagne had come to be regarded as symbolical. Although they may fittingly be included under the general term "Romance," they were usually called, not "romans," but "chansons de gestes,"[1] and the best of them are songs designed to inspire warriors, rather than pleasant tales of adventure and love to be read at the fireside.

By the twelfth century Charlemagne and Roland had ceased to be of national significance, and only the one poem, "La Chanson de Roland," reflects traditions which had been profoundly inspired by Charlemagne's greatness. But, although Charlemagne had ceased to be an inspiring force at this stage, he had been during his lifetime an impressive figure, and well known throughout Western Europe. He was not only the greatest warrior prince of Europe, but also the most zealous patron of learning. His encouragement of scholars, whom he invited to his Court from all parts of the world, made Alfred the Great regard him as a model king. But in an unlettered world it is inevitable that memories even of the greatest men should become confused and dimmed with

---

[1] "Songs of great deeds."

the passage of time, especially when circumstances and national ideals have so changed that they cease to symbolise the spirit of the nation. By his campaigns against barbarian Saxons, Charlemagne had not only established the security of his own realm, but also secured Christianity against the inroads of Paganism. But by the eleventh century, the Saxons, converted from Paganism, had ceased to be a constant source of peril to Southern Europe, and so Charlemagne's campaigns must have had little deeper significance to Frenchmen of the twelfth century than those of Marlborough have for us to-day. Only one existing poem, by Jean Bodel of Arras, has for its theme his conflict with the Saxons, and so little impressed was the poet with this piece of barbarian warfare that he made of it a romance of chivalry, infusing into his narrative that spirit of gallantry and etiquette which reigned in the twelfth century.

In the eleventh and twelfth centuries it was not the Saxons but the Saracens[1] who inspired France and Europe generally with fear and hatred. During the eleventh century there had been a steadily increasing tide of hatred towards the Saracen rulers of Palestine, culminating in the First Crusade of 1096. And since Charlemagne had fought one campaign against this common foe of all Europe, it is not surprising that poems written to celebrate his prowess in war should be almost entirely restricted to his strife with Saracens. In 777 Charlemagne was asked by a Saracen prince, Ibn al Arabi, to assist him against the Caliph of Cordova, also a Saracen. In 778 he entered Spain, subdued a few unimportant towns, but failed in his real object, the subjugation of the Caliph. This expedition was not, in any sense, a religious war, since Charlemagne was concerned primarily with assisting one Saracen against another, and secondarily with furthering his own aggrandisement. Furthermore, he besieged and captured, during his campaign, a Christian city, Pampeluna, and treated

[1] A general term for all Mohammedans and allied races—Turks, Arabs, Moors, Persians, etc.

the Christian Basques of the Pyrenees as enemies. But the intense hostility between Christians and Saracens of the eleventh century made men distort his campaign into a Holy War against infidels and the retaliatory vengeance of the Basques on his rearguard as a treacherous attack by Saracens who had signed a truce. This distortion was assisted by the fact that two of his predecessors, Charles Martel and Pippin, had actually saved Europe from the menace of Saracen conquest by their defeat of two Saracen armies, at Tours and Narbonne respectively. Popular tradition frequently credits the greatest of its heroes with the most famous exploits of his predecessors, and, by confusing Charlemagne's expedition to Spain with the services of two earlier monarchs, came in time to exalt him as the great champion of Christendom.[1]

Long before the First Crusade, warfare against Saracens had come to be regarded as the noblest of all conflicts, and this religious fervour made men focus their attention on this one phase of Charlemagne's warfare, because the traditional and poetic history of a great man comprises not the deeds which caused his greatness so much as those which appeal to popular sentiment as being important; and popular sentiment naturally changes as conditions change. Charlemagne's fame as a warrior rests upon his defeat of Saxons; the only warfare which fired the imagination of Frenchmen in the eleventh and twelfth centuries was Saracen warfare; Charlemagne, therefore, was regarded by Frenchmen as a great religious champion who had saved Christendom from Saracen aggression.

"La Chanson de Roland" reflects something of the spirit which must have animated the Franks during and shortly after the reign of Charlemagne, but it is an epic of France, not of the Franks; it hymns the hatred against Saracens of the eleventh century, not that against Saxons of the eighth. The later Charlemagne romances reflect the same

---

[1] The correspondence of names—Charles Martel and Charles the Great (Magnus)—made it easier to confuse the exploits of these, the two greatest of all Frankish kings.

hatred, but not the same national spirit; Charlemagne is the symbol neither of the Franks nor of France, but of all Christendom. The direct inspiring forces seem, therefore, to have been traditions which arose from popular sentiment of the eleventh century, not those which obtained during the rule of Carolingian kings; they do not presuppose a continuous oral literature extending back to Charlemagne's own time. The deeds of great men in heroic periods are commonly extolled in song and anecdote during and immediately after their lifetime, and at a later period these oral traditions become distorted and confused, owing partly to lapses of memory and partly to the habit of incorporating new elements which will be more significant and therefore more interesting to the audience. During Charlemagne's lifetime Latin poems were written to extol his fame, but not designed for the entertainment of the general public, who knew no Latin; shortly after his death a biography was written, also in Latin—the "Vita Caroli"—but whether popular songs or poems were also composed at this time, and whether his fame continued to be extolled in popular songs without a break until the eleventh century, is still unknown. Even if there was an unbroken chain of oral literature, very little of it appears to have been incorporated into the romances which now exist, which reflect only the conditions and spirit of the tenth and eleventh centuries, neglecting those features of his character and career which must have predominated in Frankish traditions. Apart from the one isolated poem which celebrates his Saxon campaigns, the Charlemagne romances may be classified into four groups according to their themes:—

(1) Religious warfare against Saracens.
(2) Feudal warfare against rebellious vassals.
(3) Narratives of the life and deeds of supposed relatives of Charlemagne.
(4) Romances of adventure attached with little or no reason to his name.

The romances of the first and most important group were inspired by the crusading fervour of the eleventh century, and relate partly true and partly fictitious campaigns against religious foes in various countries. Four distinct themes are presented.

(1) A wholly fictitious journey of Charlemagne to Palestine.

(2) Warfare against Saracens in Italy, based on fact, but greatly distorted.

(3) The campaign against the Saracens of Spain, less distorted, but still widely divergent from historical truth.

(4) The defeat of the rearguard in the Pyrenees, and the death of Roland, reflecting historical truth more closely than any of the others.

The wide divergence from historical truth, the consistent reflection of conditions not existing before the tenth century, the constant reference within the poems to relics possessed by various religious houses, and to chronicles emanating from those houses, all seem to indicate that the traditions on which these romances are based were not genuine popular traditions handed down from Charlemagne's own time so much as spurious legends deliberately manufactured in churches and monasteries. Charlemagne's valuable services to Christianity, even where only incidental, would naturally enhance him in the eyes of the Church, and religious fervour would easily lead to wholesale distortion of facts, and give rise to innumerable stories of miracles and divine favours. The "Vita Caroli" naturally could not satisfy ecclesiastics who wished to present Charlemagne not only as the great champion of the Christian faith, but also as the patron of their own individual establishments; they therefore amplified and distorted to suit their own ends. Even as early as 968 he was represented in the chronicle of a monk called Bénoît as the champion of the Christian faith, and from that time on there arose a steadily increasing desire to place under his auspices as many religious foundations as possible, actuated by the same spirit which in various periods and countries has caused several different towns to be acclaimed as the birthplace of the same famous poet or artist of obscure birth. Both the town and cathedral of Zurich ascribed their foundation to Charlemagne; Aix-la-Chapelle claimed to have the Persian scimitar which, according to legend, was given to him by Haroun al Raschid; and both Toulouse and Roncevaux claimed to have Roland's horn. In Italy many monuments were erected in honour of both Charlemagne and Roland, one in Florence claiming to have been erected by Charlemagne and consecrated by Turpin, Bishop of Rheims 753-794 Churches situated on the chief routes to Palestine and Spain asserted that they had either been founded by or received patronage from Charlemagne. Most of these claims are now known to be false, but they serve to show that ever-increasing religious fervour which culminated in the canonisation of Charlemagne in 1165.[1]

The medieval Church well knew how to maintain and extend its privileges and powers by the use of judicious propaganda, as may be clearly illustrated from a typical anecdote. Charlemagne dreamt that he was attacked by a wild boar and promised aid by a naked boy if he in return would provide him with clothing. He made the required promise, and the boar was killed. The bishops who were asked to interpret this dream stated that the boy represented the ruined chapel of St. Cyr in the Cathedral of Nevers, and that the clothing promised signified restitution and endowment of that chapel. The widespread belief that dreams were prophetic presented astute ecclesiastics with many a golden opportunity.

The first episode, the journey to Palestine, is represented in only one French poem, "La Pélérinage de Charlemagne à Jérusalem," of which no English version exists. Since

[1] The installation of Charlemagne in 1478 as Patron of the University of Paris reflects the earlier and more genuine tradition of him as a patron of learning.

Charlemagne never went to Jerusalem, this poem is of importance as showing that romances could be composed without any historical basis whatsoever.[1] This poem names as its source the Abbey of St. Denis, which claimed to have in its possession the Crown of Thorns and other relics brought back by Charlemagne from Jerusalem. This legend must obviously have arisen long after his death, and presumably at a time when pilgrimages to Jerusalem had become common. During the tenth and eleventh centuries pilgrims from France were constantly passing through various Italian ports on their way to Palestine; the monasteries and churches situated on the pilgrim routes would naturally vie with one another, each striving to attract most of the pilgrims in order to enhance its reputation and increase its revenues. The two greatest attractions which a religious house could offer to pilgrims were famous relics which men would desire to see and traditions of some great man—the supposed founder or patron of the house—which men would desire to hear. And just as modern tourists will flock to any inn which is credited with having housed Queen Elizabeth on her travels, so medieval pilgrims would flock to a monastery which claimed to have had Charlemagne as a guest during his pilgrimage to Palestine. If a church or monastery could also show relics that he had brought back from Jerusalem the attraction would be all the greater. Relics could easily be manufactured, but unfortunately Charlemagne had never undertaken that particular pilgrimage, so the history had to be manufactured also. Popular traditions cannot grow from nothing; they must be based on either historical fact or deliberately concocted legend, and the story must have been deliberately fabricated, and presumably by an ecclesiastic. Charlemagne, like most pious kings of the Middle Ages, had collected a large number of relics, most of which he gave to the cathedral of Aix-la-Chapelle. A

---

[1] It has frequently been considered that writers in the Middle Ages were incapable of inventing a pseudo-historical story without some historical basis.

chronicle of the twelfth century, obviously emanating from the Abbey of St. Denis, asserted not only that Charlemagne had voyaged to Jerusalem and founded churches there, but also that the relics which he had brought back had been transferred from Aix-la-Chapelle to St. Denis. The romance of "Fierabras" also states that Charlemagne had brought back from Jerusalem the Crown of Thorns and other relics, all of which had been deposited in the Abbey of St. Denis. The Crown of Thorns was the most valuable and coveted of all relics, and therefore a certain baït for credulous pilgrims; the chronicle would be written to bolster up the claim to this relic, and the romances—"La Pélérinage de Charlemagne à Jérusalem" and "Fierabras"—both naming St. Denis as their source, would extend this propaganda still more widely. Since different churches often claimed to possess the same unique relic, constant advertisement was essential to any religious house which desired to prevent its claim being refuted and therefore disbelieved. Even if the romance relating Charlemagne's pilgrimage was written merely for entertainment, the legend on which it was based seems certainly to have been deliberately concocted as propaganda for one or more churches, notably that of St. Denis, and it became so firmly established that the crusaders of the First Crusade firmly believed that they were following the actual route of Charlemagne.

The themes of both the second and third group, the campaigns in Italy and Spain, are based on history, but history so much distorted as to become almost pure fiction. Neither campaign was strictly religious warfare, and only the latter against foes of a different religious faith, but both are presented as Holy Wars in defence of Christendom. To the people of France, and indeed of all Western Europe, Charlemagne was no longer a mere Frankish monarch; he was the supreme champion of the Christian faith.

In 773 Charlemagne went to Italy to assist Pope Hadrian against the Lombards, and from that historic fact arose spurious legends of a Holy War apparently invented in religious houses which had been established for the accommodation of pilgrims to the tomb of St. Peter at Rome. The large numbers of Frenchmen who undertook this pilgrimage presented a potential source of profit to the monasteries, which no doubt vied with one another in their endeavours to attract these pilgrims, and fostered legends about Charlemagne by way of propaganda. On his return from defeating the Lombards, Charlemagne became the guest of the Abbey of the Novalese, near Mt. Cenis. Early in the tenth century Saracens invaded Piedmont and forced the monks to flee temporarily from this Abbey. During the eleventh century a Latin chronicle was written purporting to record its history, and distorting the campaign against the Lombards into a religious war against Saracens. There is not the least evidence that the fusion of these two distinct events was the result of popular tradition. The Abbey had enjoyed the patronage of Charlemagne, the monks knew that pilgrims would take no interest in a campaign against Christian Lombards, but would flock in large numbers to a monastery whose monks could describe a conflict with Saracens. Charlemagne had fought in Lombardy, so had Saracens; they had only to fuse the two together, present Charlemagne as a Crusader, and the prosperity of their Abbey was assured. As a final realistic touch to stifle all dispute, they claimed to have in the Abbey the tomb of Charlemagne's wife, though no wife of his was ever buried there. It therefore seems fairly certain that the monks, or even the chronicler alone, had concocted this legend simply as advertisement. In the section of the "Liber Pontificalis" which recounts the life of Pope Hadrian were also incorporated legends about this Lombard campaign, and from this basis arose traditions and chronicles which represent Charlemagne as the defender of Rome against Saracens. This legend also, like the former, arose from the blending of isolated historic facts. In 846 Rome was captured by Saracens, and Charlemagne's campaign of 773 as an ally of the Pope was easily distorted therefore into a conflict with Saracens and the reconquest of Rome. The dissemination of this legend would attract larger numbers of pilgrims than perhaps any other, because the only deed which could conceivably rank higher than the preservation of the head-quarters of Christianity would be the capture of Jerusalem, and that was still to come. The French romance, "La Destruction de Rome," which relates this legend, was probably based on traditions fostered by one or more monasteries situated on the main routes to Rome. "Fiera-bras" deals in part with the same theme, but names as its source the Abbey of St. Denis, and therefore presumably was designed to advertise that Abbey, though the legend or legends on which it is based may have originated in Italy.

Charlemagne's expedition to Spain was no more religious warfare than that against the Lombards, but could easily come to be regarded as such in popular tradition, because his opponents were certainly Saracens. Yet even here the distortion and exaggeration seem largely, if not entirely, to have been due to ecclesiastical propaganda, designed to enhance the reputation of the churches in Galicia, and chief of all that of St. James at Compostella. The route from France to the shrine of St. James was also the chief route through the Pyrenees to Spain. It would therefore be easy to persuade pilgrims that Charlemagne had followed that route in his invasion of Spain and had patronised the religious houses situated on it. The pil-grims of the Middle Ages would know, even less than modern tourists, the date of foundation of churches and monasteries which they visited, and were unable even to consult guide-books. They would obtain their informa-tion, as do most modern tourists, from the monks, and blindly accept all statements; any monk could, therefore, assert with safety that his monastery had been founded before this invasion and patronised by Charlemagne. During the tenth and eleventh centuries the monasteries situated on this route had zealously fostered raids against the Saracens, raids which came to be regarded as Holy Wars approved by God.[1] This encouragement of the Church was natural, since Saracens actually held part of the route and from time to time attacked bands of pilgrims,[2] even capturing Compostella on two occasions—in 944 and 988. By making liberal use of the names of Charlemagne and Roland, by fostering legends which would enhance their own reputation, and by displaying spurious relics of the campaign, these monasteries, and particularly the church of St. James, also attracted large numbers of pilgrims. In 1108 some Arab ambassadors found the road to Galicia completely blocked by large bands of pilgrims journeying to St. James' shrine. To authenticate the various legends invented, and to establish still further the security of St. James, a Latin chronicle was written during the eleventh century and added to at intervals. Since Bishop Turpin was claimed to be the author, it is now called the Pseudo-Turpin Chronicle. Charlemagne's campaign in Spain and the defeat of the rearguard by the Basques had been recorded in the "Vita Caroli"; the Pseudo-Turpin Chronicle, using this as basis, exaggerated and distorted to enhance the fame of Compostella and to make pilgrims regard it as the Mecca of all devout Christians. This chronicle was the source of the romances which narrate events of this campaign, the greatest of which is "La Chanson de Roland." This poem, the only one which exists in an English version, concentrates on the final episode, the attack upon the rearguard and the death of Roland; "L'Entrée en Espagne" and "La Prise de Pampelune" narrate the earlier events.

"La Chanson de Roland," written apparently at the end of the eleventh century, is the only remaining relic of the

---

[1] Raids of Frenchmen into Spain are recorded under the years 1018, 1033, 1063.

[2] The romance "Fleure et Blanchefleure" (see Chapter VIII) opens with the defeat of a band of pilgrims by Saracens in Galicia and the capture of a French lady whose daughter becomes the heroine of the story.

heroic tradition which, arising with the Carolingian dynasty, seems to have been almost exhausted by the end of the tenth century. The preservation of the earlier heroic spirit in this poem is due to the fact that it is not based merely on the Pseudo-Turpin Chronicle, but drew inspiration from earlier poems or songs upon the same theme. It is known that a Norman minstrel sang of the death of Roland at the Battle of Hastings, but whether similar songs had been composed at an earlier date has not yet been discovered. It is quite probable that there were fragmentary traditions of all the great events of Charlemagne's reign in addition to the legends concocted by the Church, and that these traditions were made full use of both by chroniclers and poets. "La Chanson de Roland" is the most epic of all extant French poems; it stresses Roland's heroic fight as a great and disastrous national event, and makes Roland symbolical of French ideals and aspirations. Far from seeking to rouse interest by heaping adventure upon adventure—so common in romance—the poet concentrates upon one episode, the last and greatest action of the campaign, the rearguard's heroic stand against overwhelming odds. This is portrayed as a great national tragedy, and a tragedy enhanced by treachery; Ganelon, sent as ambassador to the Saracen Emir of Saragossa, incites him to attack the rearguard and wreak his vengeance upon Roland and Oliver. That the details of the story are almost wholly fictitious matters little; the merit of the poem lies in its vivid reflection of French national sentiment and the crusading fervour of the eleventh century. It stresses the duty of men to sacrifice themselves for their country and their Faith, and presents Charlemagne as the symbol of Christian kingship, Roland as the great Crusader. It welds together the spirit with which Charlemagne must have animated the Franks and the dominating ideal of Frenchmen in the eleventh century—to crush the Infidel in Holy War. Its deeply patriotic spirit is shown by the fact that it describes, not victory, but honour, courage, and sacrifice. Wherever patriotism is a real inspiring force it is the spirit of the fighters which rouses fervour, not the mere winning of victories; a dogged defence stirs deeper chords than a brilliant cavalry charge; the defence of Lucknow and of Verdun are more profoundly moving than the victories of Balaclava and Messines.

The national sentiment, however, is that of France in the eleventh century, not that of the Franks in the eighth. Charlemagne is the champion of Christendom rather than the King of France, fighting not a national foe, but the forces of heathendom. He is no longer the mere ally of an exiled king striving to regain his conquered realm; he is the servant of God bidding Saracens choose "between death and baptism." Bishop Turpin is a warrior bishop fighting by Roland's side and promising that those who die shall have the martyrs' reward in Heaven; and when he dies Roland exclaims, "Turpin is dead—dead in the service of Charlemagne, he who by great battles and by beautiful sermons was ever a champion against pagan foes. Never did man more willingly serve God, never since the Apostles was such a prophet for maintaining Christian law and attracting men thereto." When Roland dies, his body is carried to Heaven by the angels Gabriel, Raphael, and Michael, and when Charlemagne, who has returned too late to avert defeat, asks God to stay the course of the sun until all the infidels are killed, his prayer is answered; at sunset not one remains alive. Yet, in spite of its heroic spirit, the poem is marred in places by the introduction of fantastic details which were to become so common in later romance; Charlemagne is represented as two hundred years old but still a vigorous warrior, his campaign of a few months becomes one of seven years, and the direct intervention of God detracts from the realism and the intensity. It marks the transition from epic to romance, from the realistic portrayal of great national events to the telling of marvellous and incredible stories designed for the amusement of a bored and *blasé* audience.

The Pseudo-Turpin Chronicle presented Charlemagne's

voyage to Spain as the result of a vision from St. James in which he was ordered to free Compostella from Saracen rule. This deliberate distortion caused him to be regarded not merely as a crusader, but even as the exclusive champion of St. James rather than of God. Astute propaganda attracted pilgrims, and made the church of St. James so famous that it was made first into a bishopric and later the head of a number of bishoprics.

The activity of monasteries in producing chronicles and fostering legends which would enhance their reputation seems to have been on a par with the practice of modern tourist resorts which seek to attract visitors by building up legends on a slight basis of truth. It is also difficult to resist the inference that the continual boosting necessary to attract pilgrims from other routes and from attendance at other shrines, and especially the wrangling of churches, each of which claimed to possess the same unique relic, must have fostered scepticism amongst thinking men and assisted to some extent that disintegration of the Roman Church which openly began in the fifteenth and sixteenth centuries. One Spanish writer, tired of hearing Charlemagne so extravagantly praised for an action in which he had really failed, and disgusted with the wholesale distortion of truth, pretended that the "Vita Caroli" contained evidence that Charlemagne had been bought off by his Saracen foes.

Of the English Charlemagne romances four, "The Sowdone[1] of Babylon," "Sir Ferumbras," "The Destruction of Rome," and "The Siege of Melayne,"[2] narrate episodes on the Italian campaign, the first two being based on the French "Fierabras," the third on "La Destruction de Rome," and the fourth—relating a brief expedition to Milan undertaken during his campaign in Spain—having no existing French original. One only, "The Song of Roland," deals with the Spanish campaign, and, though based apparently on the French poem, adds some further details from the Pseudo-Turpin Chronicle—the defeat of

[1] Sultan.   [2] Milan.

the rearguard is partly attributed to the debauchery of the soldiers occasioned by Ganelon bringing back from Saragossa wine and women slaves; the French poem concentrates wholly upon the treachery. Three other romances, "Otuel," "Duke Rowlande and Sir Otuell of Spayne," and "Roland and Vernagu," present only duels between Frenchmen and Saracens, portraying episodes of neither campaign. Of the third no French original exists; the other two are both based on the French "Otinel." Since the most famous episode in "Fierabras" was a duel between Roland and the Saracen Fierabras, it is thought that the stories of Otuel and Vernagu may be simply imitations of this combat, having no basis in tradition whatsoever.

Just how much of each legend is to be attributed to the deliberate fabrication of monks and how much to genuine popular traditions cannot be known. But whatever the chief cause of the distortion may have been, the romances of the twelfth and later centuries reflect neither the true greatness of Charlemagne nor the national sentiment of France. They reflect only a faint religious sentiment, too shadowy to arouse deep feeling. Charlemagne becomes so nearly perfect as to be unhuman, he is portrayed as a devout and saintly king, praying continuously and rewarded by numberless visions and miracles; he lives in a society of guardian angels, is guided to Galicia by a line of stars, and when he prays to God the walls of Pampeluna fall miraculously, like those of Jericho. It is impossible for us to know just how much of the supernatural and miraculous a medieval audience could stand without losing interest, but since the rapid declension of romance in the thirteenth and fourteenth centuries seems to have been largely due to excessive sensationalism and lack of human interest, it is probable that the audience of these romances would have preferred Charlemagne to be a little less saintly and a little more human.

Of the three great themes of France, Germany, and Britain, this of France was by far the most heroic in its original spirit, but has aroused least interest in modern times, that of Germany, the "Nibelungenlied," is less heroic but more human, while the Arthurian Legend is the least heroic of all, but in the hands of able writers has been made the most human, and therefore the most interesting of the three.

The second group of romances, composed to extol the fame of great baronial families under whose patronage and protection the poets lived, reflects neither national nor religious sentiment; they represent instead the disintegration of national unity, that strife between monarchs and their feudal vassals which became so marked a feature of the reigns of the later Carolingian and the Capetian kings. Even Charles Martel, though he could vanquish the most feared of all foes, the Saracens, could not maintain absolute discipline in his own realm, and a celebrated rebel of his reign, Renaud de Montauban, became the most famous of rebel heroes in romance. These feudal rebellions became far more frequent under Charlemagne's successors, who were relatively mean and petty monarchs utterly unable to keep the vassals in check—their very nicknames indicate their feebleness: the Pious, the Bald, the Stammerer, the Simple, the Fat. These romances, two of which, "Les Quatre Fils d'Aymon" and "Huon de Bordeaux," were later translated into English,[1] particularly serve to show how little national feeling was aroused by Charlemagne's deeds and reputation. The weakness of Charlemagne's successors aroused the jealousy of the barons, who came to regard them as merely nominal heads to whom a slight formal allegiance was due, but whose attempts to wield absolute power it was not only necessary but a merit to oppose. The Capetian kings[2] fanned this jealousy into open revolt by striving to increase their powers and by seeking to support the citizen classes in furtherance of this aim. Authors who depended on

[1] "The Four Sons of Aymon" by Caxton in the fifteenth century. "Huon of Bordeaux" by Lord Berners in the sixteenth century.

[2] Hugh Capet, Count of Paris, was elected king in 987, thus ending the Carolingian dynasty.

these feudal vassals for their existence naturally sought to extol their patrons at the expense of the king, and, in writing romances, naturally chose that king who was familiar to all, Charlemagne. To follow current traditions, whether of popular or ecclesiastical origin, was to extol monarchy, a power which their patrons were trying to reduce. They therefore chose as heroes, not Charlemagne and his peers, but barons who had rebelled against some earlier king, it did not matter which, and who, in some cases, would be related to the family under whose patronage the author wrote. And just as Charlemagne had been credited with all the merits of his predecessors and successors in the romances which narrate his Italian and Spanish campaigns, so in this second group of romances he is endowed with all their demerits; just as Charlemagne had been extolled as the saviour of Europe from Saracens when Charles Martel had really done the work, so Charlemagne replaced Charles Martel as the tyrant king against whom Renaud de Montauban rebelled. "The Four Sons of Aymon"[1] portrays him as continually guided by evil counsellors, railing at his vassals, whining miserably when he suffers defeat, and consenting to treacherous attacks on men to whom he has promised safe conduct. The four sons are all rebels, and the eldest, Renaud, became such a popular figure that even to this day the chimneys of many French peasants' homes bear pictures of him. The Church of St. Reynold in Cologne was named after him, and has upon its walls a painting of the four rebel sons, Renaud being distinguished by an aureole, the sign of saintship.

It is very significant that, though Charlemagne is degraded, Roland is not; the author was interested only in proclaiming the independence of barons, and had no desire to belittle other heroes in order to enhance his own. So careful was he to maintain Roland's prestige that he presents him as equal in prowess to Renaud. In the duel between these two champions neither is victorious, nor is

[1] The French original is a free prose rendering of an older poem "Renaud de Montauban."

Roland scorned because of his loyalty to Charlemagne. Loyalty was the duty of all vassals except when the king sought to exercise tyrannical powers; Renaud and his brothers do not rebel until they become the victims of injustice and have to flee to avoid death; furthermore, Renaud finally undertakes a pilgrimage to expiate his sin of rebellion and dies at Cologne. The injustice which he suffers is somewhat crudely presented. Renaud had killed Charlemagne's nephew with a chess-board in return for an angry blow; Charlemagne naturally wished for vengeance, and so the revolt began.

Huon of Bordeaux is the only other rebel represented in English as well as in French romance. In this romance the feeling of hostility towards kings is exemplified not only by the degradation of Charlemagne, but also by the portrayal of King Arthur childishly disputing with Huon the realm of Fairyland, being chided by Merlin for his wrangling, and finally pacified by being made ruler of the fairies of Tartary. It is, however, more a pure adventure story than a romance of rebellion; it concentrates chiefly on the adventures of Huon and his children, where "The Four Sons of Aymon" concentrates on the hostility between king and vassal.

The great difference in spirit between these two groups of romances is well illustrated by two statements of Roland. In "La Chanson de Roland," of the first group, he says of Charlemagne, "Never was man who prevailed against him"; in "Gui de Bourgogne," of the second group, "Let us leave this old man who is doting." Both groups arose from traditions which existed side by side. The first, based on combined ecclesiastical and popular traditions, presents him as a great religious monarch, and reflects the crusading fervour of the tenth and eleventh centuries. The second, based on traditions cherished and fostered among the feudal barons, presents him as a capricious despot, and reflects the feudal jealousy and strife of the same period. The two statements of Roland are, therefore, thoroughly symbolical. In all the romances

D

he is a loyal follower of Charlemagne; in the first group there is only one cause and absolute unity, in the second, baronial independence must be maintained, so Roland remains loyal in his service, but has little or no respect for his feudal overlord.

The third group consists of romances which narrate fictitious accounts of supposed relatives of Charlemagne, the best known being "Berte aux grands pieds," which purports to relate the adventures of his mother. This group is of little importance and entirely unrepresented in English romance, so may be passed over here.

The last group consists of stories and legends which, though originally unconnected with Charlemagne, were linked to his name to enhance their interest. The most famous of all, "Ami et Amile," was translated into English, but, since it forms no part of real Charlemagne tradition, it had been left for discussion to a later chapter.[1] Since all the Charlemagne romances, however, tended to be tales of fantastic and sensational adventure rather than national epics, it will be useful to exemplify this degradation which was common to all themes of romance. The older heroic literature, recounting the deeds of heroes who were vivid personalities to the audience, had no need to rouse interest by spurious means. Its interest lives in the realism and the intensity of national feeling; and this is true largely even of "La Chanson de Roland." But in the later Charlemagne romances fantastic adventure ceases to be a mere incidental excrescence and becomes the vital theme; it is no longer the character, but the adventures of the heroes that attract. "Huon of Bordeaux" affords the most vivid illustration of this hopeless distortion. Though based on the rebellion of a vassal, it depends for its interest, not upon strife with Charlemagne, but upon reckless deeds and hairbreadth escapes, most of which have not the slightest connection with the basic conception. Oberon,

---

[1] "Amis and Amiloun." See Chapter VIII, "Miscellaneous Themes of Romance."

king of the fairies, becomes Huon's adviser, and is later succeeded by him in his kingdom; King Arthur is introduced merely to dispute the claim to kingship with him; and many of the voyages of Sindbad the Sailor are attached to Huon's name. From time to time sequels were added, each further removed from the original theme; authors who despaired of finding any new adventures with which to enhance his fame relate the deeds of his children and grandchildren. The climax is reached when Huon's granddaughter, Ide, serves in the Roman Emperor's army disguised as a man, receives his daughter to wife, and has her sex changed by Divine decree in order that the marriage might be consummated.

One English romance, "The Taill of Rauf Coilzear,"[1] is a frank burlesque, and reflects the attitude of shrewd and intelligent working men towards the fantasies of knight errantry. Charlemagne, following the well-known example of Haroun al Raschid, disguises himself in order to inspect his subjects in secret. He becomes for one night the guest of a collier, who insults and buffets him, turning all knightly etiquette into sheer farce by his remarks. Charlemagne desires Ralph to go first into supper, and hesitates to take the head of the table. Not only does Ralph box his ears, but reproves him for his lack of etiquette in not doing as he is bidden. Ralph is persuaded to visit Charlemagne the next day to sell him some coal, and goes, quite unconscious that his guest was the king. Meeting Roland on the way, he speculates whether the glittering armour covers a real "manly man." Charlemagne, who has recovered his good humour, knights Ralph and gives him sixty squires. On his return home he fights a Saracen knight. By means of these and various other episodes the author provides an amusing burlesque of the chief features of feudalism, knighthood, and warfare as they were portrayed in romance.

The degradation in spirit of these stories, their increasing

[1] "The Tale of Ralph the Collier."

lack of any national sentiment or ideal, their concentration on the coarser aspects of warfare, combined with the increase in refinement during the twelfth century and the growing patronage of women,[1] all contributed to an increasing distaste for these romances, which reflected too much the rough and brutal manners of an earlier period to compete against the recently invented romance of chivalry, which concentrated upon knightly etiquette, gentleness of manners, and, above all, upon love and devotion to women. The Charlemagne romances became an entertainment only for the lower classes, except for a temporary revival during the fifteenth century, when prose versions were made and printed in sumptuous editions for the barons. It was these prose versions that formed the basis of the translations made by Caxton and Lord Berners. Boiardo in his "Orlando Innamorato" and Ariosto in his "Orlando Furioso" attempted to give the story of Roland a permanent place in poetry, as Spenser later did with the Arthurian legend. But later poets were not sufficiently interested, and whereas the Arthurian legend has won a permanent place as a poetic theme of universal interest, the Charlemagne legend has died a natural death. It still remains popular among the peasantry of Europe, especially the episodes of Roland's duel with Fierabras and his death at Roncevaux—the latter because "La Chanson de Roland" made Roland rather than Charlemagne the symbol of Christian leadership and courageous martyrdom, the former because symbolical of that great conflict of the later Middle Ages, between Christendom and Islam.[2] As late as 1833 a historical drama on Fierabras was acted by villagers in the Pyrenees, and even more recently a traveller to the Faroe

---

[1] See Chapters IV and XIII.

[2] It has been stated that the stories of Otuel and Vernagu were probably invented because duels between Christians and Saracens made a wide appeal. So in Arthurian romance duels with Saracens may have been invented in imitation of that with Fierabras—in "Morte Arthure" Gawain fights a Saracen prince called Priamus.

Islands, seeking at a bookstall for some literature in the Faroese language, was offered a ballad of Roncevaux, while another traveller saw an Italian peasant weeping because he had just heard of the death of Roland, recited by a professional story-teller.

The English Charlemagne romances, except for the two translations made by Caxton and Berners, were designed only for the lower classes, and suffered the double disadvantage of being based on French poems written long after Charlemagne had ceased to be an inspiring force, and of being composed by men who neither belonged to nor were under the patronage of the knightly class. No trace of either national or religious sentiment is therefore to be expected; they are simply exciting stories of adventure of varying merit—"The Sowdone of Babylon" being perhaps the best told, "Roland and Vernagu" the worst. To the authors the heroes possessed neither any national nor personal significance. Their inability to appreciate fully the French originals is well illustrated by their use of the French term "douze pairs"—the twelve chief vassals of Charlemagne, of whom Roland and Oliver were the most famous. To English romancers, who had no intimate knowledge of French, the term came to signify merely great men or champions. In both Charlemagne and Arthurian romances the words "duzzepeers," "duspers," and "dosiperes" are used as terms of rank, as we would use the word "noblemen," or "champions." In "Otuel" one sultan is called the "duzzepeer" of another sultan, from which we may conclude that the poet realised that "pair" indicated a vassal, but did not know that "douze" meant "twelve." Even Spenser adopted the English mistake in his line,

"Bigge looking like a doughtie Doucepere."[1]

Regarded simply as adventure stories, "The Sowdone of Babylon" and "Sir Ferumbras" are thoroughly interest-

[1] "The Faerie Queene," Book III, canto x, stanza 31.

ing, but reflect nothing of the spirit which had inspired the first French poets, and especially the author of "La Chanson de Roland." "The Four Sons of Aymon" and "Huon of Bordeaux," though far more interesting, are merely close translations of the French, and cannot be regarded strictly as English romances.

CHAPTER III

ORIGINS OF THE ARTHURIAN LEGEND

THE ARTHURIAN LEGEND, THOUGH INCOR-porated into literature later than that of Charle-magne, quickly overshadowed it, and became the greatest theme of medieval romance, because adopted by able poets who realised how easily it could be adapted to suit contemporary interests. The traditions of Charle-magne and his peers had become too crystallised, too definitely symbolical of religious and feudal warfare to suit the increasing desire for tales of chivalry which arose in the twelfth century. Even if Arthur represents some historical British leader who successfully opposed Saxon invaders, both he and his followers by the twelfth century must have been nebulous figures in popular tradition, capable of adaptation to any purpose; not only would the greater lapse of time have rendered any oral traditions vague and fragmentary, but, in the absence of written records, all national significance must have been lost far more completely than with Charlemagne, whose fame had been carefully fostered by the Church.

Although crusades were undertaken at various times throughout the later Middle Ages, interest in religious warfare seems to have waned rapidly after the first,[1] and increasing refinement, together with the growing patro-nage of women, compelled poets to compose romances which stressed the ideals, not of organised warfare, but of chivalry and love. Their audience no longer wished to hear the deeds of feudal monarchs, but of young knights-errant, not of warfare undertaken to crush a heathen foe, but of sacrifices made to win a woman's love. Charlemagne was too definitely a warrior monarch and religious champion

[1] The necessity of raising enormous taxes for the second crusade of 1146 caused serious riots.

to become President of a Board of Chivalry; Arthur was
but a shadowy figure of confused popular traditions, ready
to fit any part, as the poet and his audience required.

Arthur was first introduced into literature by Norman
chroniclers of England, who presented him as a great
religious warrior and a national hero. A few, but very
few, romances were based on these chronicles, but the
earliest, and those which have given rise to our modern
conceptions of the legend, record the exploits of single
knights, lay little stress upon King Arthur, and derive
little if any material from the chronicles. They must
therefore be considered separately. It is necessary also to
remember that the Britons, from whom the Arthurian
traditions have descended, were divided into two distinct
groups, one remaining in Britain, chiefly in Wales and
Cornwall, the other fleeing to and settling in Brittany.
Arthurian traditions circulated in both countries, and
must have become widely divergent by the twelfth century.

The origins of the legend are too confused and offer too
difficult a problem to be fully discussed in a work which
aims only at a general brief survey, but a short review of
both the oral traditions and the chronicles is essential.
Whether Arthur represents any historical figure of early
British history is still unknown, but by the twelfth century
at latest there existed a widespread belief that a British
king, named Arthur, had defeated invading Saxons in
many battles, and that, whenever a great national crisis
should arise, he would again return to help his country's
need. The earliest record of his victorious career is to be
found in the Latin chronicle of Nennius of the tenth century, which is, however, but a late version of one or more
earlier histories of the Britons. Its composite nature is
shown by the fact that in an early section 858 is given as
the year of composition, while in a later section it is stated
that 976 years had passed since the death of Christ. It has
been considered that the Arthurian material dates back to
a seventh-century record, but it is by no means certain that
Nennius made no addition to the earlier sections of the

work. Very little is said of Arthur—merely a reference to his supreme command over all the British kings and his victories against the Saxons on twelve occasions. This seems to imply that he had come to be regarded as a national hero, and from the further statement that he bore an image of the Virgin Mary on his shoulders it may be implied that he was also regarded as a champion of the Christian faith. Since the Virgin Mary held no definite place in religious worship as early as the seventh century, it is probable that this latter statement is an interpolation made during the ninth or tenth century, when Mariolatry had become widespread. This religious feature was later emphasised in both chronicles and romances, even being extended to other characters, such as Gawain.[1] This chronicle of Nennius is so untrustworthy in those details which can be tested from other sources, that no reliance can be placed upon its statements concerning Arthur, and no other chronicles earlier than the twelfth century make any reference to this legend. There is, however, other evidence sufficient to show that before the twelfth century Arthurian traditions were widespread, extending even to Italy. In two Lombard documents of 1114 and 1136 are recorded the names Artusius and Galvanus, which are simply the Latin forms of Arthur and Gawain. As both refer to full-grown men, the former at least was born before the twelfth century, and both before any chronicle, except that of Nennius, had been written to relate their exploits. These records seem to imply that Arthur and his chief knight were well-known characters to the people of Lombardy, and it must be remembered that this adoption of the names of historical or legendary heroes has far greater significance than those modern instances in which parents have named their unfortunate children Mafeking or Ypres. The prevailing custom was to name children after patron saints, and medieval parents would not depart from a deeply respected traditional practice unless the names had

[1] Gawain bears an image of the Virgin Mary in "Sir Gawain and the Green Knight."

acquired a significance equal to that of saints' names. At the very least it must be assumed that Arthur and Gawain were widely famous, and that implies a tradition of long standing. This evidence seems to testify to a knowledge of Arthurian traditions upon the continent too early to have been brought from Wales or Cornwall by the Norman conquerors of England. There is also not the slightest trace of British tradition in Anglo-Saxon literature, and even if oral traditions had circulated amongst the Angles and Saxons, it is hardly possible that they were transmitted to Italy.

These two documents of Lombardy are by no means the only evidence of early and widespread traditions of King Arthur. Alanus de Insulis, writing in the twelfth century, stated that a belief in Arthur's eventual return was so widespread in Brittany that denial of it might have cost a man his life, and of the same century is recorded a dispute at Bodmin in Cornwall because a servant of some monks from Laon in Brittany had denied that Arthur still lived. Such firm beliefs could not have arisen in a few years or from one source, but indicate old and widespread traditions; how old cannot be known.

The earliest Anglo-Norman [1] chronicler who refers to Arthur was William of Malmesbury, in his Latin Chronicle of the Kings of England, completed in 1125. He made no attempt to give a historical account, merely referring to the many traditions current in his time. "It is of this Arthur that the Britons tell so many fables, even to the present day; a man worthy to be celebrated, not by idle fictions, but by authentic history. He long upheld the sinking state, and roused the broken spirit of his countrymen to war."[2] This implies that he regarded Arthur as a historical character, but considered the oral traditions too distorted and fantastic to be reliable. The next and most important account is that given in the Latin "History of

[1] Anglo-Norman is the term applied to Normans resident in England, and to the Norman language spoken and written in England.
[2] Giles' translation, Bohn Library.

the Britons," written by Geoffrey of Monmouth, and completed in 1147 or 1148. This chronicle presents the earliest connected account of Arthur still extant, and offers such a wealth of material that romances could be composed from it without the aid of any other source. Although intended to be a systematic history of the Britons from their origin to their final subjugation by the Saxons, it devotes more space to Arthur's career than to that of any other king or period of equal length. This seems to imply that Geoffrey had found material either in writing or in oral legends sufficiently detailed and impressive to fire his imagination and make him regard Arthur as supreme among British kings. He claims to have based his work upon an ancient book given to him by Walter, Archdeacon of Oxford, but no evidence remains of any such book. Some of his details agree with those earlier recorded by Nennus, others are contradictory, but those portions of his history that can be tested from reliable sources contain such absurd statements that his account of Arthur cannot be regarded as of any historical value whatsoever. One illustration alone will serve to show how valueless is his work; it is stated that two British kings, Belinus and Brennus, conquered Gaul and Rome when Porsena was consul. This fiction is simply a distortion of two unrelated historical events transferred from Roman to British history; Brennus was a leader of that Gaulish host which sacked Rome, Lars Porsena an Etruscan who also nearly destroyed Roman supremacy. Geoffrey of Monmouth must therefore be dismissed as a sheer romancer, who, in his ability to concoct a realistic narrative from very little evidence, was a worthy forerunner of Defoe.

King Arthur is portrayed as a typical Norman king, ambitious of conquest and of military fame. Not only does he defeat the Saxons, Picts, and Scots, the most dreaded foes of the Britons, but he also overruns the whole of Gaul and even subjugates Rome itself. His marriage with Guenivere is recorded, and three well-known knights of romance, Gawain, Kay, and Bedivere, are members of his

army. The most popular knights of romance—Lancelot,
Tristram, and Galahad—are never mentioned. The
Arthurian section of the history concludes with Modred's
usurpation of the kingdom, the battle between Arthur and
Modred, and the translation of Arthur to Avallon. Although it is highly probable that Geoffrey invented many,
perhaps most, of the details he records, he was a historian,
not a romancer. Like most men of his race, he was more
interested in facts than in romance, and though he would
not hesitate to invent where there were gaps in his oral or
written sources, he made no attempt to cast a romantic
glamour over his work. He supplied admirable material
for romances, but not romance itself.

In 1155 this chronicle was translated into Anglo-Norman
verse by Wace, and his version into English verse by
Layamon in 1205. The great respect paid to Latin learning
during the Middle Ages and the consequent reverence
accorded to all people descended from the Romans, made
the chroniclers distort the origins of the British race so
drastically as to eliminate almost all historical truth.
Instead of portraying the Britons as a mere subject race of
Rome, they ascribed to them actual Roman origin from
Æneas through a descendant called Brutus.[1] This name,
which was given to the alleged founder of the British race
simply to account for the names Britain and Briton, which
could not be explained away, caused Wace and, after him,
Layamon to call their chronicles "The Brut." In keeping
with this claim of Roman origin, Guenivere is described as
the daughter of an old Roman family, which would not be
impossible, since Roman officers would no doubt be
regarded as the aristocracy of Britain in the days of Roman
rule. If ever there was a historical character as basis of
King Arthur, he too would probably be of Roman origin,
since the Britons would naturally prefer, in times of war,

[1] It is possible that the popularity of Arthurian romance was largely
due in the first place to this assumption of Roman origin. Not only
did Arthur thus become the descendant of a Trojan, and therefore
suitable as a popular hero, but the conflict between Britons and Saxons
was regarded as a conflict between Romans and Germanic heathens.

to give the supreme command to a member of the greatest military race in history; it has been suggested that the name Arthur may derive from Artorius, the name of a Roman clan.

These chronicles did not, however, form the chief basis of romance, partly because they presented a conception of Arthur not adapted to the changed French tastes of the twelfth century, and partly because the poets had available other sources which could be more easily adapted to these tastes. Geoffrey's conception of Arthur was typically Norman—a universal conqueror and crusader, as Charlemagne had been presented, and therefore unsuited to the romance of chivalry and knight-errantry which was more and more demanded from the middle of the twelfth century. The earliest French romancers, therefore, ignored the chronicles and drew from popular traditions. When, during the thirteenth century, long prose romances came to be composed, dealing with the whole or large portions of Arthur's life, instead of with the exploits of individual knights, the chronicles had to be used to supply material lacking in oral traditions and in the earlier poems. One early verse romance, the "Merlin" of Robert de Boron, of which only a fragment remains, was probably based upon the work of Geoffrey, who had given elaborate details about Merlin in his chronicle, but others, relating the adventures of Eric, Lancelot, Tristram, and Percival, who are not even named by Geoffrey, had to be based entirely on other sources. The prose romances were almost all composite works, each incorporating the adventures of several knights and giving a prominent place to Arthur's war against the Saxons; the authors, therefore, found the systematic accounts given by the chronicles a very useful supplement to the early verse romances.

Some of the details in romance differ drastically from the chronicler's statements; Bedivere, stated by Geoffrey to have been killed in the campaign against Rome, becomes in romance the last knight to remain with Arthur after Modred's defeat, and the birth of Arthur is made a

mystery by delaying Uther's marriage with Igerne so long
after his conception that he has to be born in secret, and
therefore experiences great difficulty in establishing his
claim to the throne. By means of these distortions—
apparently deliberate—the realistic accounts of the
chroniclers were suffused with a spirit of mystery and
romance. Layamon's chronicle contains details not recorded by Geoffrey; Arthur's marriage is described as a
love-match, his battle with Modred and his translation to
Avallon are expanded, and an attempted explanation of
the Round Table is offered.[1] He offers the rational explanation that Arthur's table was made round to prevent
quarrels over precedence amongst the knights, though no
table could be so shaped as to prevent all disputes, since
the places nearest to the king would be the most coveted.
The prose "Merlin" states that it was made by Uther at
Merlin's command, in imitation of the Table of the Last
Supper. Both of these explanations are simply inventions,
having no reference to any possible British or Celtic customs. But since Posidonius, writing in the first century
B.C., records that the Celts of Southern Gaul were accustomed to sit in a circle during feasts, the possible origin of
the Round Table, if it belongs to very early traditions,
might have been simply the custom of sitting round a camp
fire. Writers of the twelfth century presumably had heard
oral stories of a round table, and proceeded to offer their
own explanations. Whatever the origin of these further
details, unrecorded in Geoffrey, they were found useful
by romancers and incorporated into their work.

Although Welsh traditions may have formed the basis of
many incidents recorded by Geoffrey of Monmouth, they
probably exerted no influence at all upon the first romances. The earliest Welsh literature is too late and
makes too little mention of Arthur to have been the
stimulus of French romancers, and the oral traditions of

[1] These additions may be inventions of his own or the result of his
own researches into oral traditions. It has also been suggested that all
of them may have already existed in an earlier version of Wace's
chronicle, now lost.

Wales and Cornwall could hardly have become familiar to Frenchmen as early as the twelfth century. Oral traditions can be gleaned by a foreign race only after a period of close intimacy, and the long-continued hostility between the Welsh and Norman peoples prevented any such intimacy until long after the Conquest.[1] The traditions which circulated in Italy and the earliest French romances must both have originated from the only other possible source of British legends, Brittany. Hostility between Welshmen and Normans was still active as late as the twelfth century, but from the tenth century the Bretons had been vassals of Normandy, and supported William in his invasion of England. They must have been thoroughly familiar with the Norman language, and continual intercourse would allow Breton legends to penetrate into Normandy and from there into all Norman domains, including many parts of Italy. They would also be more accessible to French poets than Welsh or Cornish legends.

The Bretons not only escaped Roman rule and civilisation, which allowed them to retain their legends uninfluenced by that Latin spirit which dominated French literature, but had also remained independent of all foreign control until the tenth century, and so were able to foster their traditions untainted by any foreign influence. These legends would almost certainly have maintained that spirit of boundless imagination common to all Celtic races, and would therefore appeal by their novelty to French poets seeking new subjects for romance. Both the Charlemagne and the most famous classical legends would be far better known and of deeper significance, but too definitely crystallised to be easily adapted to new sentiments and ideals. The very formlessness of Celtic legend and its concentration upon individual characters instead of upon grandiose national themes must have contributed largely to the eventual supremacy of Arthurian

[1] It would be possible for men who, like Geoffrey of Monmouth, lived on the Welsh borders to collect oral traditions, but difficult for any traditions unrecorded by such men to become well known to Continental poets.

romance. It must not be concluded that French romancers drew inspiration from Breton legends only; the original stimulus would come from Brittany, and at a later date Welsh and Cornish legends would also be adopted as they became familiar to the Normans in England.

Many of these Breton legends would, no doubt, be mere anecdotes handed down orally, and suffering drastic changes from generation to generation. Whether any of them entered France in a definite literary form cannot be known, although it has been thought that some were introduced in the form of songs or poems. Towards the end of the twelfth century a French poetess, Marie de France, wrote a number of short poems, called "lays," purporting to be based on Breton themes. At this early date "Breton" may mean no more than Briton, and so refer to either Brittany or Wales. But since scholars have asserted that some of the names[1] mentioned in these lays are distorted forms of Breton words and could not have come from any other Celtic forms, it seems highly probable that some of her lays were based on Breton themes. Marie states that the Bretons themselves had made lays on the themes which she narrates,[2] that she had heard them recited,[3] and that men recited them to the accompaniment of harps and rotes.[4] In some of the Celtic races prose tales were told by professional story-tellers,[5] so it is possible that the lays referred to by Marie were lyrical verses chanted at intervals during a prose narrative, and embodying the most highly emotional episodes. There is no evidence that this custom was ever followed, and the only French romance which consists of a prose narrative interspersed with songs was probably an artistic innovation of its author uninfluenced by the practice of any minstrels.[6]

---

[1] Bisclavret, Laustic.
[2] In the lays of "Guigemar" and "Eliduc."
[3] In the Prologue to the Lays.   [4] In "Guigemar."
[5] Called in Wales "Mabinogi," and a famous collection of such tales called the "Mabinogion," of which there is a translation in the Everyman Library.
[6] "Aucassin et Nicolette." See Chapter VIII.

It is not, however, unsafe to assume from Marie's evidence that songs or poems relating Breton legends were chanted by minstrels; whether her statements refer to Breton songs chanted in Brittany and later in France, to Breton songs translated into French by French poets, or to French songs relating Breton themes chanted by Bretons who had learned French, it is impossible to ascertain. Marie's service was to transform what were probably crude compositions into artistic poems, adding to an already inherent glamour the poetic artistry which would make them attractive to a cultured audience. Her lays are narrative poems rather than songs, but some of them are essentially lyrical and could appropriately be set to music. The term "Breton Lay" does not always indicate Breton or even British origin. Marie de France seems to have been inspired by Breton songs, but the term itself was later used for various types of poems; poets apparently hoped to enhance the interest of their works by giving them a popular title, as they also did by incorporating King Arthur into all types of unrelated stories.

If those lays described by Marie as being chanted to the accompaniment of a harp or rote were genuine Breton songs, they may first have won fame through the charm of the music. Just as in modern times many people have been attracted by the melody of Maori and Hawaiian songs, though ignorant of the language, so Frenchmen may first have been attracted by the melody of Breton songs and then become interested in the themes. Arthurian stories may have been the most prominent themes, and, in addition, some of the French poets would be familiar with the chronicles of Geoffrey or of Wace. This double influence alone would be sufficient to make the Arthurian legend supreme, apart from any inherent superiority of interest in the stories themselves. Thomas, author of the earliest existing romance on Tristram, seems to have been deeply inspired by the melody of these lays, and embodied his appreciation in his description of the chanting of a lay by Queen Iseult.

E

"La reine chante doucemente,
La vois accorde à l'estrument;
Les mains sont belles, le lai bon,
Douce la vois, et bas le ton."

Although it is uncertain in what form and through what channels Breton legends entered France, there can be little doubt that Arthurian romance was chiefly inspired by the oral traditions of Brittany rather than by those of Wales and Cornwall. Whether Geoffrey and Wace drew their materials from British or Continental sources matters little; the earliest romancers not only made little use of the incidents they record, but relate the adventures of knights who are not even mentioned in the chronicles.[1] The works of Geoffrey, Wace, and Layamon were freely used only by later romancers, whose object was to relate the whole, or large portions, of Arthur's life. Similarly, also, Welsh, Cornish, and Irish legends came eventually to be well known, and were incorporated into French romance. This would partly account for the variations of the same legend in different romances, since they must often have offered variants of the themes already known from Breton sources. But if oral traditions had circulated in France for some generations before being adopted by the poets, they would gradually suffer changes, and two poets, in relating the same theme, might easily have widely different oral versions on which to base their work. If, moreover, these stories were circulated in prose form, with or without verse passages, the variations would be all the greater. To improvise during a verse recital is difficult, because all improvisations must be fitted to the rhyme and rhythm of the neighbouring passages; the minstrel would therefore memorise more thoroughly than he would a prose recital, in which improvisation would be relatively easy.

The development of Arthurian romance probably followed this course :—

(1) Breton legends told in prose or verse.

[1] Tristram, Lancelot, Percival.

(2) The composition of French poems relating the same legends.

(3) The composition of long verse romances based on materials which had become familiar through these short lays, and incorporating elements from various other sources. These include the romances of Thomas, Chrétien de Troyes, and Robert de Boron,[1] the most famous poets of Arthurian romance.

(4) The rise of romances which offered different versions of the same theme owing partly to the natural variations in oral tradition, partly to variant legends existing in different localities—Brittany, Wales, Cornwall, Ireland—and partly to the incorporation of extraneous elements to arouse interest in an audience which had possibly heard already one or more versions.

(5) The ascription of the term "Breton Lay" to romances on any subject, and the incorporation of King Arthur into completely unrelated stories to enhance their interest.

(6) The composition of long prose romances, relating the careers of several knights and, by freely using the chronicles of Geoffrey and Wace, offering a composite narrative of Arthur's career wholly or in part. This stage witnessed the culmination of a tendency which had existed from the beginning, to add more and more fantastic episodes until the basic conceptions of character and moral ideals were almost completely lost and the whole subject degraded.

(7) The permanent revival of the theme by great writers like Malory, Spenser, and Tennyson, each preserving the essence of the best medieval romances, but adapting the subjects to suit their own particular aims.

[1] See Chapters IV and V for these poets.

Breton Lays and the Lays of Marie de France

"Breton Lay" seems to have been a well-known and popular term from the earliest period of romance. Thomas portrays Tristram as an accomplished harpist charming King Mark and all his Court by chanting the lays of Brittany. It is therefore evident that Frenchmen were familiar with the term before Marie de France composed her poems. But it so quickly became a conventional term applied by poets to every type of poem in order to attract attention that it ceased to have any significance at all. Even in the romance of Thomas, one of the earliest of all Arthurian romances, the story of Pyramus and Thisbe is the theme of one of Tristram's lays. This makes it clear that the term "Breton Lay" was no longer regarded as having any relationship with Breton or even Celtic themes generally. Before long the term was applied so indiscriminately as to become entirely meaningless; the French romances of King Horn and Havelok the Dane[1] are both called Breton lays, though relating purely English traditions and direct narrative poems, not lyrical songs.

It is probable that the prevailing theme of the original Breton lays was love, that the demand by French ladies for tales of love would give them an enduring popularity, and that eventually "Breton Lay" became a conventional term for any lyrical love poem. This would account for the ascription of the term to a song which hymned the tragic love of Pyramus and Thisbe. The later custom of calling any type of poem a Breton lay would be stimulated by the desire of poets to call attention to their works, since well-known titles have proved a good advertisement in all periods and countries. The English romance of Sir Orfeo[2] opens with a general account of Breton lays, which shows that, although a multitude of types had come to be included within their scope, the most prominent theme was love.

[1] See Chapter VII for these romances.
[2] See Chapter VIII for this romance.

"The lays that are of harping
Are found of frely thing.[1]
Some are of weal, and some of woe,
And some of joy and mirth also;
Some of treachery, and some of guile,
And some of haps that fall by while;[2]
Some of bourdes[3] and some of ribaldry,
And some there are of faerie.
Of all things that men may see,
Most of love forsooth they be,
In Brytayn these lays are written."

The stress upon Breton (or British) origin, harping, and the supremacy of love may be owing to the prevalent type of the original Breton lays, but may even more be due to the influence of the romance of Thomas, which had caused Tristram to become renowned for his skill in harping and established the name "Breton Lay" as the conventional term for any song of love.

Although the credit of popularising Breton lays is apparently due to Thomas, Marie de France was the first poet to give this type of work a literary form. The absence of reliable written records makes it impossible to determine how far her evidence can be trusted, but it is probable that her lays more closely approach the form in which oral traditions were circulated in Brittany than the Arthurian romances which were being composed at the same time. Although they clearly reflect French sentiment of the twelfth century, they are more deeply imbued than are the romances with the romantic glamour which suffuses all known Celtic legends. Their brevity and simplicity of diction also afford an admirable opportunity to those readers who wish to acquire a direct knowledge of some French romance but are unfamiliar with the languages of medieval France.

In spite of the extensive researches and ingenious suggestions of many scholars, her identity still remains uncertain. Although the term "de France" could strictly be used only by a personage of royal blood, it is too vague to offer any definite knowledge. There is a growing body of

---

[1] "pleasant things."   [2] "at times."   [3] "jests."

opinion that the king to whom her lays were dedicated was Henry II of England (1154–1189), and, from her knowledge of English and her reference to France in one passage as "les terres de là," it has been suggested that they were written in England. This would not, however, necessarily imply English nationality,[1] or even permanent residence in England; visits of French people to relatives in England must have been very common at this period. Another interesting suggestion, though based on no more reliable influence than the above-mentioned hypothesis, is that she was the Countess Marie de Champagne. This lady was of royal blood, stepdaughter to King Henry, and the most famous patroness of romance in all France. She had sufficient ability, knowledge, and literary taste to write poems of this kind, and may even have done so, but none of these facts offers any evidence that she composed these particular lays.

Though based on legends drawn from various sources, two being certainly, and others possibly, of Breton origin, they all reflect clearly and vividly the courtly sentiment which animated French aristocratic society of the twelfth century. The ideals of knightly conduct chiefly stressed are courtesy and loyalty in love. The reader is not, however, overwhelmed with the formal stateliness of aristocratic life, as he often is in reading the romances; elaborate description and ornament are avoided, the simple charm of old folk-tales is preserved far more closely than in the romances, and the stress is almost entirely upon character and the spirit of chivalry and of love. Marie was a skilful narrator who knew the value of suspense in telling tales of idealistic love—not the conventional courtly love so prevalent both in life and romance during this period, but passionate love which triumphs over all barriers of duty and of social law, love in which the woman makes the sacrifice, and therefore best portrayed by a woman. The emphasis laid upon the sacrifices which women must make

[1] *I.e.* membership of the Royal Family of England, which was, of course, French in origin.

in the name of love imbues them with a tragic or rather a pathetic spirit, though none of her stories has a tragic end. Love is always triumphant, not merely because regarded as supreme in itself, but because considered as the most ennobling of all influences upon character; the triumphs become therefore triumphs of character, harassed but not dismayed by hardship and suffering. Denis Pyramus, writing early in the thirteenth century, testified to the great popularity of these lays among both men and women. They offered a peculiar appeal to women, because romance too often represented the lover as undergoing all the hardships and making all the sacrifices. Ladies who could look forward to nothing more than the deadly routine of castle life desired to hear of heroines who did something more than sit quietly at home waiting to be wooed by lovers who first had eliminated all the hazards. Not that every romance portrayed love thus—Iseult alone is a standing refutation—but Marie's lays reversed the position; they made women the active agents, willing to accept any hardships in the name of love.

Although the lays were ostensibly based on Breton lays, which also presumably inspired the first Arthurian romances, none of them deals with specifically Arthurian stories. King Arthur's name is mentioned casually, but no more, Guenivere appears but once, and there represented as a type of "Potiphar's wife,"[1] and one lay relates an episode in the story of Tristram and Iseult.[2]

They became so famous that, in the thirteenth century, a translation was made into Norwegian by order of King Haakon IV, and called "Strengleikar." English translations exist of two—"Lai le Freine" of the fourteenth and "Launfal" of the fifteenth century—and there also remain other English poems, called Breton lays, and similar in form and spirit to those of Marie, but of which no French originals have been discovered.[3]

In spite of changed ideals, Marie's lays still retain their

---

[1] In "Lanval." [2] "Chièvrefeuil."
[3] "Emare," "Sir Orfeo," "The Earl of Toulouse."

interest, because they so deeply reflect the romantic charm
of medieval popular traditions, a charm which, though
inherent in the legends on which most medieval romance
was based, is rarely reflected in the romances themselves.
They present simple, direct stories of passion, and efface
the boundary between real life and fairyland. There is no
ulterior motive such as duty to King or Faith, no seeking
of adventures for adventure's sake, but simply an idealisa-
tion of honour and of love set in a dream world of faerie
and romance.

CHAPTER IV

GENERAL SURVEY OF ARTHURIAN ROMANCE

THE FRENCH ARTHURIAN ROMANCES, though offered and accepted as genuine historical accounts of Arthur and his knights, were designed to entertain rather than to instruct. In no period and to no people have accounts of unfamiliar customs of alien races been so interesting as those which reflect national sentiments and ideals. An audience loves to hear of strange events in far-off lands and distant times, but expects to have the narrative coloured with its own ideals and sentiments; the poet too will usually be unable to avoid endowing the persons of his story with the characteristics peculiar to his own nation. French poets, therefore, sometimes deliberately, sometimes unconsciously, adapted old Celtic legends to the tastes of twelfth-century Frenchmen, distorting and adding to their basic material without hesitation when opportunities offered. Although possibly very little may be attributable to the poets' own invention, it is impossible to ascertain, in any romance, how much is based on Arthurian or even British tradition and how much on other sources—classical literature and general European folk-lore—which would make the story more attractive.

The chronicles concentrate upon the deeds and character of Arthur, the earliest romances upon individual knights, most of whom are not even mentioned in the chronicles, and therefore, presumably, formed no part of original Arthurian tradition. Some of them, like Tristram, were certainly, others, like Lancelot, were possibly heroes of Celtic legends, but whether any or all of them had already been linked up with Arthur in oral tradition before the period of romance still remains unknown. In Geoffrey's chronicle, and possibly in early popular tradition, Gawain

is represented as Arthur's foremost follower; in the earliest
romances also he ranks supreme above all other knights,
although the hero of no single romance by any of the well-
known romancers.[1] He was, however, quickly ousted from
this place by Lancelot, and became steadily degraded in
French, though not in English romance, until it was
possible for Malory and Tennyson, who based their work
almost entirely upon French sources, to make him the
symbol of fickle and licentious love. This drastic change in
attitude serves to show how completely the earliest romancers ignored the chronicles and, as will be shown, how
greatly traditions were distorted to suit contemporary
sentiment.

In all periods the character of literature designed for
entertainment is determined by its patrons. In modern
times the extension of education to all classes has produced
a large reading public willing not only to read, but to buy
books; the invention of printing made it possible to sell
books at a low price, and therefore in large numbers; the
result has been that there now exists such a wide variety of
tastes that any author of merit may follow his own inclina-
tions and yet find sufficient readers to support him. Neither
of these advantages existed in the Middle Ages, and so the
character of romance was determined by the Court—the
courts of kings, barons, or of powerful ecclesiastics—
because the authors had to depend upon the patronage of
men and women who were both able and willing to maintain them. The position may be well exemplified from the
conditions which obtained in England. Before the Norman
Conquest many highly artistic poems were composed,
presumably encouraged by the patronage of Anglo-Saxon
kings or powerful ecclesiastics. After the Conquest French
became the official language, and French literature was
demanded by the higher classes, even those of Anglo-
Saxon stock. In the fourteenth and fifteenth centuries
good English romances were written under the patronage

[1] He is the hero of later romances of uncertain date and authorship.
See the Gawain section of Chapter V.

of knightly families, but until then English had remained the language of the lower classes, and the romances written in English were nearly all of little merit. Furthermore, although the tastes of the higher and lower classes were very different, the latter had to rest content with hashed-up versions of romances originally written for the high-born ladies of France. Creative work was impossible to authors who had no patrons to support them; such authors could do no more than make a hasty translation of a French romance, omit what they thought would not be understood or appreciated, and hope to earn a living by reciting their work in public places.[1]

The romancer, therefore, had to frame his work to suit the taste of his patrons. The chansons de gestes were mostly composed in Northern France, and largely stimulated by the patronage of warrior barons who had little culture or refinement and who, no doubt, took keen delight in exciting narratives of bloody fights and dare-devil deeds. Arthurian romance received its greatest stimulus from the Court of Troyes in Champagne at a time when culture and refinement were fast increasing and under conditions which obtained at first in very few other places. The First Crusade had not only opened up new sources of learning in the East, which stimulated a temporary renascence in scholarship, but had also introduced, largely as a result of contact with Byzantium, a desire for luxury and refinement. Men, and particularly women, came to realise that mere brute strength was not man's greatest attribute, and that gentleness and courtesy, apart from any fundamental moral value which they might possess, were at least essential to harmonious social life.

Even Geoffrey of Monmouth, though stressing so heavily the Norman ideal of warfare and conquest, represents Arthur as introducing, after the Saxons had been defeated, such politeness and refinement that men were attracted from all parts of Europe to his Court, and strove to reproduce them in their own homes. But the

[1] See Chapter IX for a detailed analysis of this contrast.

chief reason for the great difference in spirit between the chansons de gestes and Arthurian romance was the sudden rise to prominence and power of women, partly as a result of the First Crusade and partly because of increased education. The prolonged absence of many great feudal lords—first fighting and then ruling in Palestine—made it necessary for their wives to assume control, sometimes for long periods, and for dependants to seek their favour and patronage. The new impetus to learning also encouraged women to seek a liberal education and, when they had been educated, to demand literature suited to their tastes. Under normal circumstances women both had more leisure and lived more confined lives than did men. They were therefore able to extend their education further, and frequently became far more learned than was considered necessary for any man who was not destined for the Church; they also required more entertainment, and therefore more literature. Hitherto literature had been designed for men; during the twelfth century romancers were obliged to adapt their work to suit the tastes of women, and from then until the present day writers of fiction have had to suit a female rather than a male audience.

Although it must not be assumed that men ceased to be patrons of literature—they continued to patronise some types for centuries—women became the chief patrons of literature which was primarily designed to entertain. It was this transference of patronage which stimulated poets to incorporate those elements of refinement which had just begun to enter France, and to stress in their heroes those features of gentleness and courtesy which would appeal to a female audience.

This transference of patronage and introduction of refinement would not operate immediately in every Court in France, nor did romance of chivalry immediately supersede all other types. Chansons de gestes and romance of chivalry existed side by side throughout the period of romance. But great impetus was given to this newer type, because one of the ablest of French medieval poets wrote at the beginning of this period and under the patronage of the most refined Court and perhaps the most intellectual lady in France. The Court was that of Troyes, the lady Marie, Countess of Champagne, and the poet Chrétien de Troyes. In 1152 Aliénor of Guyenne, the repudiated wife of Louis VII of France, married Henry Plantagenet, later Henry II of England. To his possessions of Anjou, Touraine, Maine, and Normandy she brought Poitou and Guyenne, thus knitting together in a firm bond the North and South of France. In the South of France a courtly literature had already begun, and had by this time reached its greatest heights. The refined and sentimental love-lyrics of the troubadours,[1] composed for the ladies of Provence, fired the imagination of ladies in Northern French Courts, who insisted that the poets under their patronage should incorporate the same spirit of love, courtesy, and devotion to women into their romances. The Countess Marie was a daughter of Aliénor, and thoroughly familiar with the literature of Southern France; she therefore naturally became the most enthusiastic patroness of chivalrous romance. Under her guidance Chrétien, though probably not the first author of Arthurian and certainly not the first of chivalrous romance,[2] established courtly love and chivalry as the enduring themes, and by choosing Arthurian traditions as his subject, made them the most popular topics of succeeding poets. It is impossible to give any dogmatic reason why he chose the comparatively unfamiliar British rather than the well-known Charlemagne or classical legends, but possibly the greater scope permitted by their unfamiliarity and lack of definite form roused his ambition, and the atmosphere of mystery and sentimentalism which must have existed in

[1] See Chapter XIII for their influence upon the love-element in romance.
[2] The fragmentary romance of "Tristan" by Thomas—see Chapter V—was probably written earlier, and the earliest romances on classical themes—see Chapter VI—were certainly earlier than any of his.

the Celtic oral traditions would make them seem eminently adaptable to feminine tastes.

The French race, deeply imbued with the Latin spirit, had become an intellectual race, and, although devoid of deep passion, was enthusiastic, somewhat sensual, and analytical rather than imaginative. The chansons de gestes, apart from their other disadvantages as entertainment for a female audience, retained too much of the old and alien Germanic spirit and depended too much on action to excite a fervent interest under the changed conditions of the twelfth century. The Arthurian stories would already in their oral forms depend for their interest upon sentiment, and could easily be framed to give full play to that analysis of character and emotions which is peculiarly attractive to the French mind, and particularly to an analysis of love sentiment which would appeal irresistibly to the new patrons of romance. Analysis of character and of sentiments can only arise from individualistic authors, never from those who seek only to express national ideals. It will therefore play little or no part in heroic literature, and requires for its cultivation a well-educated audience. It must for this reason be a late development in any country, but will arise much earlier in a nation like the French, whose character is adapted to it from historical causes, than in a nation like the English, whose predominating spirit is Germanic rather than Latin.

Courtly and chivalrous romance originated, therefore, from many causes—the introduction of luxury and refinement, the patronage of women, the rise of frequent intercourse between the North and South of France, and the intellectual character of the French nation. In searching for material to suit the tastes of their new patrons, romancers not only adopted Arthurian and general Celtic legends, but also incorporated elements from widely varied sources—Classical and Biblical sorties, European folk-lore and popular legends, and Eastern legends and literature. Although courage and skill in arms still necessarily commanded great respect, mere physical strength was no longer regarded as supreme, but in its place courtesy, gentleness, and service of others before self. The defence, not of king or Faith, but of the weak and helpless, became the supreme duty of knighthood, and the women of romance were no longer mere wives and mothers, but mistresses to be adored and served. Not that it implies disparagement of women to portray them only as wives, and particularly as mothers of heroes, but restriction to this aspect usually means that they play only a subordinate part; in all the romances of chivalry they are frequently supreme, the adventures undertaken and the hardships suffered by knights being usually in their service alone. A great and even exaggerated respect is paid to them, and they become not merely the inspirers, but the very pivot of men's lives and deeds. The knights of the chansons de gestes may have reflected life more truly, but those of Arthurian romance reflect what women wished men to be, and literature, if it is to please, must reflect the ideals of the readers, not the actual.[1]

Chrétien de Troyes, the most famous author of Arthurian romance, began his literary career between 1160 and 1170 with a translation of Ovid's "Art of Love" and "Metamorphoses." He then wrote a romance on Tristram, now lost, and four other Arthurian romances, "Erec," "Lancelot," "Yvain," and "Perceval," the last being still uncompleted when he died about the year 1180. All except the last are simply tales of love, in which pseudo-Arthurian stories are used, and to which fantastic adventures are added to enhance the love theme. Whether Erec, Lancelot, or Perceval were attached to Arthurian legend in popular traditions before he wrote, or whether he attached them himself from unrelated sources is still unknown; Yvain, brother of Gawain, is mentioned in Geoffrey's chronicle. "Erec" and "Yvain" present examples of conjugal love disturbed by human weakness or

[1] This problem has remained to authors throughout the ages. Many a book—*e.g.* "Tom Jones"—has portrayed men who are convincingly realistic to male readers, but considered coarse and *unnatural* by many women.

misunderstanding.[1] "Lancelot" presents the courtly love theory of the troubadours,[2] the love of a knight for a married woman, to whom he vows unswerving loyalty, and "Perceval," which has only a slight love element, narrates the career of a young man brought up by a widowed mother far from Court, but ultimately attaining the greatest heights of chivalry—this theme of sudden rise from obscurity to fame was very popular, even Arthur and Tristram being endowed with the same feature in later romances, and similarly Roland in the later Charlemagne romances. Into "Perceval" was incorporated a version of the Grail Quest,[3] which later became the most prominent theme of Arthurian romance.

The influence of female patronage is clearly evidenced by Chrétien's statement that he received from the Countess Marie the material for his "Lancelot," the most courtly of all his romances. It also serves to show that this conventional courtly love between a bachelor and a married woman was the most absorbing of all topics, at least to Marie, if not to most high-born ladies of the twelfth century. The absence of this type of love from his other poems, and the portrayal of conjugal love in two of them, seem to show that it was not so congenial to the poet as to his patroness.

The chief feature of his work is a formal, conventional, and systematic analysis of love; every emotion and sentiment of the lovers of both sexes is fully analysed,[4] and the courtly spirit is enhanced by detailed descriptions of armour and dresses, of tournaments and adventures, and of the scenes where the main incidents occur. By these four poems Chrétien became the founder of modern romantic

---

[1] The story of the first is given in Tennyson's "Eric and Enid," of the second in the Middle English romance "Ywain and Gawain."
[2] See Chapter XIII for a full discussion of this.
[3] See Chapter V.
[4] In "Cliges" both the hero and the heroine fully describe their emotions in passages extending to several hundred lines. This romance, though dealing with King Arthur's Court, has not been included in the list of Chrétien's Arthurian romances, because the hero is obviously unrelated to the original Arthurian tradition.

fiction, especially of romantic love-fiction. The main features of the structure and spirit of his work are still preserved in most European and many English love stories.

The great achievement of Chrétien de Troyes was to establish securely the romance of chivalry and love; that of Robert de Boron, who wrote about the same time, was to provide the chief stimulus for romances on the Holy Grail, which later became the most absorbing topic of Arthurian romance. Unfortunately very little of his work remains. In the Huth MS. is a statement that he made his work in three parts—the first ending at the beginning of the Grail Quest, the second at the finding of the Grail, the third at the death of Lancelot. This appears to indicate that Boron formed a far more ambitious design than Chrétien—instead of a series of poems dealing with the adventures of isolated knights, a cycle of poems relating the whole career of Arthur and of his most prominent followers. His first romance, "Joseph d'Arimathie," ends at the beginning of the Grail Quest, and his third, "Perceval," now lost, presumably ended with the finding of the Grail, since Perceval had already been made the hero of this Quest by Chrétien. But of no romance ending at the death of Lancelot has any trace been found. One other poem of his, "Merlin," still remains, but both this and "Joseph" have come down only in a fragmentary condition. This romance, like all those on Merlin, relates the early history of Arthur's career. Since it refers to the romance of "Joseph," already written, and states his intention of writing "Perceval" his design of writing a composite cycle seems to be even more clearly established; "Joseph" relates the early history of the Grail before the days of Arthur, "Merlin" relates the early career of Arthur, and "Perceval" presumably the quest for the Grail, which he would consider the most important event in Arthur's reign.

Although probably not the first, Chrétien and Boron are the most important authors of Arthurian romance; they prescribed what were to be the chief topics, they estab-

F

lished the form and spirit of Arthurian stories, and so paved the way for innumerable others. They made the Arthurian legend the most popular theme of romance and established Lancelot, Tristram, and Perceval as permanent symbols of courtesy and chivalry. Not only was this theme adopted by poets of nearly every country in Western Europe, but it has exercised a profound influence upon modern writers. Nearly every great English poet has been inspired by it, though not all of them have made it the subject of a poem. The absolute predominance of Arthurian legend as the great symbolic theme of chivalry inspired Malory to adopt it in his magnificent attempt to instil the principles of true chivalry into the decadent nobility of his time,[1] and the poems of Spenser and many nineteenth-century poets, the allusions to it by others like Milton who never used it as a theme, and the operas of Wagner[2] all serve to show how fascinating the subject has been throughout the ages. Long before the close of the Middle Ages Arthur was ranked as one of the nine Worthies, though the only one of modern times who is not certainly a historic character;[3] the romancers had made him such a vivid personality that he became as real as Charlemagne or Alexander, and more famous than either. Yet in the early romances he plays little active part; his knights undertake the adventures, while he becomes a kind of President. He decides which knight shall undertake each quest, receives the defeated captives, and gives his blessing to the hero and heroine in such romances as culminate in marriage. He is the universal protector, but in keeping with his position as a great king, he performs his services through the agency of vassals. There were two distinct circumstances which would tend to prevent him being the active hero of any early romance: vassals and knights would be more attractive heroes to the average audience than would kings, whose lofty station made them more

[1] In the "Morte d'Arthur."
[2] "Tristan und Isolde" and "Parzifal."
[3] The others were Hector, Alexander, J. Caesar; Joshua, David, Judas Maccabaeus; Charlemagne, and Godfrey of Bouillon.

remote from human interests, and whose activities in romance would relegate all other heroes to a subordinate position; the prevalent demand for tales of love would also disqualify a king already married, since a liaison with a lady of inferior rank could only degrade him, while a liaison with a queen would actually exalt a knight of meaner birth. But in the later prose romances these disadvantages no longer obtained; kings had become of greater interest, and the early craze for courtly love had been modified, so that Arthur, lacking the blemishes of a Lancelot or a Tristram, came to represent all the qualities of chivalry combined, and as such was chosen by Spenser as hero of the "Faerie Queene." In that poem, as in the romances, the individual knights symbolise individual virtues; Arthur combines them all and represents perfection.

Every period of true romance is necessarily followed by one of sham romance. Subjects or types of literature inspired by national or class sentiments must change in spirit as the sentiments change, or they will decay. If continually revived by able writers who can adapt them to suit any conditions and any ideals, they may endure indefinitely. If not they will become more and more superficial, less and less significant, until the patrons lose all interest and seek for entertainment in other fields of literature. The chansons de geste had first been inspired by fervent ideals, of religious and national unity, or of feudal independence. When those ideals decayed, imitations followed, similar in form, but lacking their inspiring force; they therefore ceased to attract the knightly classes for which they had first been composed. So, too, Arthurian romance began by reflecting fervent ideals, not of national unity, but of chivalry and courtesy. The Arthurian knights, symbolising the most ideal virtues of knighthood, became guiding stars to a whole nation, and must have been a great stimulus to true chivalry in actual life. The topics of Arthurian romance also became hackneyed, as author after author made the same familiar knight the hero of his work; changes in treatment therefore became necessary, not only to suit changes in sentiment, but also to avoid monotony. The later romancers were faced with the problem that confronts a modern novelist from whom an admiring public demands sequels to a favourite story. He has already given a completed work and cannot possibly make any sequel equally significant. The medieval audience demanded the heroes with whom they were familiar, and the romancer had to relate their exploits with sufficient novelty to attract interest. With every distortion and addition the ideals originally stressed became more faint and emphasis upon mere fantasy more marked. When all available traditions had been exhausted, the romancer had to rely on his own invention or seek material in totally unrelated sources. Thus pure romance of chivalry was succeeded by sham romance of adventure, which brought the whole Arthurian legend into disrepute until it was revived again by Malory and Spenser.

Even the earliest romances had never been so fervently inspired by ideals as the older heroic poetry. The epic poet concentrates upon his hero and frames his narrative to make him symbolical of national sentiment; the author of romance is more concerned with the entertainment of his audience. The primary object of the romancer was to tell a story, and Chrétien himself had been content to relate adventures for adventure's sake. The best romances had as central theme some ideal or problem of chivalry and knightly conduct, but very few present truly inspiring conceptions of character. The two great German poems, "Tristan und Isolde" and "Parzifal"[1] present heroes who are deeply significant of human character—its weakness and its strength—but French romance never reached these heights. The conception of character or conduct which the authors aimed at is nearly always clear, but they rarely troubled to select just such incidents as would present it most vividly. From every available source they extracted adventurous incidents, episodes and objects of magic and

[1] See Chapter V for these romances.

of mystery, no matter how incongruous they might be to the theme in hand—enchanted gardens and fountains, fairies, giants, dwarfs, magic rings and jewels; and it is these features which most please the modern reader and which no doubt were most prominent to a medieval audience. From the beginning the world of Arthurian romance was an unreal world, of magic and witchcraft, and of endless exciting adventures, with a maiden to be wooed at the conclusion. But in the early romances this atmosphere of adventure and of mystery does not disguise the essential spirit of courtesy, chivalry, and faithful love. Though basing their work on Celtic oral traditions, the romancers were not primarily concerned with reflecting the spirit of Celtic legend; they professed to relate British history, but in reality they merely used these legends as the basis of stories meant to please a French audience, and so expressing French ideals and sentiment, not Celtic. Most of the material used would be of Celtic origin, but their habit of drawing upon all available sources makes it difficult to separate the Celtic from the non-Celtic elements.[1]

In the thirteenth century, when ability to read had become fairly general in the knightly classes, at least amongst women, prose versions were made of all the Arthurian stories. The earliest seems to have been the "Lancelot" of about 1210, but others quickly followed. Most of these romances form part of two great cycles, each of which aimed at presenting a complete account of Arthur's career along with the most important adventures of his chief knights. The first and best, called the Vulgate or Walter Map cycle, makes the Quest of the Holy Grail the central theme, and round it weaves the whole Arthurian legend. It consists of five parts: (1) The History of the Holy Grail, (2) The History of Merlin, (3) The Book of Lancelot, (4) The Quest of the Grail, (5) The Death of

---

[1] Any attempt at a full discussion of this formidable subject—the influence of Celtic folk-lore and mythology upon Arthurian romance —would be out of place in a general survey like this. Readers are referred to the works of J. D. Bruce, A. Nutt, and J. Rhys. See Bibliography.

Arthur. By making all the well-known knights partici-
pators in the quest of the Grail, the cycle offers a reasonably complete story of the legend as far as it had been used
by earlier French poets. The second cycle, called the
Pseudo-Robert-de-Boron cycle, is merely a derivative of
the first, and of little importance. The names originated
from the belief that Walter Map and Robert de Boron
respectively had been chiefly responsible for their compilation. Although Walter Map may have composed part
of the first cycle, it is now known that Robert de Boron had
nothing to do with either beyond being, like Chrétien de
Troyes, one of the originators of Arthurian romance.

It was these prose romances that chiefly distorted the
spirit of Arthurian romance; composition in prose proved
so much easier than in verse, and the desire for literature
increased so rapidly that the authors rambled on and on,
adding adventure after adventure, until all unity and all
traces of a basic ideal or conception utterly vanished. The
climax was reached in the immense romance of "Pala-
mède," which claimed to relate the history of the generation preceding Arthur's reign. The Charlemagne legend
had come to the same inglorious end, with narratives of
fictitious ancestors. When this stage is reached, when
romancers despair of arousing interest by narrating the
deeds of men whose names have become household words
and have to invent relations and ancestors to throw to the
lions ever hungry for fresh prey, then the spirit of true
romance is dead. As far as France is concerned, Arthurian
romance did die, never to revive; but it was French, not
English romance that inspired Malory and Spenser, and
through them our nineteenth-century poets. It was left to
French poets to establish the glory of these British legends,
but the credit of immortalising them is due to English
writers and, chief of all, our poets.

CHAPTER V

THE CHIEF CHARACTERS AND TOPICS OF ARTHURIAN ROMANCE

IT HAS BEEN STATED THAT THE CHRONI-
clers gave a composite account of Arthur's career, and
that the romancers drew most of their material from
other sources, even portraying as heroes men who are
not mentioned in the chronicles. No composite romance
on the whole Arthurian Legend has yet been found, nor is
there any reason to believe that one was ever attempted.
Chrétien de Troyes wrote a number of poems, each of
which relates the deeds of some one knight, but each
entirely independent of the others. Robert de Boron
apparently aimed at writing a cycle of poems which
should relate the whole Arthurian story as then known,
and possibly he completed this task; the cycles of prose
romances were obviously designed to give a composite
account, but, being based on the early verse romances,
could only do so by recounting the exploits of all the well-
known characters, each in turn. Thus from the beginning
Arthurian romance consisted of a galaxy of isolated personages, each the hero of a series of adventures, having
little or no connection with the others. The only episode
which made it possible to link these personages together
was the quest of the Holy Grail. This in the early verse
romances was, like all other quests, the quest of but one
knight, Percival; in the prose cycles all the well-known
knights take part, and so some unity was achieved.
Merlin's position as principal adviser to the king inevitably
made romances dealing with his life narratives of Arthur's
early career, and the disaster wrought by Lancelot's unlawful love of the queen tended to make romances dealing
with that love accounts of Arthur's later career and death.[1]

[1] The prose "Merlin" ends with the birth of Lancelot.

The combination of a prose "Merlin" and a prose "Lancelot" yields an almost complete account of Arthur's life from birth to death, while the prose romances of the Holy Grail weld the principal knights of his Court together into one unified company animated by one common aim.

The principal personages of Arthurian romance are Merlin, Gawain, Modred, Percival, Galahad, Lancelot and Guenivere, Tristram and Iseult, and since they were isolated in romance, it will be most profitable to isolate them in discussion. Percival and Galahad will be discussed in the last section of this chapter, which deals with the Grail Quest, the others will be discussed in turn in the sections bearing their names. Whether any or all of these prominent figures were inherent parts of Arthurian legend in oral tradition is uncertain, since the written records of the Celtic races are too late to be of any use as evidence, and those of French and Anglo-Norman writers too untrustworthy. The use of Gawain's name along with Arthur's as a baptismal name in Lombardy makes it possible that Gawain at least formed a genuine part of the legend. Even Geoffrey's chronicle makes mention of only four, Merlin, Gawain, Modred, and Guenivere; it is therefore probable that the others were attached by the romancers themselves, although all may belong to early Celtic, though not necessarily Arthurian legends.

MERLIN

Merlin differs from the other prominent figures of Arthurian romance in that he was not employed to symbolise some ideal of courtly sentiment; his prominence was due to his position as adviser and chief wizard of the king. Geoffrey portrays him as the chief agent in Arthur's birth, arranging the plot whereby Uther Pendragon, king of the Britons, was enabled to beget Arthur upon Igerne, the wife of one of his vassals. It still remains uncertain whether he represents some historical character, although eight Welsh poems attributed to a bard called Myrrdin have come down to us. But since all of them were probably written later than Geoffrey's chronicle, it is just as likely that Myrrdin is an invention coined from Geoffrey's Merlin as that Merlin represents a genuine historical bard. There still also exists a "Vita Merlini," probably written by Geoffrey also, which links Merlin not only to Arthur, but also to Taliesin, the most famous of all Welsh bards. That there was a Welsh tradition of a bard bearing this name is certain, but whether a historical character or even independent of Geoffrey's Merlin cannot be ascertained.

The first romance was the verse "Merlin" of Robert de Boron, written late in the twelfth century. Of this poem only a fragment remains, but since a prose version of it was made soon afterwards and two continuations were composed a little later, Boron's conception of the story has been faithfully preserved. He altered Geoffrey's account by representing Arthur's birth as a mystery. In Geoffrey's chronicle Igerne's husband dies immediately after her adultery with Uther, which was very convenient for all parties; Uther is enabled to marry Igerne immediately, Igerne is saved from disgrace, and Arthur, bearing no stain of illegitimacy, is able to inherit his father's kingdom without dispute. But, however satisfactory this may be in real life, it does not yield good romance. Boron, by permitting the husband to live for two months longer, makes Arthur's birth as romantic as his death. The marriage is delayed two months, Arthur has to be born in secret to avoid scandal, is later viewed by the barons as a bastard, and wins his throne only after prolonged disputes and with the aid of Merlin. This alteration enabled romancers, and even more so Malory and Spenser, to cast a deeply romantic glamour over the whole of Arthur's career, arising mysteriously, and mysteriously departing—so well expressed by Tennyson:

"From the great deep to the great deep he goes."

It also made Merlin the most important character of the legend, because he not only was the cause of Arthur's con-

ception, but had to provide for his secret birth and training, win his kingdom for him and help him to defeat the
Saxon invaders.

Merlin is, therefore, the magician, or wizard, of Arthurian
romance, and, as a natural corollary, is represented as of
supernatural origin. Nennius relates that the advisers of
King Vortigern prophesied that he would be unable to
build his citadel unless he first sprinkled upon the ground
the blood of a child who had no father, and that a boy
called Ambrose was found who fitted this condition, but
was so well versed in magic that his life was spared.
Geoffrey relates the same story, but calls the boy Merlin,
and presents him as the son of a virgin and a devil. This
belief in the power of devils to beget children upon mortal
women was not only very popular in the Middle Ages,
but was often turned to practical use. The term usually
applied to such a supernatural father was "incubus," and
unmarried girls frequently evaded punishment by plead-
ing that their illegitimate children had been fathered by
an incubus. Superstition is a double-edged weapon, for
people who were gullible enough to believe that this was
possible, but shrewd enough to suspect each individual
alleged case, could not reasonably refuse to discredit these
excuses. This same plea was also useful in religious
houses, made sometimes by the authorities, who naturally
wished to avoid public scandal, and sometimes by the
nuns themselves, who knew that the penalty of illicit love
was usually death. To Geoffrey's conception Boron added
the popular superstition about Antichrist; just as Christ
was represented as the Son of God and a virgin, and therefore omniscient of good, so in the Middle Ages men
believed that the Antichrist who was to come would be
the son of Satan and a virgin, and therefore omniscient
of evil. This conception was adopted by later romancers
also, and is clearly reflected in the opening passage of the
English prose "Merlin," which describes how the devils
gathered together after Christ stormed Hell and discussed
how they might again subjugate mankind. They decide

to create a man after their own nature by means of a devil and a human virgin. The result is Merlin.

Since it would have been unseemly to represent Arthur's chief adviser as a fiend, Geoffrey invented or introduced a priest named Blase, who shields the mother from death and later becomes Merlin's tutor. Thus was the design of the devils defeated, and Merlin, instead of being a tor-mentor of men, becomes their friend and guide, possessing all the knowledge and cunning of Satan without his evil nature. Blase was also made useful in still another way; he is said to have received instructions from Merlin to record his deeds in writing, and this apocryphal book is represented as a proof of Merlin's authenticity. The author of the prose "Merlin" boldly states that the book of Blase is the source "whereby we now have our know-ledge."

The supernatural powers attributed to him included not only the ability to perform magic feats which made Saxon opposition to Arthur as futile as criminals' attempts to baffle Sherlock Holmes, or even as Satan's war in Heaven, but also ability to predict the future. This tradition or invention gave Geoffrey a magnificent chance to pretend that he had found a British book of Merlin's prophecies which he felt obliged to incorporate into his history; the prophecies naturally extend no further than Geoffrey's own time, and are therefore reasonably accurate. These prophecies were introduced into romance, and also inspired later writers to compose books of prophecies which they ascribed to Merlin.

Merlin's fame as a wizard of supernatural origin became so widespread that authors of romances unrelated to the Arthurian legend attempted to enhance their stories by portraying men of similar origin and presenting them as Merlin's half-brothers. The romance of "Sir Gowghter"[1] opens with the statement that devils occasionally beget children upon mortal women, and then proceeds to relate how an Austrian duchess was deceived by a devil who

[1] "Sir Walter."

masqueraded as her husband. The child resulting from
this embrace, though half-brother to Merlin, was, unfortunately, not provided with a priest as tutor, and therefore
kills several nurses, burns a convent, and violates the nuns,
before he is brought to do penance and so eradicate the
evil from his nature.

The common tendency of late romancers to add to existing material in order to retain interest in themes already
hackneyed led to an unintentional degradation of Merlin's
character. He is made to fall in love with Nimiane,[1] and
to instruct her in his own magic powers. The climax is
reached when he is represented as imprisoned by Nimiane,
who employs the magic which he himself has taught her;
the wizard, capable of any magic feat and able to foretell
the future, becomes unable to foresee his own impending
fate and so weak that he can neither win a maiden's love
nor protect himself with all his magic art. This story, first
related in the prose "Lancelot," was based on a common
Eastern theme—the deception of a wise man by woman's
guile. The story of Samson and Delilah is the best-known
example, but Aristotle, Virgil, and Hippocrates were portrayed as similarly deceived. The legend of the last-
named is related in "The History of the Holy Grail"; he
makes a magic cup in which no poison can remain, but,
like Samson, could not keep his secret from his wife, who
substitutes a similar cup and then proceeds to poison him.
In the prose "Merlin," Nimiane is described as the
daughter of one Dionas, godson of the goddess Diana, who
had promised that his daughter should be loved by the
wisest man in the world. In the same romance it is stated
that Nimiane was a Hebrew word meaning "I shall not
lie." Under such circumstances Merlin is perhaps to be
excused; he would not expect that a lady bearing a name
of that significance would make the telling of falsehoods
the chief business of her life.[2] Nimiane herself acquired

---

[1] The Vivien of Tennyson's "Idylls of the King."
[2] Tennyson's poem "Merlin and Vivien" accurately reflects the
character of Nimiane in romance.

still greater fame by being called the "Lady of the Lake," and thus identified with the foster-mother of Lancelot.

The three existing English romances of Merlin derive from the prose version and the two continuations of Boron's poem, called the "Vulgate Merlin" and "La Suite de Merlin" respectively. Two of them are verse romances—"Arthur and Merlin" of the fourteenth and Lovelich's "Merlin" of the fifteenth century; the third, also of the fifteenth century, is a prose romance, and called simply "Merlin."

Another famous supernatural character in Arthurian romance, though less prominent than Merlin, is Morgan, usually called "le fé" or "la fée." By some writers, as, for example, Giraldus Cambrensis in "Speculum Ecclesiae" and the author of the English romance "Sir Gawain and the Green Knight," she is called a goddess, and has therefore been identified by some scholars with the Celtic goddess called Morrigain, who is represented in Irish literature as the enemy of the epic hero Cuchulainn, just as Morgan, in some romances, is portrayed as hostile to Arthur. In "Sir Gawain and the Green Knight" she arranges the whole adventure in an attempt to bring discredit upon Arthur's Court, but is frustrated by the courage and chivalry of Gawain.[1] In none of the romances, however, is she represented as a goddess, but simply as a magician. The term fé, though often translated as "fairy," corresponds more closely to the "jinn" of Eastern stories than to the modern conception of fairy, and could represent either a good or an evil spirit. The double appellation of Morgan—"le fé" and "la fée"—seems to indicate a legendary spirit of doubtful sex. In the prose "Merlin" it is stated that she gained her knowledge of magic from Merlin, and it is possible that she and Nimiane are but variants of the same traditional character.

[1] See the next section of this chapter for this romance.

GAWAIN AND MODRED

Gawain's early fame in Lombardy and great prominence in Geoffrey's chronicle seem to indicate that he was not only a popular figure in early oral tradition, but also intimately connected with the Arthurian legend for a long time before the earliest written records. He seems even to have been of mythic origin, because in various romances his strength is reported as waxing and waning at different hours of the day; at daybreak he had merely human strength, from 6 to 9 a.m. it doubled, and at noon it again became normal. The impossibility of ascertaining precisely what details of any legend existed already in oral tradition, and what was added by the earliest writers, makes it unwise to say dogmatically that this attribute must have been accorded him in popular tradition, and not engrafted by romancers; but it very possibly is a relic of a genuine solar myth, in which Gawain represented the sun-god.

In written records he is first mentioned by William of Malmesbury in his chronicle in 1125, and is portrayed by Geoffrey of Monmouth as Arthur's most important follower. As nephew to a king who had no sons he would naturally rank first, and in the romances based on Geoffrey's chronicle he is represented as the queen's knight, even though Chrétien had earlier established Lancelot as her lover. In the chronicle of Wace and in most of the prose romances he is presented as a model of courtesy and chivalry—"One of the best knights, and wisest of the world, the least mis-speaker, and no boaster, and best taught of all things that belong to worship or courtesy."[1] Yet in spite of the tradition which led to this high praise, he seems to have had little attraction for the early verse romancers; Chrétien at first ranked him supreme among Arthur's knights, but neither he nor Boron

[1] English prose "Merlin," almost literally translated from the French prose "Merlin."

made him the hero of any one romance. When Lancelot, to suit the new craze for courtly love, had been made by Chrétien the courtly lover of the queen, he ousted Gawain from his position of supremacy, and remained the chief knight throughout the period of romance.

Gawain had to yield place to Lancelot, but he did not sink merely to second place; he gradually became more and more degraded, with the result that many people of modern times who are thoroughly familiar with the names of Lancelot, Tristram, Galahad, and Modred have never even heard of him. The probable reason for his loss of fame was his chastity. One French poem, "Messire Gauvain," presents him as the hero of various adventures designed to protect helpless damsels, but invariably refusing the reward usually offered by rescued maidens to their knights, their love. This poem and the many English romances which go even further, and make Gawain the subject of deliberate chastity tests, afford reasonable evidence that Gawain had early become the symbol of physical purity and abstention from sexual love.[1]

French romance was, however, almost entirely love romance, written to please ladies who regarded love as supreme and wished every knight to be a devoted lover; under such circumstances chastity, in the rigid medieval sense, is naturally at a discount. It was not that the virtue of chastity was distasteful or regarded with contempt, but that the rigid medieval conception of chastity, embracing absolute celibacy as well as purity of mind, was incompatible with sexual love of any kind, married or illicit. Lancelot superseded Gawain simply because portrayed as lover of the queen, and Tristram likewise became famous as lover of Iseult. To high-born ladies, like the Countess Marie, Gawain would appear a dangerous character, since the stress upon his chastity might at any time endanger the popularity of courtly love; a wave of

[1] Unfortunately the French originals of these English romances no longer exist.

religious fervour would have been sufficient to destroy the fame of Lancelot and Tristram, and exalt Gawain again above all other knights. Romancers, therefore, who wished to please a patroness of this type would be compelled to ignore Gawain altogether, or present him as an inferior knight. And the boldest of poets would shrink from the task of making hero in a love-story a knight who refused to offer or accept love under the strongest provocations, and had to be hard pressed before he would even accept a kiss.[1]

When the Grail Quest became a prominent theme of Arthurian romance—in the prose cycles—there would have been an opportunity to exalt Gawain once more, because of all the virtues essential to the successful questor, chastity was supreme. But Gawain had not been consistently portrayed as absolutely chaste and, furthermore, a hero had already been provided by Chrétien and Boron, namely Percival.[2] Percival was later superseded by Galahad—represented as the son of Lancelot—since Lancelot's prestige would not suffer so much from the success of his own son as from that of an unrelated knight. But Gawain was protected by no such vested interests as was Lancelot, and so not only was prevented from being the hero of this quest, but had to face two hostile bands of romancers. One group, the authors of love-romances, viewed Gawain's chastity as dangerous, because a standing reproach to their heroes; another, relating the quest for the Grail, viewed Gawain as a serious rival to their heroes, Percival and Galahad. Since in both cases his chastity was the stumbling block, the only possible resource of romancers was to deprive him of his chastity, and so render him harmless. He was permitted to retain his reputation for courtesy, but was more and more portrayed as licentious, until he became the supreme type of fickle and licentious love. His wantonness is emphasised

[1] See passage on "Sir Gawain and the Green Knight," p. 82.
[2] A German poem, "Diu Crône," portrays Gawain as successful in the Quest.

in the continuations of Boron's "Merlin," in the prose "Lancelot" and "Tristan," and in the Grail sections of the Vulgate Cycle.

To Englishmen, especially of the lower classes, this very chastity would make him popular. Stories of courtly love make no appeal to the lower classes of any country, and to all classes of Englishmen, inheriting a strong vein of Puritanism from the Anglo-Saxon stock, chastity would be a highly reverenced virtue. Since most English romances were fashioned to suit the lower classes, it is not surprising that where Tristram is the subject of one, and Lancelot only of two, Gawain is the hero of ten. In most of these he is made not only the symbol of purity, courtesy, and valour, but even the subject of deliberate chastity tests. The teachings of the Church would naturally be more respected by the lower classes than by high-born ladies living in an atmosphere of gallantry and love, and so the stress upon chastity would make Gawain supreme among heroes of romance. The inherent Puritanism of the English race would also make Gawain popular to the higher classes in England, when once French influence had ceased to dominate.

Of the romances written for the lower classes the best is "Ywain and Gawain,"[1] in which, though Ywain is the nominal hero, Gawain is portrayed as the greatest and most courteous of all knights. In "The Wedding of Sir Gawain and Dame Ragnell" his courtesy is so great that he consents to marry a hideous old hag in order to free Arthur from a temporary embarrassment; his courtesy, however, is fittingly rewarded, for in the bridal chamber she becomes again young and beautiful. Most of the romances make him the subject of chastity tests, but often very crudely; the authors frequently considered chastity as mere abstention from adultery; he is portrayed as spending a night with the wife of his host, and steadily refusing all her offers of love, only to be rewarded the following night by the offer of his daughter, which he accepts. The original

[1] Adapted from Chrétien's "Yvain."

G

conception may have been either absolute celibacy allied with complete devotion to his knightly profession, corresponding to the monk's self-dedication to the service of the Church, or it may have been merely abstention from adultery as a counterblast to the theory of courtly love between a bachelor and a married woman. English romances reflect both these conceptions, but none portrays him as a libertine, although one, "The Jeaste[1] of Sir Gawain," ignores the question of chastity altogether and presents him as other knights, amorous but not openly licentious.

The only romance which clearly stresses absolute chastity is "Sir Gawain and the Green Knight," written in the fourteenth century for a cultured audience, and by far the best of all English romances. Those written for the lower classes would all be mere adaptations from French originals, and therefore could not portray him as celibate without drastic alterations; and such originality could not be expected from the limited ability of writers who catered for the lower classes. "Sir Gawain and the Green Knight" may also have been based on a French original, but need not be considered as a faithful rendering, since the great ability of the author would enable him to make an entirely fresh story, if necessary and desirable.

Gawain in this romance is the symbol of both courtesy and chastity, the incidents being so arranged as to lay great stress on both. Although the adventure which he undertakes is one of sheer magic, there is no straining after sensationalism, and the supernatural element is so depicted as to emphasise these two traits of his character. A stranger, called the Green Knight, enters Arthur's hall and issues a challenge, which Gawain accepts on the king's behalf. The challenge is simple and straightforward —Gawain may strike the challenger one blow on the neck with his axe, provided he is willing to receive a similar blow himself one year later. The Green Knight then bows his head to receive the blow and has his head struck off by

---

[1] Geste=deed or adventure.

Gawain; but instead of dying he merely picks up his head, reminds Gawain of his pledge, arranges a meeting-place and departs. This crude episode is described very briefly, and then, by emphasising Gawain's fixed resolve to keep his contract, although it seems to entail certain death, the poet makes this very crudity enhance his nobility of character. For Gawain becomes, not a knight-errant seeking joyous and exciting adventures, but a high-principled knight facing certain death from a supernatural foe rather than break his knightly pledge and disgrace his profession. This episode emphasises his valour and his fidelity. The second episode, featuring a deliberate chastity test, emphasises his purity. On his way to meet the Green Knight he spends three days in a strange castle, where he is thrice offered and thrice refuses the love of his host's young and beautiful wife, who tempts him under the most provoking circumstances, visiting him in his bedchamber and dressed in the most alluring possible manner. This was a test deliberately arranged by husband and wife, who had heard of his great reputation for chastity. His courtesy and truthfulness are also clearly stressed in the same episode, for his host has made him promise to give him whatever he wins from his wife; Gawain is too honourable to take advantage of his host's absence in the hunting field to make love to his wife, but, when asked by her for a kiss on each occasion, he cannot in courtesy refuse, and so gravely returns the kiss to his host on his return each night from hunting. On the last morning he receives from his hostess a girdle, which she said would make all weapons powerless against him. This he naturally retains instead of giving it to his host, but later bitterly laments his lapse from knightly conduct. The poet thus arranges incidents to reflect clearly his courage, courtesy, chastity, and fidelity to knightly bond. Since of course the chastity test is concerned with a married woman, even this poet may have primarily aimed at showing him free from adultery, rather than from all sexual intercourse, but since it is also stated that he has no lady-love, it may be inferred that Gawain was intended to symbolise absolute chastity.

The proof that English audiences seem to have been more attracted by the representation of chastity rather than by that of courtly love lies not so much in any difference between the English and French versions of Gawain romances, which the loss of the French versions makes impossible to compare, but in the large number of existing English romances on Gawain and the small number on the two great lovers Lancelot and Tristram. These, the two greatest lovers in romance, were both heroes of stories of adulterous love. In a period when marriages were purely business contracts, in which love had no place, a love-story, to reflect life, must be either tragic because unfulfilled, or else portray illicit love. The ladies of French society would not relish the former type, but took great delight in the latter, not because they desired salacious stories, but because they revelled in the analysis of passions and emotions, in which French romancers were so skilful. The English mind does not readily appreciate this analysis, and the average Englishman, not only of the lower classes, but even of the higher classes, when they had ceased to be dominated by French influence, would tend to see in the stories of Lancelot and Tristram only the stark fact of adultery. At a later stage Malory was to make these two stories of lasting significance by emphasising the tragedy and guilt, but this conception had only faintly been realised by French writers. It was natural, therefore, that Gawain should be the most popular of Arthur's knights to Englishmen, and very fitting that he should be the hero of the greatest of all English romances.

The development of Gawain's character in French romance is of great significance. It has been shown that a romance could be composed relating exploits which had no basis in historical fact, even though the hero is a historical character;[1] the attitude of romancers towards

[1] Cf. "La Pélérinage de Charlemagne à Jérusalem," discussed Chapter II.

Gawain similarly shows how readily they ignored tradition. It matters little what part he played in oral legend; the fact remains that he at different times and to different authors was both the symbol of chastity and the supreme type of fickle and licentious love. The aim of romancers was to adapt the legends which they found to suit contemporary conditions and the tastes of their audience. It is therefore unwise to consider that any detail in romance must necessarily have a basis either in history or in oral tradition, unless definite supporting evidence can be adduced. It is unfortunate that Malory, and, after him, Tennyson, adopted the later French view of Gawain, and that the resultant modern conception of him should be the extreme reverse of that reflected in the greatest of English romances and presumably in the earliest French traditions.

Modred, another of Arthur's nephews, was portrayed in Geoffrey's chronicle, and possibly in tradition, as a typical traitor. Whatever the origin of this conception may be, it is a pleasing antithesis to have one nephew presented as the staunchest champion of the king, and another as his bitterest foe. Left behind as regent of Britain during Arthur's campaign, he betrays his trust, marries Guenivere, and usurps the kingdom. The only reference made to this marriage, the messenger's report that the queen had wickedly married Modred, is not certain evidence that Geoffrey intended to portray her as a willing adulteress; but since no statement is made in contradiction of this report, it may reasonably be assumed that such was Geoffrey's conception. A Welsh folk-song represents her as willingly accepting Modred's love, and calls her "Naughty young, more naughty later," but it is unknown how far back this tradition extends. It has been suggested that in popular tradition Modred was regarded as the queen's accepted lover, and that French romancers substituted Lancelot and made Modred a forcible abductor, because of his treacherous character. French sentiment demanded that the queen should have a lover, but would not tolerate that lover being a traitor; the only possible solution, therefore, would be to invent, or incorporate from another source, another knight more worthy of her love.[1]

It has also been suggested, though with less reason, that Gawain and Modred were originally one and the same person, and that, to remove the incongruity of presenting the same man as first the king's chief supporter and then his betrayer, the dual personality was sharply divided. Since none of the written accounts yields any satisfactory evidence in support of this view, it must remain merely as an interesting hypothesis.

LANCELOT AND GUENIVERE

In all literature it would be difficult to find any clearer illustration of the influence wrought by racial sentiment upon legend and romance than in the story of Lancelot. His origin is unknown; his name is never mentioned in the chronicles that introduced Arthurian legend into literature; he is the subject of no popular tradition now known; in the bas-relief of the cathedral of Modena, which presents many famous Arthurian knights, he has no place. Yet in one of the earliest romances he is portrayed as Arthur's greatest knight, and within half a century he had won a supremacy which has never been disputed. Other heroes rose to fame, only to be superseded, but from the thirteenth century at latest no writer of any period dared do otherwise than rank him first. The earliest romance in which his name occurs[2] ranks him third, only Gawain and the hero ranking higher. In Chrétien's "Lancelot" he is not only the hero, but ranks higher than Gawain, who hitherto had held first place, though the subject of no one romance. But since this is the worst constructed and the

[1] Modred's fame as a traitor would render it impossible for romancers to change his character, and therefore the creation of a new lover would be easier.
[2] Chrétien's "Erec," in a list of Round Table Knights.

least inspiring of all Chrétien's poems, and since Chrétien barely mentions him elsewhere, we may assume that his interest in Lancelot was but slight. Whether he was the subject of early oral legends or the mere creation of some poet it is impossible to say. It has been suggested that the thirteenth-century German romance "Lanzelet" was based on a lost French poem of an earlier date than Chrétien's; this romance, though relating that Lancelot had been fostered by a fairy in the Land of Maidens from early childhood, makes no reference to any love between him and Guenivere. It is therefore probable that the story of his love for the queen is simply an invention of Chrétien or of his patroness. It was a common belief that fairies not only stole children, but also enticed to their abodes full-grown men to be their lovers; Lancelot may therefore have been the hero of some popular legend which symbolised one of these superstitions, and incorporated by Chrétien when a lover had to be found for Guenivere.

Whatever his origin may have been, Chrétien was apparently compelled by circumstances rather than by personal interest to make him hero of a romance and rank him supreme amongst Arthurian knights. He definitely states that Marie of Champagne gave him the material, and we may therefore assume that she commanded the romance. Deeply interested in the courtly love poems of Southern France, she seems to have been obsessed with the idea of presenting Arthur's queen with a lover, and a lover who should rank above all other knights. Chrétien's poem established him in this unenviable situation, and the ever-spreading craze for courtly love amongst high-born dames ensured a lasting reputation. This sudden rise from obscurity to enduring fame and supremacy among all the heroes of romance is due neither to tradition nor to chronicles, but entirely to French sentiment of the twelfth century. A female audience wished for tales of love, prevailing sentiment demanded courtly love between a knight and a married woman, the lover of the queen must rank above all other lovers, and therefore above all other knights, and any poet who dared to dispute this supremacy could expect no hearing. Crusading fervour and feudal warfare had re-fashioned the exploits of Charlemagne and of Roland; courtly sentiment changed Celtic legends into French romance of chivalry, and made an unknown figure the greatest hero of them all.

No romance dealing with Lancelot alone could ensure absolute supremacy, for all writers wished to make their heroes prominent. His fame was permanently established only by the prose "Lancelot," which is a composite romance narrating also the deeds of Gawain and other knights, the quest of the Holy Grail, and the death of Arthur. By stressing Lancelot's supremacy over all others in all quests, the author of this romance established his fame for all time. And the drastic change in the form of Arthurian story by this distortion is well exemplified in the narrative of Arthur's expedition to Gaul; in Geoffrey's chronicle Lancelot plays no part, in this romance the expedition has but one purpose—to win back Lancelot's patrimony from a usurper.

Only two English romances present Lancelot as their hero, "Le Morte Arthur"[1] and "Lancelot of the Lake," both being based on sections of this prose romance. Reasons were advanced in the preceding section of this chapter why Lancelot should exercise less attraction in England than did Gawain. Unlegalised love has apparently always been viewed by the English race with deep distrust, and even to this day the average Englishman is frequently amazed at the judgments of French law courts and the attitude of French writers in the question of unlawful love. The theme of Lancelot's love for Guenivere seems to have become famous and popular in England only when it had come to be viewed as a tragedy—the primary cause of the disruption of the Round Table and of Arthur's death.

---

[1] "Le Morte Arthur" and "Morte Arthure" must not be confused. They are distinct romances, and Malory's "Morte d'Arthur" is again distinct from both these. Its title alone shows that the author of this poem was more inspired by the story of Arthur's death than by the love of Lancelot.

French society of the twelfth century did not, however, view illicit or even adulterous love as necessarily alien to the spirit of chivalry and courtesy. The courtesy of a knight was primarily reflected in his devotion to some one particular woman, and this devotion must be something more than the feudal service which he owed his lord; devotion implied adoration, and adoration desire; the knight must love his mistress as well as serve her, and the lady must reward his service with her love. Adultery may to some extent have been condoned by society, but was still an offence against feudal law, if the lover was also a vassal of the lady's husband. Some romancers, therefore, in order to exonerate Lancelot from any charge of treachery, portrayed him as an independent knight, and not as a vassal of Arthur. By vowing himself to the queen's service only, Lancelot evaded any possible imputation of disloyalty. Modred, the traitor, had lost his position as the queen's accepted lover, and Lancelot is carefully portrayed as a noble character, the perfect symbol of chivalry and of love. The theory of courtly love, both in real life and in romance, laid chief stress upon service; it was the lover's·duty to obey his mistress implicitly, but it was not her duty to yield herself to him; that was a purely voluntary favour. No lover could expect a reward until his devotion has been fully proved, nor had he any right to complain if he received no reward; similarly, no lady who lightly gave her love could hope for great respect.

It was this quality of service and devotion that made Lancelot famous and caused him to be regarded as the great exemplar of chivalry. Chrétien's poem reflects the essence of the theme. Lancelot's service is his rescue of the queen from an abductor, and is performed only after great hardships, deadly peril, and deep humiliation; to achieve his purpose he has to ride in a common cart, and thereby sacrifice his knightly dignity and suffer the mockery of other knights. The essence of the theme is service and the reward is love; the lover must be prepared to make any sacrifice, to risk his life or his reputation, to undertake what may seem shameful tasks and suffer mockery and contempt, but he must not fail his mistress; the lady in her turn can show appreciation only by accepting him as her lover. But where a modern writer would choose a heroine whom the hero could marry, and therefore present a love story approved by convention, French sentiment and medieval conditions demanded a married heroine, and therefore illicit love. "The Life of Gildas," written about 1150, relates the abduction of Guenivere by Melvas, ruler of Somersetshire, and her restoration through the intercession of the Abbot of Glastonbury. This represents ecclesiastical ideals; courtly sentiment demanded that the rescuer be a knight and a lover.

This craze for courtly love as a topic of romance seems to have been but transient, because in the thirteenth century romancers began to regard this love-story as a tragedy. Lancelot still remained the symbol of chivalry, but his devotion to the queen was regarded less as an outstanding example of chivalry than as the direct cause of faction amongst the knights of the Round Table, which ultimately led to the disruption of the realm. "La Mort Artu," the first romance to concentrate upon the death of Arthur, was also the first romance to present this view of Lancelot's love. But neither this nor any other romance portrays the disruption of the Round Table as arising from moral guilt. It was not indignation at moral sin, but jealous regard for feudal prestige that caused dissension, and so prevented complete unity of effort against the traitor Modred; Arthur's most loyal vassals, especially Gawain, became incensed because of their queen's love for a knight of inferior rank; the evil lay not in adultery, but in difference of rank and the jeopardising of the king's honour. "Le Morte Arthur" relates the flight of Guenivere with Lancelot, because their liaison has been betrayed, the besieging of Lancelot's castle by Arthur, and the Pope's intervention and insistence that Arthur should make peace and receive Guenivere as his wife again Malory, in keeping with English tradition, stresses the moral guilt, but in no narrow Puritanical spirit. He presents him as an essentially noble character marred by one weakness, a weakness that provokes great tragedy; Lancelot and Guenivere both do penance for their sin, but cannot avert the suffering they have caused. Guenivere thus has come to rank with Helen of Troy as an enduring symbol of the disaster that may come upon a whole nation from illegal love.

In its early form the story of Lancelot really marks the decadence of romance, as Chrétien seems to have perceived. Introduced simply to reflect an artificial social craze, he symbolised no national ideal and no enduring aspect of human nature, as did the heroes of Chrétien's other poems. But the craze remained sufficiently long for this artificial courtesy to become ennobled and refined, until Lancelot became the symbol of true chivalry. And finally, by stressing the tragedy which must inevitably result from unlawful passion, romancers made the love-story of Lancelot and Guenivere deeply and permanently symbolical.

Lancelot therefore presents a paradox unique in the history of romance. The most obscure in origin of all the famous figures in Arthurian legend, he became the most renowned. He supplanted Gawain as chief knight and Modred as queen's lover; he became the model of chivalry, the father of the Grail hero, Galahad, and finally a warning to all unlawful lovers, simply because a temporary craze demanded that the queen must have a lover, and that lover first among men. In early romance he won his fame because of his love and service to the queen, in modern literature his fame remains because his love was guilty love and caused the greatest tragedy in the history of romance. The modern conception in early romance would have killed his fame, the early conception in modern romance would drive him into obscurity, if it did not present him as a villain.

TRISTRAM AND ISEULT

Not only does this theme in popular tradition seem to have been as completely divorced from Arthurian legend as that of Lancelot, but it did not become an integral part even in medieval romance; the modern conception of him as one of Arthur's knights is almost entirely due to Malory. But Tristram, unlike Lancelot, was almost certainly a well-known figure in Celtic legend, and his love for Iseult may possibly have been the most famous example in Celtic tradition of tragic passion, as it became the most outstanding in European romance. It is not surprising, therefore, that the rise of romanticism in the nineteenth century and the consequent desire for stories of romantic love won for it an enduring fame through the work of poets and through Wagner's opera, "Tristan und Isolde."

It represents an elopement legend, a common theme of Celtic traditions, the most famous being the Irish legend of "Diarmaid and Grainne." Although the subject of this type of story was usually a married, not a single woman, the design was not to enhance or even merely portray adulterous love, but love made irresistible and therefore tragic by supernatural influence. It was common belief that certain men and women were fated to exercise irresistible fascination over all members of the opposite sex who came in contact with them; this influence arose either from a love-spot on the man's body, or from a mysterious charm, called "geis," inherent in the woman. This superstition is but one of many which have arisen from the exaggeration of natural causes; there always exist men and women who can exercise a powerful fascination over others, and little exaggeration was needed to interpret it as of supernatural origin.

From the beginning Tristram was represented as a vassal of King Mark of Cornwall, and in most romances as either his nephew or grandson, his mother being portrayed in some as sister, in others as daughter of the king. This attachment to King Mark probably had already existed in legend, and would alone be a primary factor preventing complete incorporation into Arthurian legend. Whether the Mark of romance represents the Mark who was king of Cornwall in the sixth century it is impossible to say; all that can safely be assumed is that the legend of Tristram had very definite shape in oral tradition, possibly more definite shape than any of King Arthur. For where Arthur and his knights became typical Frenchmen of the twelfth century, Tristram throughout romance retained characteristics which harmonise more with primitive than with feudal and aristocratic conditions. He was more famous for his skill in outdoor sports, his knowledge of forest craft, his nimbleness and feats of strength, than for the knightly exercises of feudal France or the courtly etiquette of French society. Romancers emphasised this difference in type by making these very attributes the means of his betrayal; his secret visit to a house later became known because he had amused himself with throwing rushes, so that the first stuck in a curtain, and each successive one in the one preceding. Similar feats with knives, spears, and arrows are common in primitive races, but not a knightly exercise of feudal France; Tristram, therefore, was not only betrayed by his skill, but by it also offers evidence for the belief that he is a creation of Celtic legend, not of French poets. He also spends his exile in a forest, where any ordinary exiled knight would have sought shelter in another castle and service with another lord. It seems fairly evident, therefore, that this legend had already been highly developed before it was incorporated by romancers; if it had been nebulous or fragmentary, the romancers would have had to shape it and the characters for themselves, and would almost certainly have made Tristram a courtly knight like Lancelot or Gawain. But from what division of the Celtic race it originated is unknown; different scholars have assigned to it such varying localities as Brittany, Wales, Cornwall, Ireland, and Scotland.

Marie de France in one of her lays[1] relates an isolated episode of the story, an episode far more in keeping with the spirit of popular legend than with that of courtly sentiment. Tristram, exiled by King Mark and hiding in the forest, hears that Iseult will pass that way returning to Tintagel, and, in order to attract her notice, cuts a wand from a hazel tree, peels off the bark, carves his name upon it with his dagger, and leaves it on the track. Iseult, seeing the wand and then her lover's name, leaves her escort and enters the forest to meet him. This lay may have been based on one of those early romances of Tristram which have either been lost or left only in a fragmentary condition, but may equally well have been based on some oral story, perhaps even a Breton lay. But, as with other stories of romance, lack of knowledge on oral legends makes it impossible to know what form this story had in popular tradition.

Poetic versions of this legend were composed by at least three of the earliest Arthurian romancers; that of Chrétien de Troyes has been completely lost, and those of the Anglo-Norman poets, Thomas, and Béroul, remain only in a fragmentary condition. Of the three, that of Thomas is probably the earliest, and he not only states that various stories were told of Tristram, but mentions an unknown writer called Bréri as the source of his romance. Of five known copies of his poem there remain only eight fragments, gathered from various parts of England, Germany, and Italy, and totalling 3144 lines, all of the latter part of the romance. Of Chrétien's "Tristan" nothing is known, but Béroul's poem offers a different version of the story from that of Thomas. Thus from the beginning two versions of the story existed, so preventing consistency amongst later romancers. Since the work of Thomas formed the chief basis of later romances, Bédier, one of the greatest French authorities on medieval romance,[2]

---

[1] "Chièvrefeuil."

[2] Bédier's principal work is "Les Légendes Épiques," which gives a full review of the Charlemagne romances, and forms the basis of part of Chapter II in this book.

attempted to reconstruct the story as told in his poem; but although his work is valuable as a consistent version of a confused and widely-varying theme, it would be unsafe to assume that it is an accurate reproduction.

The long prose "Tristan" of the early thirteenth century established Tristram's fame as the prose "Lancelot" had established Lancelot's, but in different romances the conception varies widely from conventional courtly love to frank libertinism. The original conception, however, was one of irresistible and therefore tragic love, and it was this conception that made Tristram and Iseult famous throughout Europe. As symbols of tragic though noble love they became the most famous lovers of romance; their passion was extolled by the greatest troubadours of Provence,[1] referred to by many early poets—Dante, Petrarch, Chaucer, Gower, Lydgate, and Ariosto—and frequently made the subject of poems in the nineteenth century.

In Celtic legend this type of elopement story was made symbolical by attributing the love to supernatural influence; in French romance the love of Tristram and Iseult was ascribed to an influence more adapted to the time, that of a love potion. Throughout the Middle Ages and for long afterwards men believed that potions could be brewed which would inspire a deep and lasting love; by substituting this tradition romancers avoided the absurdity of the primitive superstition without destroying the symbolism of the theme.[2] Belief in love-potions was equally a superstition, but based on reality; potions can be brewed which will arouse sexual passion, and no doubt have been brewed from the beginning of history, but illiterate people would naturally regard them as works of magic.[3] Since, however, neither man nor woman could resist the influence of a love-potion, the drinking of it by

[1] Such as Bertrand de Born and Bernard de Ventadour.
[2] The original Celtic legend may also have ascribed their love to a potion. The "geis" and love-spot were the usual traditions, but may have played no part in this particular story.
[3] This basis in reality is partly reflected in the reference to this love-potion by Gower, the great moral poet of the fourteenth century; he instanced it as a warning against indulgence in intoxicating drink.

Tristram and Iseult freed them from all guilt and made an otherwise sordid story of adultery and feudal treachery symbolical of the eternal sex problem, conflict between resistless natural instincts and rigid social laws, which has been perhaps more productive of tragedy than any other element in human character.

The theme of the two Iseults is also of deep significance—his hopeless love for one and marriage with the other. Many romances present a similar problem, conflict between love and duty, or between love and expediency. King Horn, Bevis of Hamtoun, and Guy of Warwick[1] were each betrothed to one maid and later offered another, the daughter of a king, so pointedly that refusal was very difficult and even liable to be dangerous. The proverb says, "Hell hath no fury like a woman scorned," and the immortal story of Joseph and Potiphar's wife offers a well-known example of its truth.[2] But in the Middle Ages it could be at least as appropriately said of feudal barons whose offers of daughters or sisters in marriage were rejected by men of inferior rank. Tristram's problem was made of greater significance than any of these because bound up with the theory of courtly love. This ideal was far removed from libertinism; it was not the sacred duty of a husband to remain faithful to his wife, but it was the sacred duty of a lover to remain faithful to his mistress. He could go through the formal ceremony of marriage, but he could not consummate it without breaking faith, unless his mistress absolved him from his allegiance. The whole fabric of feudalism was based on faith and loyalty, and though the theory of courtly love presented only an artificial and bizarre aspect of feudal service, it was a refined and cultured aspect in its best forms, symbolising, even though in a distorted manner, the noblest ideal of chivalry, unswerving faith. The two Iseults, therefore, present a double tragedy reflecting not merely an artificial medieval

---

[1] See Chapters VII and VIII for these romances.
[2] See Chapter XIII for examples in medieval romance, in "Lanval" and "La Chatelaine de Vergi."

conception, but life as it is in all periods. The modern significance of this tragedy is the misfortune of a man who loves where he cannot marry and later marries where he cannot love. The story of Tristram and Iseult is therefore symbolical both of the sacredness of loyalty and of the tragedy that may arise from overwhelming passion.

The stories of Lancelot and Tristram are by no means parallel illustrations of the same ideal. In essence that of Lancelot is one of conventional courtly love and service, that of Tristram one of elemental passion. Both symbolise the same idea of loyalty, but that of Lancelot at first reflected nothing more, and later became significant of the tragedy that may come upon the whole realm from a queen's infidelity, while that of Tristram from the first symbolised the tragedy that may overwhelm, not a kingdom, but simply the lovers themselves, as a result of overmastering passion. This clear distinction was not, of course, rigidly maintained by all romancers; the two themes became intermingled, and Tristram was sometimes portrayed as a mere courtly lover, even for long refraining from adultery, Lancelot sometimes stressed rather as a passionate adulterer than as a courtly servant of the queen. Guenivere and Iseult are also usually kept distinct; Guenivere is not imbued with that sublime passion which is the outstanding feature of Iseult; she is the stately queen throughout, surrendering herself to Lancelot, because he has rescued her and become her champion, but never overmastered by passion. The love-potion alone would necessarily differentiate the two types of love; as long as Lancelot strictly followed the rules of courtly love, concerned primarily with serving the queen, not with winning her love, he could be portrayed as noble and chivalrous; Tristram could also be portrayed as noble, even though his sole aim in life was to enjoy the love of Iseult, because he was the victim of a magic potion;[1] but

---

[1] Neither he nor Iseult drank this potion deliberately. It was brought by Iseult's maid in mistake for wine.

H

without some such reason no knight could be regarded as a model of chivalry who would endanger a lady's reputation merely to gratify his own desires. Apart from this, the two stories represent distinctly different stages of civilisation—that of Tristram the natural, elemental, and passionate, that of Lancelot the artificial, complex, and courteous. The latter was fashioned entirely by French poets and reflects French social ideals of the twelfth century, the former had apparently been shaped already in Celtic tradition and reflects the natural impulses and supernatural beliefs of a primitive race. The only English romance, "Sir Tristrem," probably derives from the poem of Thomas. The writer states that his original was written by Thomas of Erceldoune, but he probably confused the French Thomas with the well-known English Thomas. It is not impossible that the existing version is a copy of an earlier lost English poem actually written by Thomas of Erceldoune, and that he based his work on that of the French Thomas. The only certain fact is that it follows the version of the French Thomas, but whether it was adapted from that poem, or from a later French version, or whether it is a copy or rendering of an earlier English poem by Thomas of Erceldoune, it is impossible to say. It is one of the poorest of English romances, written in entirely unsuitable verse and full of obscurities. The audience for which it was composed would be little attracted by such a theme; the lower classes preferred that every hero of romance should be a lover, but not that the heroine should be already married, nor that the love theme should swamp the adventures. The English adapter, whether the author of this or of some earlier poem, probably attempted to suit the theme to this different taste, and had too little ability to succeed. No attempt was made to stress the moral significance which might have appealed, and it therefore became merely a story of illicit love between lovers employing any fraud to encompass their desires. Even if the author of the existing poem was not responsible for the clumsy distortion of the story as fashioned in French romance, he certainly must be accused of being one of the worst poets who ever wrote a romance.

The greatest of all the romances on this theme is the uncompleted "Tristan und Isolde" of Gottfried von Strasbourg, written early in the thirteenth century and based on the poem of Thomas. By infusing into it a loftier spirit than appears in any other version, and by portraying delicate and subtle shades of sentiment to enhance the tragedy and to depict the mental agonies of the lovers, he made it the greatest theme of medieval romance.[1]

THE GRAIL QUEST

This theme, which was apparently no more attached to the Arthurian legend in oral tradition than the stories of Lancelot and Tristram, is but one more, and the greatest, of those elements which transformed a few popular stories of a pseudo-historical king into the greatest romance in history. The earliest existing versions are the "Perceval" or "Conte del Graal" of Chrétien and the "Joseph d'Arimathie" of Boron. The former, left unfinished by Chrétien, was continued by different romancers at a later date; of the latter only fragments remain, but Boron's conception of the story can be gleaned from a prose version of it made later. The Welsh romance "Peredur,[2] Son of Evrawc," is based partly on Chrétien's poem and partly on further Welsh legends, but makes no reference to the Grail Quest.

Chrétien seems therefore to have been the first writer to relate both the deeds of Perceval and the quest for the Grail, but of his sources nothing is known. Since he did not complete his work it became not only possible, but even necessary for the continuators to incorporate further elements either of their own invention or from other sources, and this resulted eventually in such a confused

[1] It was presumably this poem which inspired the opera of Wagner.
[2] = Perceval.

medley of ideas that it is impossible to estimate whether there ever had been a Grail legend.

About the year 1240 was written a long prose romance called the "Grand Saint Graal," which both amplified and modified Boron's story and formed the basis of the English romances. Modern versions have concentrated upon only one element, the quest of the Grail itself, a mystic vessel of divine grace, which could be neither seen nor found except by one who was absolutely pure both in body and in spirit. But medieval romance offers no such clear-cut conception; other themes were mingled, some appearing to have not the slighest relationship. Yet in spite of the varied and even contradictory elements, the essence of the whole theme was a quest for wonder-working talismans—of various kinds and for various purposes— the possession of which would bring success and happiness to the finder. And the very medley of elements fittingly symbolises the medieval craving for mysticism, magic, and the sensational.

The earliest versions present two distinct themes, both of which remained throughout the period of romance— the early history of the talismans and the search for them by various knights. The first is merely pseudo-religious history; the second, more interesting because the stress is upon the questors' character, is imbued with a religious spirit, but must have derived at least some elements from traditional lore. Chrétien's poem deals only with the Quest; Boron's combines both themes, and the sources of the first have been discovered. He relates that Joseph of Arimathea had preserved in a vessel the blood shed by Christ when crucified, had been thrown into prison by the Jews, and left to starve. Fed miraculously for forty-two years, he was at last freed by Vespasian, who had invaded Palestine to avenge Christ's death. The vessel containing Christ's blood had also been preserved, and was eventually brought to Britain; as the most sacred relic of the Church it remained invisible to all impious eyes, and the finding of it naturally became a test of character.

In the "Life of Vespasian" written by Suetonius mention is made of a noble captive called Joseph; in another unrelated work, the "Narratio Josephi," it is stated that Vespasian invaded Palestine to avenge Christ's death; and the Gospel of Nicodemus records that Joseph of Arimathea was imprisoned by the Jews and visited by Christ in his dungeon. Boron incorporated into his poem the essence of all three works, and identified the Joseph of Suetonius with Joseph of Arimathea, although they were totally distinct personages.

No source has yet been found for the most important details of this legend—the preservation of Christ's blood in a vessel and its translation to Britain. In Boron's poem the history of the Grail became a conversion legend, in which Joseph of Arimathea is represented as founder of the British Church. There is no historical evidence that Christianity existed in Britain before 200 A.D., but there may have been a popular belief of long standing that Joseph was the first missionary. The source of this conversion legend as represented in Boron was a series of documents connected with Glastonbury Abbey, which may have been based on popular traditions or may record legends deliberately manufactured to enhance the Abbey's fame; this legend would also suit the Plantagenet kings, who seized every opportunity of gaining an ascendancy over the people of Wales. There may also have begun during the twelfth century a determined effort by ecclesiastics to claim for the Church of Britain an origin as illustrious as that of the Roman Church. If so, no better plan could have been designed than to make Joseph its founder and Britain the repository of the most sacred of all relics, the blood of Christ. A statement in the English romance called "The History of the Holy Grail" seems to indicate ecclesiastical zeal; the assertion is there made that Christ Himself wrote the story of the Grail, that He *wrote no other book*, and that if anyone denies this he is a liar. This theory would, of course, explain only the legend and Church documents. Romancers were not interested in

Church propaganda, and would use the legend only if
they thought it would appeal to their audience. The
stimulus to poets may have been the religious zeal
awakened by the Second Crusade of 1146, although it is
questionable whether the zeal would have remained for
the thirty years or more which elapsed between the
Crusade and the earliest romances. Perhaps, too, the
audience, though chiefly interested in love-stories, may
also have been attracted by religious romances, provided
that the stress was laid upon miracles and mysteries, not
upon moral instruction. But this conversion legend deals
only with the *history* of the Grail, which is neither an
essential nor a significant feature of the Grail romances.
It serves only as an explanation of the mysterious object
for which the knights went questing. The interest of the
authors, and presumably of the audience too, was focussed
on the *quest* which, though not catering for the chief
demand of the time, a love-story, yet supplied in full
measure that other, and nearly as urgent demand, a
record of sensational and mysterious adventures.[1]

Although the romancers claimed historical truth for all
they wrote, it need not be assumed that poets as able as
Chrétien were not astute enough to invent details or even
compose a whole story from a few slight hints. The story
of Charlemagne's pilgrimage to Palestine, and the
Spanish romances of the fifteenth and sixteenth centuries,
which caused the mental aberrations of Don Quixote, were
pure invention, and surely Chrétien and Boron were as
capable as ecclesiastics and Spanish romancers of weaving
a story from a very slight basis, or even without a basis at
all. Their frequent references to Latin originals prove
only an anxiety to be believed, and even Horace Walpole
in the eighteenth century claimed an Italian original for

[1] Though Boron's "Joseph d'Arimathie" is primarily concerned with
the history of the Grail, it also relates a quest for it, and another of
Boron's poems, now lost—the "Perceval"—was presumably concerned only with the Quest. Since he is recorded as having written a
regular series of poems, "Joseph d'Arimathie" may have been
intended chiefly as an introduction to "Perceval."

his "Castle of Otranto" till its popularity made him realise that he would gain greater fame by admitting his authorship; Cervantes in "Don Quixote" not only parodied the fantasies of romance, but also, by claiming for it a Moorish original, the conventional solemn pretence of an early unimpeachable source.

To invent a quest for some mysterious object would present no difficulty, because the wanderings of knights in search of adventures formed the usual subject of romance. That any definite legend of a vessel filled with the blood of Christ ever existed is rendered improbable by the fact that in different romances the term "grail" has different meanings; in Boron's story it is a vessel, symbolical of the Eucharist, in which, according to Catholic doctrine, the bread and wine were transformed into the flesh and blood of Christ; in the German "Parzifal" it signifies a stone, and in some romances it is merely a vessel containing an inexhaustible supply of food. This last version has parallels both in folk-lore and in the Old and New Testaments.

It seems highly probable that the story contains elements both from religious and from Celtic popular traditions. But from which source, if from either, the primary essence of the Quest has come is still hotly debated, and the impossibility of giving any concise statement here may be seen from the fact that the opinions of scholars range from the one extreme that Celtic origin is improbable to the other that it is almost certain and Christian origin untenable. No story similar to the Grail Quest has yet been discovered in Celtic legend, but various isolated elements have parallels in both Irish and Welsh traditions, the chief example being the magic cauldrons which contain inexhaustible supplies of food. This existing state of uncertainty makes it not impossible that Chrétien from a few isolated objects and incidents in both ecclesiastical and popular legends composed the story of a quest to please an audience temporarily interested in religious questions.

The fragmentary nature of the two earliest versions,

allied to the fact that Boron's "Perceval" must also have related a quest for the Grail, makes it impossible to know how many of the elements contained in later romance were included in its earliest stages. The later romances combine three distinct themes which seem to be completely unrelated—a religious quest, the restoration of an invalid to health by supernatural means, and a vengeance story, in which the hero seeks revenge for a murdered father. The first theme, the quest for a holy vessel symbolical of Christ, may be the primary theme, and therefore of religious origin, or it may have arisen simply to give a religious colouring to a theme of non-religious character, and become the most stressed because the best understood. If the history of the Grail was from the first an integral part of the story, then the quest for the Grail must have been the primary theme and of religious origin. But this is by no means certain. The second theme probably derives from folk-lore, and presents an invalid king, usually called the Rich Fisher, whose restoration to health depends on a stranger asking him the cause of his illness. Upon the king's health also depends the fertility of his realm; when he is ill the land becomes a desert, when he is well, it again becomes fertile. This dependance of the realm's fertility on the health of its ruler has been widely believed among primitive races, and in some so firmly that the king was put to death at the first sign of failing health or sexual impotence. Chrétien and Boron both made the Rich Fisher keeper of the Grail and symbolical of Christ, and in some romances the name is explained by stating that he had caught a fish large enough to feed the whole company. The latter element was obviously, and the former possibly, borrowed from the Biblical story of the loaves and fishes. The third theme, that of vengeance for a murdered father, is a commonplace of legend and romance, and has no bearing on the vexed question of Christian or Celtic origin. The earliest version is in a continuation of Chrétien's "Perceval" by a poet named Manessier, but it may also have formed a part of Boron's lost "Perceval."

Since Percival is always portrayed as a youth brought up far from Court by a widowed mother, the vengeance theme may have been added simply to account for the mother's widowhood and her anxiety to keep Percival from the exercise of arms. The novelty of the youth brought up in ignorance of knightly exercises, and later becoming the pattern of chivalry and renowned in warfare, would be the primary element, the vengeance theme being added merely as an explanation.

This quest for talismans would admirably suit Chrétien's taste, because all of his romances present quests of single champions for some definite purpose. The portrayal of the hero as an ignorant youth eventually winning great renown, and the incorporation of the story into Arthurian history would serve to enhance the interest still further. But that there ever existed any definite Grail legend, in the sense that there was a Tristram legend and a Merlin legend, is extremely improbable. It is far more reasonable to view it as a welding together of various inharmonious but exciting and sensational themes than to believe that any legend would present a magical vessel as the central object of such widely different ideas as the service of the Eucharist, vengeance for a murdered father, and the restoration of an invalid to health and of a desert land to fertility. The only French romance which presents an intelligible conception of the whole story is Boron's "Joseph," which represents a people come to destitution because of sin, a separation of the pure and impure by means of a symbol, the fish, the punishment of false disciples who seek self-aggrandisement instead of the glory of Christ, and the rewarding of the true disciples by allowing them to see the Grail. The continuations of Chrétien's poem and the prose romances present a confused medley by retaining a more primitive form of some elements, and thereby being unable to weld them into one harmonious whole. The greatest of all the romances, the "Parzifal" of Wolfram von Eschenbach, made the story both more human and more significant by ignoring the incongruous elements and by stressing Percival's character, especially the development of it by trial and temptation. Even the restoration of the king's health is made dependent upon the hero's spiritual insight, which enabled him to have full sympathy.

The Grail Quest has naturally a close affinity with the Crusades, both being religious quests. The "Parzifal" especially is thoroughly imbued with crusading fervour, not only in its general spirit, but even in many of the details; the Grail Church is guarded by a sacred order of knights, vowed to celibacy and called "Templeisen," so that both in character and in name they closely correspond to the Knights Templars who took so prominent a part in the early crusades.

The incongruity of themes, and the almost certain varied nature of the sources, upon which the Grail legend has been built, permitted adaptation in almost any direction. No one knight is the hero of the quest in all versions; in Boron's "Joseph," he is called Brons, whom some scholars have identified with Bran, King of the Underworld in Celtic Mythology; in all the other romances he is either Percival or Galahad, both of whom appear for the first time only in this story, and therefore presumably played no part in original Arthurian tradition. Chrétien made Percival the hero, and probably invented him simply for the quest. To invent a hero would be more satisfactory than to select some well-known knight, because absolute perfection was required. One tradition had made Gawain the model of courtesy and chastity, but this had probably never been a universal conception, and before "Perceval" was composed, he had come to rank lower than Lancelot, even if below no other knight. The Grail hero could not with dignity rank second to any knight, and none of the knights already famous—Lancelot, Tristram, Erec, Ywain or even Gawain—had possessed or maintained a consistent reputation for perfect chastity, and only one, Gawain, had never had either wife or mistress. Therefore a new hero was essential, and Percival was the result. But since the quest became a permanent part of Arthurian story and the greatest adventure that any knight could undertake, the hero would inevitably come to rank first of all knights, and therefore dim the glory of Lancelot, who had already been regarded as supreme. Even to maintain equality between two knights, one renowned for purity and chastity, the other for his love of the queen, would have been impossible; Percival would inevitably have been enhanced and Lancelot degraded. Lancelot's sinful relations with the queen made the quest impossible for him, so the only possible resource of romancers, by which tradition could be satisfied and Lancelot still retain priority, was to make the hero a son of Lancelot. Percival had already been described, in Manessier's continuation, and possibly also in Boron's lost "Perceval," as seeking vengeance for a murdered father, and could not therefore be portrayed by later writers as Lancelot's son; a new hero had to be created, and the result was Galahad. Since Percival had been described as marrying later in his career, Galahad may have been substituted primarily with the object of having a hero who should be always and absolutely chaste, and the portrayal of him as Lancelot's son have arisen as a secondary conception.

This attempt by romancers to maintain Lancelot's prestige provoked many difficulties; to portray Lancelot as unfaithful to the queen by marrying or taking another mistress would have been to defy the canons of courtly love, and so destroy his reputation; to portray Guenivere as the mother of Galahad would have been derogatory to Arthur's dignity. The story of Elaine was therefore invented, and Lancelot's liaison with her presented as an unconscious liaison; he steadfastly refuses to accept her love, until on one occasion she is made by magical means to resemble Guenivere. To enhance the conception further, Elaine is portrayed as one of the maidens whose duty it was to bear the Grail. The details of the Elaine story vary in different romances, the conception of her and her relationship with Lancelot largely depending on whether the romance is or is not primarily concerned with the Grail Quest.[1] Galahad is first presented as hero of the quest in the prose romance, "La Quête du Saint Graal," of the early thirteenth century, the first romance specifically designed to relate this quest. The earlier romances which had made Percival the hero were really stories of Percival, in which the Grail Quest is only one of many adventures. Then romancers began to write romances confined to the quest, to describe many knights as attempting it, and to portray Galahad as the only knight who attains success. Not all the romances made Galahad the son of Lancelot, but all portray him as the model of chastity. In keeping with the religious character of the story, his descent was also traced back to Joseph of Arimathea, and through him to Solomon; nothing less than absolute perfection could therefore be expected of him.

The outstanding feature of both Percival and Galahad, but particularly of Galahad, is asceticism. Except in the German "Parzifal," neither is much more than a mechanical symbol of the medieval ecclesiastical conception of purity, that is, avoidance of sin. Wolfram von Eschenbach was not content to stress merely this negative aspect of virtue; he stresses the development of Percival's spiritual character, made even stronger by continued resistance to temptation. The French Grail romances naturally vary in merit, but all make their heroes too nearly perfect and therefore unhuman. But in the Middle Ages this would be no bar to popularity; the people were accustomed to teaching which over-emphasised one virtue or vice at a time,[2] and did not look, as we do, for those complex figures which represent real life.

No existing English romance deals with the Grail Quest, but two—"Joseph of Arimathie" of the fourteenth and

[1] This stricture must be applied to all themes of romance. In describing the outlines of any theme, the most consistent plan must be offered, but it must be remembered that variations frequently arose from romancers embodying conceptions of their own, or incorporating elements from other sources.

[2] See Chapter VIII for romances specifically designed with this aim.

"The History of the Holy Grail" of the fifteenth century—
relate the history of the Grail and derive from the corresponding section of the "Grand Saint Graal." One other
romance, "Sir Percyvelle of Galles,"[1] has Percival for its
hero, but mentions neither the history nor the quest. It
presents the vengeance theme, and closely corresponds to
that section in Chrétien's "Perceval"; but even this
simple theme it describes very clumsily, and then wanders
off into other unrelated adventures, ending with the hero's
death in Palestine. The quest of the Grail exists in no
English version earlier than Malory's "Morte d'Arthur,"
in which Galahad is the hero.

The story of this quest, with its blending of adventure and
religious symbolism, was eminently suited to medieval
tastes, and it is difficult to account for the complete lack of
English versions in the period of romance. At all periods
a cultured audience, even though craving for sensational
narratives, desires that a story should have some underlying conception or significance. And this symbolism of
religious mysticism, of service of the Eucharist and of
Christ, must have made a strong appeal, particularly when
the craze for courtly sentiment had begun to wane or when
crusading zeal ran high.

THE ARTHURIAN LEGEND—CONCLUSION

The constant reflection of French rather than Celtic
sentiment in the French romances and the wide divergence of the early romances from the chronicles in the
incidents and characters portrayed makes it impossible to
judge what form this legend had taken in oral tradition
before first incorporated into literature. Arthur was portrayed by Nennius as the defender of Britain against invading Saxons, by Geoffrey of Monmouth as a great religious
leader and universal conqueror, as Charlemagne had been
in "La Chanson de Roland," and by the early romancers

---

[1] Galles=Wales—probably added to the title to link the story to
Arthurian legend.

as a patron of chivalry sending out knights to right wrongs and succour the oppressed.

No reliance can be placed upon the statements of either chroniclers or romancers, and even if Nennius' record is correct, that Arthur was a British king, and commander of all the British forces, he says so little of him that it would be useless as a test of accuracy in the romances. Geoffrey's conception was strongly coloured by Norman sentiment. The Normans had overrun most of Western Europe and were proud of their conquests; a Norman chronicler could therefore pay no greater homage to a king than to represent him as invincible and reducing all States beneath his sway. His portrayal of Arthur as Champion of the Christian Faith would need no basis in British history, for it simply reflects the crusading zeal of the eleventh and twelfth centuries, and was naturally incorporated by the prose romancers who drew much of their material from his chronicle.[1] In these Arthur's war against the Saxons is portrayed as a religious war, and the warriors killed as martyrs. "We may not more honourably suffer death than for the love of Jesus Christ and to strengthen and increase his law."[2] "Who that dieth in defence of the Christian faith he shall be saved from the pain of Hell."[2] The British princes who had refused to accept him as king, because of his doubtful parentage, express their willingness to join him in defence of Holy Church, but state emphatically that they do not regard him as their feudal overlord.[2] And Arthur's army carries white banners with red crosses, just as did the armies in the First Crusade.[2] The early romances, which established the supremacy of the Arthurian legend, and which first gave definite shape to those characters unmentioned in the chronicles, presented the quests of single knights, adventures undertaken in the name of chivalry—to protect the oppressed and chiefly women, or to win a woman's love. Love was usually either the urging motive of the quest or else the

[1] Or from the Norman and English versions by Wace and Layamon.
[2] The English prose "Merlin."

outcome of success. This conception reflects the courtly sentiment of twelfth-century social life and the influence of female patronage. And even the quest for the Holy Grail reflects the religious sentiment of France rather than any sentiment peculiar to the British or to any Celtic race. Welsh written versions of Arthurian stories also afford little help because many of them show traces of French influence, and all are written late enough to have been influenced by French or Norman writers.

For these reasons, the historical basis, if any, of this extensive legend, and even the popular oral traditions still remain unknown. Many brilliant hypotheses have been advanced, but none can be explicitly tested. The conceptions of Nennius and of Geoffrey are probably nearer to the truth than those of the romancers; organised warfare rather than chivalry and love would more naturally be the dominating theme of this legend in oral tradition.

But the spirit of Arthurian romance, as it has been best and most enduringly embodied, is one of chivalry and courtesy, contrasting strongly, therefore, with that of Charlemagne romance. Charlemagne throughout is ruler of a definite and limited realm, and embodies a clear-cut and practical conception—defence of Christian Europe against infidel Asia, or of monarchical despotism against baronial independence. Arthur is the supreme ruler, king of all kings,* and lord of all lords; he symbolises consistently no one definite conception. His knights, however, embody definite ideals, some of social conduct, others of human character, and though less human, are more enduring symbols than the peers of Charlemagne. It might almost be said that Charlemagne romance is based on realism, Arthurian romance on idealism. Both of these features were at once a strength and a weakness. The basis of national sentiment soon disappeared from the Charlemagne legend with the weakening of national unity, and all that remained in the later versions were racy narratives of rough-and-ready warriors fighting real foes, but with little definite purpose; they therefore ceased to mirror the sentiments of the audience, and lost still further ground when the change of patronage from men to women made any narrative which emphasised violence and bloodshed thoroughly distasteful. The Arthurian romancers tended to dehumanise their heroes by making them too nearly perfect and by straining off the realism which had been presented in the chronicles. But they did present ideals, and the ablest writers stressed character sufficiently to make their heroes both human and interesting; both quests and heroes were also adapted to suit each change in sentiment, and so remained of enduring interest.

It is not surprising that the men portrayed by Geoffrey— presumably the heroes of popular tradition—should play so small a part in romance; they had become too rigidly crystallised as national warriors, and therefore less adapted to the exigencies of chivalrous romance. Even Gawain, the greatest of them all, soon lost his priority, and was even ultimately degraded to ensure the supremacy of others; and other less famous but still doughty supporters of Arthur like Kay and Bedivere remain as minor characters throughout romance. Geoffrey's complete silence makes it highly probable that Lancelot, Tristram, Percival, and Galahad, though the most famous knights in Arthurian romance, were wholly unrelated to Arthurian legend in popular tradition. All may have been the heroes of popular legend, but it is not impossible that Percival, Galahad and perhaps even Lancelot were entirely inventions of French poets. Whatever may have been their origin, they were chosen to symbolise deep-rooted ideals of the time, and so became supreme. And the more closely a hero of romance is suited to some national ideal, the less likely is he to have been a character, at least a vivid character, in popular legends of another race, since it is easier to invent than to adapt a vivid personality to suit an alien sentiment.

The world of Arthurian romance is likewise a world of shadows in which localities count for nothing. Many of the places mentioned have been identified with sites in Wales and Cornwall, and if the romances had been based on Welsh and Cornish traditions, and Arthur a historical character, some reliance could perhaps be placed upon their accuracy. But the Bretons seem to have supplied most of the material, at least for the earliest romances which established the legend in French literature, and as they had left Britain many centuries before their traditions became available to French poets, they had probably lost all accurate knowledge of British geography. In French romance confusion between names could only increase, since its authors would be largely ignorant of geographical details and would probably not care very much where the localities were situated. Many localities in Great Britain bear Arthurian names, and many interesting hypotheses have been advanced in attempts to find a connection between the legends and history. It is impossible, however, to estimate in individual cases whether the name has resulted from popular traditions or merely from the romances; it is therefore unwise to assume that because a place-name in romance agrees precisely with the same name on the map the romance has accurately followed some local tradition, since the name may have been given as a result of the popularity of the romance. The romancers did, however, claim to relate true history, and would as far as possible retain the names of the traditions from which they drew, but the unreliability either of the romancers or of the traditions is clearly shown in the description of Winchester as a sea-port and Logres, representing England south of the Humber, as a town.[1] The authors of Charlemagne romance apparently based their work on chronicles and legends which emanated from religious houses and in which accuracy in place naming was essential, though even here accuracy only from the point of view of ecclesiastical advertisement, not from that of actual history. With the possible exception of the Grail

---

[1] In the French prose "Merlin."

I

Quest[1] there is no evidence for any vested interests behind Arthurian romance, so that geographical accuracy of any kind is not to be expected.

The decline of interest in Charlemagne, who was not only one of the greatest monarchs in European history, but could also be regarded as a French national hero, and the rapid rise to fame of Arthur, whose very origin was obscure, and who could be regarded as of national significance only because of the reverence paid to all who were reputed to be of Trojan or Roman descent, must be considered as the most remarkable phenomenon in literary history. Many protests were made against this universal popularity of an alien legend; in the prologue to "Le Chevalier au Cygne," which celebrates the deeds of Godfrey of Bouillon, it is stated that the stories of Arthur are lies, while those of Godfrey are true; and Huon de Villeneuve in his revision of the chanson de geste, "Doon de Manteuil" expresses his disgust at contemporary taste, which demanded Arthurian romance instead of more worthy poetry. But the strength of Arthurian legend lay in its capability of infinite adaptation. From the beginning it was fashioned to reflect contemporary ideals, and thus represents in a unique manner the intellectual growth of a people. It began as a symbol of national and religious warfare, possibly designed to provide the Normans in England with a rival hero to that of the Continental French —Charlemagne—and certainly reflecting the Norman militarist spirit and crusading zeal. With the rise of female patronage it was used by French poets as the symbol of chivalry and of love. In the Grail quest it symbolises the fascination exercised by religious mysticism. In Malory's "Morte d'Arthur" it reflects the aspirations of the noblest men at a time when real chivalry was dead and only its tinsel trappings remained. In Spenser's "Faerie Queene"

---

[1] See previous section. Since the conversion legend which forms the basis of romances on the history of the Grail was at least partly based on documents emanating from Glastonbury Abbey, the whole story of the Quest may have been partly stimulated by the monks of Glastonbury.

it reflects the hopes and ideals of Elizabethan England, and in Tennyson's "Idylls of the King" the ideals and failings of the Victorian era. In other words, the Arthurian legend throughout has been the mirror of men's ideals and aspirations, and particularly of their ideals of human character. No other theme of romance has proved so adaptable, and therefore no other has won the same enduring popularity.

CHAPTER VI

CLASSICAL THEMES IN ROMANCE

THE TEMPORARY RENASCENCE OF THE twelfth century is in nothing seen more clearly than in the use of classical history and legend as themes of romance. The abundant copying and enthusiastic study of non-ecclesiastical Latin works during this period opened new fields to romancers who saw that the Charlemagne legend was no longer of general interest, but had not yet realised the possibilities of Arthurian traditions. These Latin writings also presented in a definite form subjects which were consecrated both by their antiquity and by their incorporation into a literature more deeply reverenced than any other—it was for the latter reason that they were given the general title of "The Matter of Rome." This revived study, however, included little of the classical literature which inspired the scholars and poets of the fifteenth and sixteenth centuries, but was largely confined to the degenerate productions of later decadent periods; the romancers derived their knowledge, not from the works of Homer, Virgil, and the Greek dramatists, but from the works of later writers who had distorted their themes to suit personal and racial prejudices.

The most popular themes were the sieges of Thebes and Troy, and the conquests of Alexander, of which there remain numerous French and English versions.[1] The documents on which they are based diverged widely both from historical truth and from the versions of earlier writers; the romances distorted still further to suit changed ideals and conditions. The chief general reason for the superior attraction of these spurious versions over genuine classical literature was their closer approximation to the

[1] French romances were also written on other classical subjects, such as Æneas and Julius Caesar.

medieval spirit. They had changed the stern epic type into fantastic romance, and to the medieval mind fantasy appealed more than vivid reflection of past times. The romancers found in them a romantic spirit akin to their own tastes, and therefore ranked them higher than the classical writings. Just so most of us to-day consider as best those earlier works which happen most truly to reflect our present tastes. As the result of this double distortion the old heroic spirit was replaced by the spirit of fantastic adventure and courtly love. In the story of Troy, for example, the Gods, who to some extent in Homer represent destiny, were replaced by magic and necromancy symbolical of nothing. And the heroic dignity of Homer and Virgil was completely lost with the introduction of sentimental love; in the romance of "Æneas" Lavinia's love extends over 1400 lines, and Æneas is so overcome that he falls ill.

The earliest existing romance is that of "Thebes," written about 1150, and therefore earlier than the earliest existing Arthurian romances. Arthurian legends were, in all probability, rapidly becoming popular at this time, and may, of course, have actually been written up in poems now lost. The only theme of distinct priority is that of Charlemagne and from the middle of the twelfth century all the well-known themes existed side by side. The basis of this romance seems to have been a Latin prose abridgement of the "Thebaid" of Statius, the central incident of which was the long siege of Thebes, a subject which would naturally harmonise with the spirit of feudalism. The French poet made drastic alterations, enhancing those aspects which fitted in with feudal warfare, minimising the mythological element, and expanding love episodes which barely existed in the original—the French romancer dared not give a subordinate place to women. At a later period several French prose romances were written, and a Latin poem by Boccaccio, the "Teseide," best known as the basis of Chaucer's "Knight's Tale," the finest of all romances on this theme. About 1420 the poet Lydgate wrote his "Siege of Thebes," the only complete English version, for Chaucer's poem concentrates upon only one episode, a love-story barely mentioned in the original work. Lydgate's poem derives from a lost French version, but with additions from various sources, especially from Chaucer and the Bible. A little later was written a prose "Siege of Thebes," uncompleted and almost certainly adapted from Lydgate's poem.

During the early centuries of the Christian era legends of Alexander the Great became widespread throughout the East, amongst Ethiopians, Arabians, Persians, even Malayans and Siamese, but it is unlikely that any nation conquered by him would be the first to extol his deeds. The first systematic efforts to celebrate his fame would most naturally arise in Egypt, where Alexander was deeply respected both as its defender against the Persians and as the supposed founder of Alexandria; he had brought to Egypt peace and Greek civilisation, while the Persians, after their conquest, had left only misery and desolation. An account of his Asiatic campaign was written by an eye-witness, Callisthenes, who had been appointed, on Aristotle's recommendation, to accompany the expedition, but it has entirely perished. The earliest account of Alexander's life which has been preserved was written in the third century A.D. by an unknown author, now called Pseudo-Callisthenes because for a long time it was believed to be the actual contemporary account written by Callisthenes. About 340 A.D. a Latin translation was made by Julius Valerius and an epitome made of this during the ninth century. In the tenth century a Latin "History of Alexander the Great" was written by Archpresbyter Leo, who had obtained further material during an embassy to Constantinople.

None of these works has any historical value, all being attempts to magnify the fame of a great romantic conqueror, and incorporating any legends, however impossible or absurd, which would enhance the sensationalism. The version of Pseudo-Callisthenes seems to have been deliberately framed to represent Alexander as the national hero of Egypt, not as an alien ruler. Whereas he was the son of Philip of Macedon, he was presented as the son of an Egyptian king, Nectanebus,[1] by Philip's queen, deceived by magical means into dishonouring her husband. The last native king of Egypt was Nectanebus II; it therefore seems fairly obvious that the writer wished to attribute to Egypt the credit of having produced the conqueror of the world by making Alexander a lineal descendant of a native Egyptian dynasty. Greek early became the language of learning in Egypt, and so any Egyptian scholar of the third century would naturally write in Greek; Pseudo-Callisthenes must therefore almost certainly have been a native of Egypt.

The earliest extant French romance is that of Alberic de Besançon, of which only a fragment remains. During the twelfth century also was written another verse romance, and then "Le Roman d'Alixandre," the most famous of all, composed by several authors.[2] Other romances both in verse and prose followed regularly until the fifteenth century. Before the Norman Conquest an Anglo-Saxon version had been made of a supposed letter from Alexander to Aristotle, actually composed during the ninth century, but the earliest English romance is "The Life of Alisaunder," written in verse early in the fourteenth century. During the fifteenth and sixteenth centuries were written three alliterative poems, of which only fragments remain, and now usually called "Alisaunder," "Alexander and Dindimus," and "The Wars of Alexander." Also of the fifteenth century are the prose "Alexander," "The Scottish Alexander Buik,"[3] and Gilbert Hay's "Buik[3] of King Alexander."

Only the first and earliest of all these versions is of any

[1] In the English romance called Neptanabus.
[2] The use of twelve syllable lines in this poem gave rise to the term "alexandrine."
[3] A Scottish form of "book."

literary merit. The interest is sustained throughout by skilful construction, by rapid action never spoiled by digressions or undue emphasis upon isolated topics, and by suggestive and picturesque descriptions. Alexander's character is clearly portrayed through both his actions and his speeches, and he is the victim of only one slight love episode, not sentimental or courtly, but made symbolical of the deterioration in character that a man may suffer if he permits himself to be subjugated by a woman. The poet claims to have written his work as a consolation to men afflicted by care and sorrow, and he probably succeeded as far as a poet can succeed by relating an interesting and exciting story about a great historical figure. The poem is divided into sections, most of which open with lyrical passages adapted to the various seasons of the year. And Alexander's voyages into strange and mysterious lands have become so integral a part of popular tradition that the continual introduction of magic and of supernatural monsters adds to rather than detracts from the interest, even to the modern reader. They symbolise the spirit of that great king who sighed for more worlds to conquer, but found them not.

The medieval versions of the Trojan War were likewise based upon spurious documents—documents which were alien both in form and spirit to Homer's "Iliad." During the Middle Ages Homer was not only little known, but actually despised as a deliberate calumniator of the Trojans. Since Virgil's "Æneid" had portrayed the Latin race as descended from the Trojans, the medieval reverence for all things Latin could only lead to a contempt for any writer who favoured the enemies of Troy. This linking of the Latin and Trojan races alone was sufficient to make Homer's work suspect, but when writings were discovered which claimed to relate the accounts of men who lived during the Siege of Troy and which differed fundamentally from Homer's version, any slight credit that Homer may have had finally disappeared. These reputed accounts of eye-witnesses were recorded in two Latin

works, one of the fourth century A.D. and the other of the
fifth or sixth. A fragment of the Greek original of the
former has been discovered, but not of an early date, and
certainly much later than Homer's. The first claims to
present an account originally written by Dictys of Crete,[1]
a supposed member of the Greek forces which besieged
Troy; the second an account originally written by Dares
the Phrygian,[2] who in the fifth book of Homer's "Iliad" is
described as a Trojan priest of Hephaestus. That of Dictys
favoured the Greeks, and was therefore acclaimed to be the
greatest authority by Byzantine writers; that of Dares
favoured the Trojans, and was therefore ranked supreme
by the writers of Western Europe. The romancers were
able to make some use of both works, since both described
Homer as a mere inventor of lying fables, the first merely
to gain credit for itself, the second to enhance the glory of
Troy and the Latin race. The former presents a good and
well-told story, and deals only with the siege of Troy and
the homeward journey of the Greeks; the latter is far more
rambling and diffuse, beginning with the Argonauts' quest
for the Golden Fleece and ending with the fall of Troy.
The reputed version of Dares' history was naturally the
chief source of romancers, owing to its bias in favour of
the Trojans, but has much less merit than the other,
clumsily combining crudely told episodes, describing the
battles in detail, and naming all the victors and all the
vanquished, some of whom are described as killed on at
least two separate occasions, and some represented as
Trojans in one episode and as Greeks in another. Both
accounts are very crude compared with Homer's; Homer
concentrates upon the action of a few weeks towards the
end of the siege, these fail to achieve either effective realism
or intensity by including the whole period of ten years.
The "Iliad" is a dignified and artistic epic, these spurious
versions are pure romance.

The people of the Middle Ages revered historical truth,
but were very easily duped. They eagerly sought for

[1] Dictys Cretensis.   [2] Dares Phrygius.

proofs of authenticity, but, like uneducated people of to-day, were easily satisfied; where the average man of the present time will ordinarily accept any printed statement as truth, so in the Middle Ages any Latin book was similarly accepted. They also had all the prejudice and credulity of modern party politicians; they were unwilling to believe that the Trojans, ancestors of the Roman race, were inferior to the Greeks,[1] so that as soon as a book was found which portrayed the Trojans as a superior race, even though defeated, they hailed it with joy. A hundred other books championing the Greeks would have been powerless to influence their opinion. The writer of the one book had only to claim an original written by an eye-witness, and his statements were accepted with full confidence. Hence the unhesitating belief that this Latin book was not only a true copy of a history written by a Trojan called Dares, but an accurate record of the Siege. Even in the sixteenth century this belief still remained unshaken, in spite of the extensive study of Greek literature and the researches of classical scholars—Sidney in his "Apologie for Poetrie" speaks of "the fayned Æneas in Virgil and the right Æneas in Dares Phrygius," but his good taste made him consider that Virgil's account is more "doctrinable," *i.e.* of more value in instruction than that of Dares.

The earliest extant romance—and the greatest of all romances on classical themes—was the "Roman de Troie," a poem of about 30,000 lines, completed about 1184 by Benoît de Sainte-More. It covers even more ground than the Latin original, beginning with the Argonautic voyage and ending with the wanderings of Ulysses. In 1287 Guido delle Colonne made an abridged translation into Latin prose, called "The Destruction of Troy." Although a much inferior work, this became the popular authority, again because in Latin, and the basis of all later romances. Benoît's romance was the basis of Boccaccio's "Il Filostrato," from which Chaucer drew the material for his

---

[1] A belief fostered by early Latin writers and immortalised in Virgil's "Æneid."

"Troilus and Criseyde," which, like his "Knight's Tale," concentrates only upon one episode, the love of Troilus for Criseyde, which is not mentioned in Homer and hardly at all in Dares.

From "The Destruction of Troy" derived eight English versions, of which only the first can strictly be called a romance—"The Gest Historiale of the Destruction of Troy," written late in the fourteenth century. It mentions Guido delle Colonne as its authority, expresses contempt for the falsehoods of Homer, and is imbued with a thorough medieval spirit. The most famous version is Caxton's "Recuyell[1] of the Histories of Troy," translated from the French "Recueil de Troyennes Ystoires." In 1420 Lydgate, author of "The Siege of Thebes," also wrote a poem called "The Troy Book."

As a result of these spurious works claiming to relate the accounts of Dares and Dictys, the medieval romances became long and diffuse accounts of many different incidents, more discursive even than their originals, and utterly lacking in either realism or intensity. They portray the Trojans as a noble and valorous race, the Greeks as mean and treacherous; Hector as the hero and as a mighty champion who could be defeated only by foul means, Achilles as an ignoble prince, destitute of honour and unable to overcome Hector except by stabbing him from behind.

In addition to this distortion of the facts as recorded in the "Iliad," the whole spirit of the story was completely changed; in place of an epic celebrating national heroes, the romancers present a tale of sentimental love. The "Iliad" has for its central theme the Wrath of Achilles, the stubborn refusal of Achilles to continue fighting because of a high-handed action by Agamemnon. As their share in some booty taken from the Trojans these two leaders had each a captive maid—that of Achilles called Briseis, and that of Agamemnon, Chryseis. Agamemnon returns Chryseis to her father Calchas, a Trojan priest, and, with

[1] Collection.

the consent of the Greek leaders, takes Briseis from Achilles in return. Homer portrays this action simply as the reason for discord in the Greek forces, but gives no hint of any love-story. In medieval romance these two captives became confused, and the daughter of Calchas, called sometimes Briseis, sometimes Chryseis, is portrayed as heroine and the lady-love of Troilus, one of Hector's brothers. This love theme eventually became so prominent that Chaucer in his "Troilus and Criseyde," a work nearly as long as the "Iliad," concentrates upon it alone; to him the Siege of Troy was of secondary interest, and the tragic love of a Trojan for a woman who is compelled to leave him the supreme topic.[1] This conversion of an epic account of national warfare to a sentimental love-story illustrates how drastically themes were changed in the later Middle Ages to suit contemporary tastes. Here the versions may be compared, because both exist in writing. It may therefore be seen how unwise it is to assume that any romance directly or even indirectly reflects the spirit of oral traditions which are no longer known, unless con-clusive evidence can be adduced. This warning is par-ticularly needed both in making and reading hypotheses on the origin of Arthurian legends, the oral traditions of which are now no longer known.

In spite of the numerous English versions of classical themes in this period, there is no reason to believe that classical history or legend played an important part in popular English romance. Apart from Chaucer's poems, only two existing versions, one on Alexander, and one on the Siege of Troy, were written before 1400. The numerous versions of the fifteenth and sixteenth centuries were no doubt due to the recent revival of classical studies rather than to the popularity of these themes in the period of romance.

[1] Calchas is represented as being with the Greek forces and insisting that the Trojans send his daughter to him. She is therefore exchanged for a Trojan prisoner, and eventually accepts the love of a Greek warrior, named Diomede.

CHAPTER VII

ENGLISH TRADITIONS IN ROMANCE

THE CLASSIFICATION BY JEAN BODEL[1] OF the three preceding themes of romance—Charlemagne, Arthur, and classical legends—as the matters of France, Britain, and Rome respectively inspired modern scholars to call all the romances based on English traditions the Matter of England. These traditions would, no doubt, appeal only to the people of England, and were not adopted, as far as is known, by any Continental romancer. But the poets who catered for English audiences not only had to learn from the French the art of romance, but seemed incapable of writing romance on any story without the aid of some foreign, usually French, original. So even English legends had to be first written up by Anglo-Normans before English versions were composed. For a long period after the Conquest literature designed for the higher classes in England was written in Anglo-Norman or in Continental French, not in English. There is no need, however, to assume that all Anglo-Norman literature was written by men of Norman descent; some of it was probably written by Englishmen. But the men who wrote romances in English seemed incapable of writing up even English legends without support, and so had to wait until the Normans had become interested in these legends, and adapt from Anglo-Norman versions. By the end of the twelfth century the Anglo-Norman and Anglo-Saxon elements seem to have become thoroughly blended to form one composite nation with common interests opposed to those of France and, even very largely, of Normandy also. It is therefore probable that the Anglo-Norman romances which relate English themes reflect a growing desire among the Normans to accept as their national traditions those of English rather than of French history.

[1] See end of Chapter II.

The romances usually grouped under this heading are those dealing with King Horn, Havelok the Dane, Guy of Warwick, and Bevis of Hamtoun. The two last, though reflecting in various degrees English national sentiment, are of uncertain origin, and, as far as can be judged at present, have no reference to earlier English history or legend. They will therefore be left for discussion to the next chapter, in which are grouped together various famous romances belonging to none of these four main categories. The two first are almost certainly based on earlier English legend, and may therefore be considered as genuine matter of England in the same way as Arthurian romance is matter of Britain.

The disproportionate attention paid to the pseudo-history of Arthur in the chronicles of Geoffrey and of Wace may have been partly or even largely inspired by an attempt of the Normans in England to foster a national hero in opposition to the French hero, Charlemagne. Anglo-Normans would not be prepared to accept as national themes genuinely English traditions until they had ceased to regard the English as a subject race. King Arthur, far from being English, was actually hostile to Angles and Saxons, and, further, was regarded as of Trojan descent. It is therefore by no means incredible that Arthur for a time was regarded as a rival national hero to Charlemagne. But once the fusion of the Norman and Anglo-Saxon elements in England was completed, Anglo-Norman poets would not scruple to regard Anglo-Saxon traditions[1] as national traditions, and to celebrate the exploits of heroes who lived before the days of Norman rule.

Most extant Anglo-Saxon poetry consists of paraphrases of Biblical stories or of other religious and moral themes, inspired by the conversion to Christianity which began in the seventh century. This religious zeal seems to have almost destroyed interest in racial themes, and "Beowulf"

[1] Except where they reflected hostility to Normans, as in the stories of Hereward. (Cf. Lytton's romance.)

is the only complete example of a national epic literature now extant. To what extent oral literature was composed to celebrate national events cannot be ascertained, but it is unlikely that the people were left completely destitute of popular national literature, whether songs or prose anecdotes. The latest traditions prior to the Norman Conquest would be those of Norse invasion and rule of England during the ninth, tenth, and eleventh centuries; these would also presumably be the most vividly remembered traditions during the twelfth and thirteenth centuries—the seed-time of romance. The only existing Anglo-Saxon poems relating episodes of this period are "Maldon" and "Brunnanburh," which give vivid descriptions of two conflicts between Saxons and Norsemen at the places after which the poems are named. But from about the middle of the tenth century Saxons and Norsemen in many parts of England lived on friendly terms, so that any oral traditions which remained in the twelfth and thirteenth centuries would probably reflect both the hostility of the earlier and the friendly intercourse of the later period. Of the two legends already mentioned, that of King Horn reflects the hostility, that of Havelok the Dane the fusion between the two races.

Of the former theme the only existing romances are the Anglo-Norman "Horn et Rymenhild" of the twelfth century, the English "King Horn" of the thirteenth century, and "Horn Childe and Maiden Rimnild" of the fourteenth century. These three poems vary so greatly that the English versions cannot have derived from the Anglo-Norman, but all three must have originated from some one or more still earlier versions, now lost. The theme of all is the same, the forced exile in youth of a king's son, expelled by an invading force, and his eventual return and reconquest of his father's kingdom. This theme of exile, return, and vengeance upon a tyrant or traitor was a favourite Germanic legend, and forms the basis of the stories of Havelok and of Hamlet. The names of both characters and places differ so widely in the three poems that there can be no certainty about either the localities or the historical incidents referred to. The theme of the English romance, "King Horn," is as follows: Horn, whose home is in Suddene (possibly Surrey), is exiled as a boy by Viking invaders, arrives in Westernesse (possibly the Isle of Man), grows up there and is loved by the king's daughter, Rymenhild. Their love having been discovered by the king her father, Horn flees to a western land (possibly Ireland), serves a king there for seven years, and returns to Westernesse just in time to prevent Rymenhild being forcibly married, and to marry her himself. It thus presents what must have been a common incident during the ninth and tenth centuries, a sudden Viking raid upon a coastal village, a general massacre, and the flight of all those whose youth or weakness spared them from death. For this reason it is highly probable that the basis was an oral legend which had been current from at least the tenth century, and possibly even an oral poem. The Anglo-Norman and second English poems, being more definitely romances of adventure, in which little national sentiment is reflected, possibly represent later or more distorted versions of the same legend.

The story of Havelok represents a later stage in English history, after hostilities had ceased. Horn is an English champion against Norse Vikings; Havelok, a Norse hero, and eventually ruler of both Denmark and England, the first by hereditary right, the second through marriage. Denmark and England are represented as ruled by treacherous regents, the first having defrauded and attempted to kill Havelok, the second having defrauded the princess Goldeburh. Havelok flees to England with a fisherman called Grim, later earns his living as a kitchen-boy, and is eventually married forcibly to Goldeburh by the English regent, who hopes by thus degrading the heiress to establish his own rule permanently. On attaining manhood, Havelok returns to Denmark, gathers round him all those who are still faithful to his father's house, defeats the regent and regains his throne. He then returns to England with his wife, rallies her adherents, and wins back her throne.[1]

There are extant two Anglo-Norman versions, one in Gaimar's "L'Estorie des Engleis"[2] of about 1150, and "Le Lai d'Havelok," written a little later in the same century. The only existing English romance is "Havelok the Dane," written about 1300, but a summary of the story is also given in Robert Manning's English version of Pierre de Langtoft's[3] chronicle. The English romance, though telling precisely the same story, gives to all the characters except Havelok and Grim completely different names from those in the Anglo-Norman versions and the summary above mentioned. No definite reason for this change has yet been discovered, but a possible reason is confusion by some minstrel or by the author of the English romance of two similar stories which would permit of unconscious interchange in names of minor characters. Havelok and Grim are probably the only personages who were of significance in the legend. The common origin of all versions, again, was probably some tradition current from at least the eleventh century, and again possibly an oral poem.

The story was localised at Grimsby by stating that Havelok's landing-place in England was named by him after the fisherman who had saved his life, and who was later rewarded by being made an earl. The town seal of Grimsby bears the figures of Havelok, Goldeburh, and Grim. Since it is claimed that this seal was struck no later than the reign of Edward I, it looks as if the romance was regarded as authentic history of the town and the seal made for that reason. This, of course, is no proof that the original story refers to Grimsby. No evidence exists as to what names were given in the oral traditions of this legend,.but the localisation at Grimsby is probably due to the earliest

[1] In the story of Hamlet as related by Saxo Grammaticus, Hamlet marries the daughter of the king of England, returns with her to Denmark, kills the usurper, and later defeats the king of England.
[2] "The History of the English."
[3] An Anglo-Norman of Yorkshire.

K

writer, Gaimar, whose patroness, Constance Fitzgilbert, was a Lincolnshire lady.

The story of Havelok probably originated from some historical incident which in the course of time became more and more encrusted with legendary material until little if anything of the original basis remained. In the Anglo-Norman poems Havelok is also called Cuaran, which, meaning a brogue of untanned leather, was a surname of Olaf Sictricson, a Viking defeated at Brunnan-burh[1] in 937. It has been suggested, therefore, that Havelok may be a variant of Abloc, the Celtic form of Olaf. But it must be remembered that the surname Cuaran, with its common meaning, might easily have been applied to other Vikings as well. It has also been suggested that the story represents a mingling of two tra-ditions, that above mentioned and another about King Swein, who became king of England in 1013. Here again it must be remembered that medieval romancers, though claiming to relate history, were quite unlike modern his-torians. They were generally only too willing to incor-porate elements from any source and to attach their stories to any well-known names. The audience would be attracted by any good story and any well-known hero, but would not trouble to inquire whether the story fitted the hero or not. The folly of taking such romances too seriously is clearly exemplified from "Le Lai d'Havelok," which is not only called a Breton lay—that is, attributed to British not English tradition—but is even linked to the Arthurian legend by representing Arthur as conqueror of Denmark and the overlord of Havelok's father. If a cul-tured audience would accept this it would accept almost anything, and even if Havelok represents Olaf Sictricson, not one single episode may have the remotest relationship with any of his deeds.

The essence of the stories of Horn, Havelok, and Hamlet

---

[1] The Anglo-Saxon poem "Brunnanburh," which relates this fight, was incorporated into the Anglo-Saxon Chronicle under the year 937, and was probably composed immediately after the battle.

is the same—forced exile followed by vengeance upon traitors who have seized the throne. The English romances of "King Horn" and "Havelok the Dane" both reflect the spirit of the early chansons de gestes, the spirit of national unity against a common foe, and may both have been attempts to establish an English national hero in opposition to those of French romance, particularly Charlemagne. Both are almost completely devoid of the marvellous and sensational elements which were incorporated into all romance themes when the original inspiring force had decayed, and therefore were probably based on traditions which vividly reflected the spirit of the period of Norse invasions and rule of England. Both are racy narratives filled with exciting incidents. The homely descriptions and the stirring accounts of hand-to-hand fighting would please an illiterate audience, and Havelok particularly is very typical of an early non-feudal age when it was considered not shameful but even meritorious for the ruler to join with his inferiors in rough manual work. The absence of rigid caste distinction is even more strongly marked by giving an autocratic spirit only to the traitors. In the romances written for the same class of audience, but arising at a later date—Arthurian and Charlemagne romances, for example—this spirit of camaraderie is not portrayed. It is extremely unlikely that in "Havelok the Dane" it was portrayed to suit any democratic feeling of hostility towards the ruling class. The audience would not appreciate a hero who tyrannised over his dependants, but they would not demand a spirit of equality. The difference in spirit between "Havelok the Dane" and romances on Arthurian themes is probably due to the dependence of the latter on French romances which reflected French aristocratic ideals of a feudal age, and the dependence of the former on a story which reflected the ideals of England in the tenth and eleventh centuries, where, as in the Iceland portrayed in the Sagas, there was a strong bond of unity between all classes of freemen.

The fact that "Havelok the Dane" and "King Horn"

were both written earlier than most English romances on Charlemagne, Arthurian, or Classical legends seems to indicate that English romancers, and presumably their audience also, were first attracted by English legends, since French versions of all these themes were available before the composition of any existing English romance.[1] The scarcity of English romances based on English traditions will be due to the lack of Anglo-Norman or French versions. The higher classes in France, and presumably in England also, quickly tired of romances based on warfare and deeds of violence. The romancers who catered for these classes had, therefore, to adopt other subjects to ensure continued patronage, and English poets were left stranded. Unable or unwilling to compose romances without a written original as support, they had to offer to their audience themes which had been framed for the knightly classes and which almost certainly would be less attractive than those based on national traditions and reflecting English national character.

[1] It is, of course, impossible to know definitely what theme was first adopted, as many romances were doubtless written, of which no evidence remains.

CHAPTER VIII

MISCELLANEOUS THEMES OF ROMANCE

THE FOREGOING CLASSIFICATION OF RO-
mances into four distinct groups is based simply on
the origin of their themes and follows accepted
tradition. There are also many romances unrelated
to any of these groups and based on legends of various
types and sources which are not so easily classified. If all
the remaining romances were to be included, some group-
ing, according to type or place of origin, would be possible,
but, as many are of little or no importance, discussion is
here confined to those English romances which are of in-
trinsic merit or reflect some significant aspect of medieval
life; for this reason, no systematic classification will be
attempted. Some of them were apparently attempts to
popularise new heroes in opposition to Charlemagne,
Arthur, and their knights, others are illustrations of some
one aspect of human nature or of conduct, and others
again are Saracen stories refashioned to suit a Christian
and Western European audience.

"Guy of Warwick" and "Beves of Hamtoun" professedly
celebrate English champions, and might therefore be
included in the "Matter of England." They do not, however, reflect any significant aspect of English life and, unlike the romances of Horn and Havelok, show no evidence
of being based on specifically English traditions; they are
simply romances of adventure, in which the whole interest
lies in the marvellous feats of knightly prowess performed
by the heroes in various European and Eastern countries.
The authors of the Anglo-Norman originals were possibly
animated by a desire to establish national heroes of their
own race and country,[1] but, in the absence of any one

[1] *i.e.* Normans resident in England.

dominating figure like Charlemagne, chose different subjects, which, by conflicting with each other, would naturally
prevent the growth of any outstanding national tradition.
The themes, moreover, of both these and the romances of
Horn and Havelok, would offer little attraction to a
courtly audience which had tired of bloodshed and violence and demanded chivalry and love. But to the lower
classes such themes would naturally be attractive, partly
because of their stress on physical prowess, which illiterate
people prize as man's supreme gift, and partly because of
their numerous stock romantic episodes—the hero's love
for a maid of superior rank, combats with knights, Saracens, and dragons, imprisonments and disguises, magic
and mystery, and then, to crown all, a wedding. Even
as late as the eighteenth century Guy and Bevis were
national heroes and vivid personalities to many children
who knew little of the most renowned Arthurian knights.

Still another national hero of romance was Richard Lion-
heart. Not only was he a famous crusader, but he seems
to have been the only one of England's early alien rulers
who strongly appealed to the English lower classes, *i.e.* to
the people of Anglo-Saxon stock. He became so popular
that he was universally regarded as the friend and supporter of Robin Hood, the national emblem of popular
rebellion against feudal despotism. He was therefore
eminently suited to become a rival national hero to
Charlemagne and Arthur. The most inspiring event of his
brief reign, his crusade to Palestine, was made the subject
of a fourteenth-century verse romance called "Richard
Cœur de Lion." Reference is made in it to a French—
probably Anglo-Norman—original, but no other evidence
remains of any such work. It is therefore unknown how
early Richard became a hero of romance or how he was
first portrayed. But no matter how drastically the English
poet may have changed the spirit to suit a different
audience, the original, in presenting a crusade, must have
largely concentrated upon fighting and deeds of violence,
and probably portrayed the same episodes and the same

type of character, even if less distorted. In all periods of exaggerated stress on etiquette the bold bluff warrior who has performed great feats in the service of his country, but who is "socially impossible," to use a time-honoured phrase, has provoked amusement rather than admiration among ladies of Society. The high-born ladies of the twelfth and thirteenth centuries would no doubt graciously admit that Richard was a worthy man, but would resolutely ban stories of his prowess from their boudoirs. The barons may have taken keen delight in a stirring narrative of bloodshed and fierce fighting, but they were not the audience which the poets were most obliged to please. And the feats of Richard extolled in the English, and probably also in the original poem, were not calculated to please a female audience. He kills the German Emperor's son with one blow of his fist, thrusts his hand down a lion's throat and pulls its heart out, transfixes seven Saracens with one arrow, and fights so ferociously that the poet relates with great relish,

> "By the blood upon the grass
> Men might see where Richard was."

Even the stronger-minded and less courtly women of to-day would derive little pleasure from the picture of Richard eating the flesh of captured Saracens to cure himself of fever, and serving before Saracen ambassadors at a banquet the heads of decapitated prisoners.[1]

This romance also reflects intense hostility towards the French, portraying some of them as more vile than the vilest Saracens. Although there had been a steadily increasing hostility between Anglo-Normans and Frenchmen from the twelfth century, it did not reach its greatest intensity until the outbreak of the Hundred Years' War; this hostile attitude in the romance may therefore have been chiefly due to the English poet, animated by this fierce national conflict. The French crusaders are por-

---

[1] Since some of the MSS. omit these cannibalistic orgies, it is probable that they were also lacking in the original, but the general spirit of violence and brutality would almost certainly be present.

trayed as cowards, the French king and barons presented as ruining all chances of success by accepting ransom for prisoners instead of putting them to death. Richard is praised because he ransomed none, but freed only those captives who accepted Christianity. This attitude, naïve as it now appears, reflects genuine medieval sentiment, which could not clearly distinguish between the letter and the spirit. No doubt in a religious war most captives of either party would regard conversion as deep dishonour and death as martyrdom; but many would also, no doubt, be astute enough to feign conversion when life and freedom depended upon such deceit. Christian captives who had been freed on their promise to take no further part in the campaign were frequently absolved from their oaths by priests, and continued fighting. It is probable that Saracens also could similarly obtain absolution from their promise of conversion. The French custom of demanding ransom did have the merit of depleting Saracen resources and replenishing their own. Richard is portrayed as the hero of the crusade, bearing the whole burden of the campaign, and repeatedly thwarted by French cowardice, treachery, and avarice. The chronicle of the Anglo-Norman Geoffrey de Vinsauf, which relates this crusade, states that he had the valour of Hector, the magnanimity of Achilles, the eloquence of Nestor, and the prudence of Ulysses. The romancer made little attempt to illustrate any of these qualities except the first, and the last he would despise as cowardice—Richard is most praised when the deeds he undertakes are most reckless and foolhardy. But all this bombast would only enhance him in the eyes of the illiterate, who would see no objection in the wholesale slaughter and cannibalism portrayed.

Reference has already been made to the great demand among the higher classes for love-themes in romance. The higher classes in England were probably as much interested in love-stories as those in France, but before English again became the national literary medium in the fourteenth century the craze for tales of courtly love was almost dead. It is not surprising, therefore, that English Arthurian romances, designed for the educated classes, whether poems like "Sir Gawain and the Green Knight," or literal prose translations from the French, like the prose "Merlin," were versions of those themes which had become of greater interest because of their stress upon character and real chivalry, or upon the deeds of Arthur rather than upon those of his knights. There still exists, however, one romance, "William of Palerne," in which sentimental love is the central theme. It was written in alliterative verse about 1350[1] and dedicated to the Earl of Hereford. The French original was written in the twelfth century, when the demand for tales of sentimental love was at its height. The dominant theme is the hero's love for a Roman Emperor's daughter, who is naturally not permitted to marry him because of his inferior rank. The lovers therefore have to flee, and so provide an excellent basis for romance. The principal character is a wer-wolf,[2] who assists them in their flight and guides them through all their adventures. This introduction of a wer-wolf as chief character and the flight of the lovers disguised in bear-skins to elude pursuit sufficiently serve to show the universal craze for novelty and sensationalism. The title of the poem and its localisation in Italy may indicate Italian tradition as the origin, but both themes were so common in European legend that no certainty can be assumed.

To the medieval mind a story which emphasised some particular virtue or aspect of human character was peculiarly acceptable. The clergy had possibly first aroused and certainly fostered this desire by using alle-

---

[1] About this time were written a number of alliterative poems, apparently a determined effort both to make English the national literary medium again and to revive the alliterative measure, the only measure of Anglo-Saxon verse. The greatest of them is "Sir Gawain and the Green Knight."

[2] A man transformed into a wolf by magic, but still preserving his human faculties.

gorical stories in their sermons,[1] and the fame of Arthurian romance was largely due to its symbolic portrayal of codes of conduct. Romances were therefore composed for no other purpose than to symbolise some aspect of human conduct. One famous group was designed simply to stress the virtue of patience and meek endurance; a man or woman is exposed to great hardship and suffering simply as a trial of patience, and happiness ensues only as a result of meek acceptance of all trials without complaint. Both in the heaping up of the miseries endured and in the common neglect to attribute any satisfactory reason for their sufferings these romances closely resemble the story of Job, and may have been influenced by it. The aim was not to show that sin entails just retribution, but that it is man's duty to suffer any trials imposed by God with resignation.

The first theme, commonly called the Eustace legend,[2] is represented in the English romance "Sir Isumbras," and presents a knight who is offered by God the choice of suffering in youth or in old age. Choosing the former, he is deprived of all his property, separated from his wife and children, and overwhelmed with disaster after disaster for over twenty years. Having endured all his woes without complaint, he is finally restored to his family, regains his wealth, and lives happily ever after.

The second theme, frequently called the "Constance Saga" because Chaucer's tale of Constance[3] is the best-known example, portrays a maiden banished or fleeing from a harsh or unnatural father, wandering in alien lands, marrying a foreign prince, falsely accused during his absence at war of having born a monstrous child, again banished, and eventually reconciled to both husband and

[1] The "Gesta Romanorum" is the most famous of collections of stories designed for the use of priests in sermons. To each story was added a moral, which made it significant of some virtue or vice.
[2] Because the earliest version is the story of St. Eustace, recorded in a Greek MS. of the eighth century. A large number of versions exist, in nearly every European language.
[3] Man of Law's Tale.

father. The original tradition is apparently of Germanic origin, and seems to have had as basis a father's desire to form an incestuous alliance with his daughter. Chaucer's tale of Constance presents the theme almost in full, while his tale of Griselda offers a different type of story, but also designed to stress the virtue of meek endurance. The basis of Chaucer's tales of Constance and of most existing versions of this theme is Nicholas Trivet's Anglo-Norman chronicle, which relates the story of a Greek Emperor's daughter forced to marry a pagan Sultan, exiled by him because of the false accusation, and eventually marrying the King of Northumbria. The substitution of an unwilling and unnatural marriage for the incestuous desire of a father made the story more artistic and less disgusting. The introduction of a Northumbrian king may indicate an English tradition as the original basis, and the Greek Emperor and pagan Sultan be substitutes to add a more romantic glamour. It has been suggested that the original heroine was a daughter of the famous Mercian king, Offa, who was overlord of Ælla, King of Northumbria, and desired to rule all England. The chief foes of Ælla and Offa were the Scots, and the Saracens of romance may have been substituted for the Scots of tradition because of their remoteness and therefore greater fascination. Apart from Chaucer's poem, the most charming English version is that of "Emare," in which the heroine flees to avoid incestuous marriage with her father, even though it has been sanctioned by the Pope. The story in general outline is otherwise the same, except that Emare is married only once, and to the King of Galicia. Great stress is laid upon the sentiment and upon courtly etiquette, the training, manners, and dress of the heroine being charmingly described. Following conventional tradition, the poet called it a Breton lay, but no French or other original has yet been discovered.

Another famous romance, "Amis and Amiloun," was designed to emphasise the virtue of firm and enduring friendship. The earliest French version, "Ami et Amile,"

of the twelfth century, was incorporated into the Charlemagne cycle of romance, but was almost certainly based
on a tradition unrelated to any definite historical legend.
Amis and Amiloun are two friends who pledge themselves
to assist each other under all circumstances. Amis later
seduces the daughter of his overlord, and is accused of his
crime by the steward. He demands trial by combat, but
cannot undertake the duel himself because, as a pre-
liminary, he would have to swear his innocence, and thus
commit perjury. Amiloun, disguised in his armour, fights
in his place, kills the steward, and thus saves his friend's
life. As a result of this deceit Amiloun is stricken with
leprosy and so becomes a beggar. Amis eventually finds
him, and does not hesitate to sacrifice his children when
warned in a vision that only by their blood can Amiloun
be cured.

It was quite in keeping with medieval sentiment that this
ideal of friendship should be carried to its logical extremes.
In almost every act of life was visualised the will of God.
As Job had suffered, so Sir Isumbras, Constance, and
Emare suffer undeserved and almost incredible misery
without complaint because God had ordained. And just
as Abraham had unhesitatingly agreed to sacrifice his
only son, so Amis agrees to sacrifice his children at the
divine command.

Such exaggerations would tend to hinder rather than to
stimulate moral progress, and the excessive emphasis of
the Church upon impossible ideals would also tend to
breed apathy rather than active virtue. The average man
and woman would deeply reverence a Constance or
Griselda, but despairing of attainment to such exalted
ideals, would be inclined to follow the line of least resistance and submit to periodical penance for their sins rather
than strive to avoid them.

All of these romances clearly reflect the essential difference between medieval philosophy and that of ancient
Greece and modern Europe—the latter stresses the need
to consider man's life as a complex whole, the former

stressed one aspect at a time. In many Arthurian romances and in these we see one ideal after another exalted, each in turn as supreme and exaggerated beyond human possibility. The exaggeration alone prevented the people from gaining a well-balanced view of life, and the isolation of these varied aspects made confusion worse confounded, because frequently one ideal of conduct was deliberately degraded in order to enhance another. For this reason men wandered in a maze of doubt, and by relying blindly on Church ritual and priestly absolution, made religion a mere mechanism instead of an inspiring force. "Amis and Amiloun" well exemplifies this clash of ideals. The ideal here isolated is that of friendship, but the example chosen is unfortunate. It was the steward's duty to expose the feudal treachery of Amis, but in order to stress the ideal of friendship, he must be killed. Not only is the first exposition of friendship based on deceit and sin, but the poet unconsciously teaches his audience that the steward is evil, not faithful and trustworthy, because he does his duty to his master. It is true that the deceit is not condoned; it is portrayed as sinful and therefore productive of misery, but not to the real offender. Amis has been guilty of feudal treachery and fraud, but suffers no punishment; Amiloun is afflicted with misery because he does his duty as a friend, the ideal which the romance was designed to enhance. The average priest may not have taught so crudely as did these romances, but the Church was responsible for this isolation of ideals which led to these distortions in literature. And morality could not be placed upon a sound footing until the teaching of the Church embraced all aspects of life in one survey, instead of isolating individual virtues and vices.[1]

One of the most charming of English romances, "Sir Orfeo," illustrates the popularity of Classical legends in this period and also clearly shows how thoroughly an alien

[1] The moral tales of the nineteenth century frequently exemplify this same mistake, which is one reason why the characters often appear so priggish. They are not human beings, but symbolical ideals on stilts.

theme could be imbued with contemporary sentiment. This Greek story of "Orpheus and Eurydice" becomes a medieval fairy tale, and Orpheus the prototype of all medieval minstrels. His wife is stolen by the king of the fairies and he wins her back only by virtue of his musical powers. But though a classical myth may have a tragic ending, a fairy tale may not; Orfeo, the harpist-king, retains his wife and enjoys with her a long and prosperous reign.

For many centuries Europeans have regarded the East as the home of mystery and romance; it was only natural, therefore, that the steadily increasing intimacy in this period between Frenchmen and various Saracen races, both in Eastern countries and in Spain, should lead eventually to the incorporation of Saracen stories into French and later into English romance. The First Crusade brought many thousands of Western Europeans not only into direct contact with Turks and Arabians, but also into far more intimate relationship than ever before with the Byzantines, who for a long time had been influenced by Eastern art, literature, and philosophy. Frequent conflict between the South of France and the Moors and Mussulmans of Spain led also to continued direct contact with still other Saracen races. The relationships in both cases would not always be of a hostile nature; for generations a large part of Palestine was governed by crusading barons, who found it expedient to live on friendly terms with their subjects, and similar friendly intercourse was no doubt common with the Mohammedans of Spain. During intervals of peace, pilgrims and crusaders would glean and bring back home oral tales from Palestine and Spain, while at all times written versions of Eastern stories were available in Byzantium. Poets were continually searching for something new, and would eagerly incorporate such stories into romance. The "Arabian Nights Entertainments" sufficiently illustrate how predominant in Mohammedan literature are the elements of mystery and love, and a romancer could desire no better source from which to introduce stories which would please his courtly and largely female audience.

The English romance which most clearly shows this new influence is "Floris and Blauncheflour," composed about the middle of the thirteenth century. It is a free and much abridged translation of the French "Fleure et Blanchefleure," the theme of which is of Saracen, probably Spanish, origin. A Saracen king of Spain, during a predatory raid in Galicia, attacks a band of pilgrims, and carries back amongst his prisoners a young French widow. Soon afterwards she gives birth to a daughter, Blauncheflour, and the Saracen queen to a son, Floris. The children are brought up and educated together, until the young prince falls in love with the French girl, who is then sold as a slave, after all other attempts to cure his infatuation have proved abortive. Floris then sets out to rescue her, and finally discovers her in the harem of the Emir of Babylon.[1] He bribes the porter to admit him to the harem and is later discovered in Blauncheflour's room by the Emir's Chamberlain. Both are condemned to death, but finally the Emir takes pity on their youth and love, marries them, and sends them safely home. Another French romance, "Aucassin et Nicolette,"[2] one of the most charming of all medieval romances, relates a similar story, in which the prince is a Christian and the captive maid a Saracen. These two romances appear to be variations of the same story, the second being adapted to suit French tastes more closely. No direct original of either is known, though Eastern stories containing similar episodes are common. Both present a simple idyllic story representing the supremacy of love over both filial duty and religious faith, and it would be difficult to conceive of any stronger representation of love's supremacy above all law than the love of a prince for a maid who is both a slave and

[1] *i.e.* old Cairo, formerly called Babylon, not the city which now bears that name.

[2] This romance and the French "Ami et Amile," referred to earlier, were made the subject of a fine appreciation by Walter Pater in his "Renaissance."

an infidel. Even in the English version the Eastern spirit of mystery and of passionate love is well portrayed, and no attempt was made to infuse the courtly sentiment so common in Arthurian romance.

INTERMINGLING OF ROMANCE THEMES

A characteristic feature of medieval romance is the wholesale incorporation of elements from widely divergent sources and the consequent linking together of originally isolated themes. Romancers drew material from the Bible, from Classical history, legend and mythology, from general European legend and folk-lore, and from one another. Where Biblical stories could be adapted to suit contemporary sentiment they were liberally adopted because of their familiarity, and Biblical characters like David and Solomon were often used both as exemplars of particular moral aspects and as ancestors of illustrious knights. The legendary conception of the Terrestrial Paradise, in presenting a wonderland of marvels and monsters, satisfied the craving for sensation, the "Apocrypha" yielded many stories suited to romance, and "Revelation" offered an almost infinite variety of gorgeous descriptions and of precious stones, which were freely used by poets as artistic embellishments. Galahad is described as a descendant of Solomon,[1] Gawain is cured by the Flower of Paradise,[2] and a battle in the "Morte Arthure" is stated to have been more terrible than that at Jehosophat.

Classical mythology supplied romancers with a list of gods and goddesses who could be used as conventional symbols, and were also used as the names of Saracen gods by romancers who had no knowledge of Mohammedanism, but had to portray its inferiority to the Christian faith as best they could. The Underworld of Classical mythology was useful as a source of magic and mystery, and could easily be blended with that of Celtic mythology

[1] In Grail romances.   [2] In the "Morte Arthure."

and the Hell of Christian belief. Where pagan gods were portrayed as deities they were fitted into Christian doctrine by being represented as the offspring of devils, which, after all, is only a cruder and less artistic variant of the conception used so magnificently by Milton in "Paradise Lost." It was probably this exploitation of Classical legend and mythology that made chroniclers and romancers portray Britain as a Trojan settlement in order to ally the British to the Latin race. In the "Morte Arthure" King Arthur is presented as a descendant of Hector, son of Priam, and Gawain is wounded by a knight called Priamus, a descendant both of Hector and of Alexander the Great. Guy of Warwick is but one of many heroes who possessed the sword of Hector and the helmet of Alexander; so many heroes were invested with these two trophies that a whole armoury could have been stocked with the gear of these two warriors alone, who were credited with as many suits of armour as Queen Victoria had dresses. Only modern sceptics, like the pilgrims of Mark Twain, become disillusioned after collecting a barrel-full of nails, all from the true Cross. Devout Christians of the Middle Ages were willing to credit an infinite number of nails and an infinite number of swords once possessed by Hector. That the medieval audience was not critical of fact is well exemplified by the prose "Merlin," in which one of Arthur's foes, King Rion, is described as a descendant of Hercules, possessing a sword forged by Vulcan, and having his banner carried by four elephants. It was probably excess of sensationalism rather than mere lack of truth that chiefly contributed to the decay of romance in the fourteenth and fifteenth centuries. The romancers were obliged to introduce novelty, but by concentrating upon the novelties, instead of upon character, they lost the interest of an audience which was steadily becoming more educated and enlightened as literary merit decayed.

Not only did these various legends and the equipment and characteristics of legendary heroes and heroines become the regular stock-in-trade of all romancers, used

L

indiscriminately in any theme, but the actual stories and heroes of romance became in time common and interchangeable elements. In one of the sequels to "Huon of Bordeaux," Clariet, the daughter of Huon, becomes the heroine of an adventure which was either adapted from "Aucassin et Nicolette" or based on a mingling of this romance and "Fleure et Blanchefleure." In the same romance Merlin is described as the son of Ogier the Dane, one of Charlemagne's twelve peers, and both the children of Roland and Charlemagne's most rebellious vassal, Renaud, were incorporated into Arthurian romance as members of Arthur's army. Arthur himself appears in all sorts of romances under the most incongruous conditions; he is overlord of Havelok's father,[1] contests with Huon of Bordeaux the realm of Fairyland, and is therefore reproved by Merlin for his wrangling. The interchange of heroes in romance is well illustrated in "Le Chevalier du Papegau"; the original verse romance has for hero a knight called Guiglos, the later prose version substitutes Arthur, presumably to enhance the interest. It was, no doubt, the same spirit that inspired the author of "Ami et Amile" to link his story to the Charlemagne legend; and the same desire still holds in modern times. The average reader of historical romance desires only a good story and the introduction of famous historical characters. He is too indolent to investigate whether the author has presented a faithful picture of the period and the characters, and, if he reads a large number of such romances, any historical knowledge that he has gained from study is eventually obliterated by the more vivid representation in romance. Few novel-readers, when attempting to judge if a particular novel presents historical truth, realise that their knowledge has largely been gleaned from romances read earlier, not from historical texts.

The authors of both medieval and modern romance have had a similar aim—to satisfy these two primary demands, a good story and the introduction of historical or supposedly

---

[1] "Le Lai d'Havelok"—omitted from "Havelok the Dane."

historical characters. The audience of both would naturally be annoyed by any obvious distortions of history —the portrayal of Galahad as an amorous libertine, of Charles II as a saintly ascetic, or of Henry VIII as an avowed celibate—but would be little perturbed by minor perversions. The only essential difference is that the modern author cannot take as many liberties, because his public is slightly better educated, more critical, and less credulous.

CHAPTER IX

THE CHARACTERISTICS OF ENGLISH ROMANCE

IN SPITE OF ITS VARIED AND INCONGRUOUS sources, French romance faithfully reflects French sentiment and ideals because it was based largely on oral legends and written by skilled poets who were able to adapt those legends to suit French tastes. English romance was written largely by poets with far less skill and adapted from the written versions of Frenchmen; for both reasons, therefore, it could not be easily fashioned to suit English tastes, and so reflects less faithfully English sentiment. French romance was also written for and reflects the ideals of the educated classes, ideals which, except in decadent periods, will reflect the genius and character of the nation more closely than those of the illiterate. The bulk of English romance was an adaptation of literature designed for the higher classes of a foreign race to suit the tastes of the lower classes in England. To reflect accurately the ideals even of his audience the romancer would need more than skill and experience in adapting themes from foreign writers; he would have to select suitable themes. Since English poets were unable or unwilling to compose romance except from a written version, their choice was limited; the result, therefore, was that they reflect English sentiment only very indirectly.

Apart from didactic treatises and homilies, very little English literature was written for nearly two centuries after the Norman Conquest, and there is no evidence for the composition of any English romance before the thirteenth century.[1] Anglo-Saxon literature had been submerged first by Norse invasions and later by Norman rule,

---

[1] Many extant romances are merely copies of earlier versions now lost. Linguistic tests frequently offer satisfactory evidence as to the date of the originals, but in no case point to any date earlier than the thirteenth century.

and when English literature again began to flourish, it was completely dependent upon French and Norman models. The higher classes of Englishmen were forced to adapt themselves to Norman customs and assimilated their learning and culture largely from France. Until the fourteenth century, French, at first Anglo-Norman and later Parisian French, was the literary medium in England, French romance the dominant literature, and English romance designed simply for the uneducated classes who were unfamiliar with any form of French. During this century hostility with France caused a great outburst of patriotism, which led many of the aristocracy to desire a truly English literature and to encourage poets to write in English instead of French. The work of Gower shows this change of attitude in its transition stage; of his three long poems one is in Latin, one in French, and the last in English.

English romance cannot, therefore, be regarded as one composite whole; three distinct divisions must be recognised. First arose in the thirteenth and fourteenth centuries English verse romances, based on French versions and altered to suit widely different tastes. Then during the fourteenth century poets composed romances for a cultured audience or for titled patrons, whose tastes closely corresponded to those of the French nobility. Finally during the fifteenth and sixteenth centuries prose translations of French romances were made, sometimes by scholars like Caxton, sometimes for patrons, and sometimes by noblemen themselves like Lord Berners. This third group may be ignored here because, being for the most part close translation, it cannot be regarded as English literature reflecting English sentiment.

Although originals of many English romances have not yet been discovered, it is practically certain that nearly all existing romances were based on French versions. Since few of them were composed earlier than 1300 and many of them much later, it is probable that the French original was often a late version not belonging to the most brilliant period of French romance, the twelfth century. The drastic alterations made by later French romancers to suit their own tastes or to retain the interest of an audience which may have been familiar with earlier versions, and the further distortions of English romancers to suit a widely differing audience make it impossible to expect either great merit or any vivid presentment of the original conception in most English romances. Even apart from this disadvantage the crudity of most existing versions seems to indicate authors of little culture, though not, of course, uneducated. Some will have been clerks, men of the lower classes educated by ecclesiastics because their intelligence was above the average, and others merely minstrels who made their compositions not from French, but from earlier English versions written sometimes in a different dialect and therefore unintelligible to the audience of another district.[1]

In France as well as in England popular versions were made of aristocratic romances to suit the lower classes, and the romance of "Fleure et Blanchefleure" offers a good illustration of the alterations made. The version written for the knightly class concentrates upon the love theme, subordinating the adventures; that written for the lower classes emphasises the adventures and subordinates the love theme. The English romance was adapted from the French aristocratic, not the popular, version, but was similarly altered, abbreviating the love episodes and exaggerating the adventures to impress illiterate minds. French aristocratic romance reflected ideals of courtliness, caste distinction, and sentimental love, which made little appeal to uncultured people, and since the most famous French poet, Chrétien de Troyes, was preeminently the poet of courtliness, it is not surprising that his work was almost entirely neglected by English poets. Only one of his poems was made the basis of an English

[1] It must be remembered that at this period there was no standard English dialect; every author wrote in his own dialect and of many romances there still exist versions which differ in very little except the dialect.

romance, and that one, "Yvain," the most adventurous of them all. It was naturally based on a love theme, but the hero's adventures, especially with a lion which he tamed, still made an admirable romance even with the love theme drastically abridged. The English version, "Ywain and Gawain," eliminated much of the love sentiment, but presented the adventures in full.

The audience of French aristocratic romance, composed largely of cultured women who lived in an atmosphere of courtliness and gallantry, were more attracted by courtly heroes than by heroes famed for physical prowess, by knights who made devotion to women their chief duty, not devotion to the service of the State. The audience of early English romance were more attracted by physical activity and feats of strength. Even to-day the Latin races stress etiquette and chivalrous conduct, where the English race stresses prowess in outdoor sports. Provided that the primary basis of courage and honesty be present, the average Englishman and even Englishwoman expresses more genuine admiration for bluntness and bluffness of manner than for courtly grace, and to such an extent that many men assume a superficial pose of bluntness and even roughness to win popularity. Lancelot was the supreme hero of French fiction, Robin Hood of English. Robin Hood was made the subject of no English romance, simply because he played no part in French romance, but he was the hero of many ballads, and quickly transcended all the Arthurian knights in popular fame.

The great contrast in taste between the audience of English and that of French romance is well exemplified in "Richard Cœur de Lion," in which the poet gives a list of famous men whose lives should be an inspiring force to Englishmen. All of them are naturally heroes of French romance, because he knew of no other source,[1] but no

[1] The same list may have been present in the original Anglo-Norman version, but as was explained in the preceding chapter, even this version could not have been composed for the usual courtly audience. It was probably composed for some bluff Norman baron whose tastes would be similar to those of the average audience of English romance.

outstanding hero of romance of chivalry is included in the list. Five are from Charlemagne romance—Charlemagne, Roland, Oliver, Turpin, and Ogier the Dane; three are famous warriors of classical history and legend—Alexander, Hector, and Achilles; and only two from Arthurian romance—Arthur and Gawain, both more noted for courage in warfare than for courtliness or devotion to women. Lancelot and Tristram, the two most famous heroes of French romance, are ignored, just as they are largely ignored in English romance. The examples named were obviously selected on the score of strength and courage, which would appeal to Norman barons and Englishmen alike.

With the exception of those romances, which are little more than direct translations from the French, and therefore offer no useful evidence as to differences between English and French tastes, detailed comparisons between English romances and French originals are impossible, because in many cases the only existing French versions are obviously not the direct originals, and in other cases the differences are sufficiently great to make direct relationship uncertain. There can, therefore, be no certainty whether differences between existing French and English versions of the same story represent differences from all French versions, including those now lost, or whether earlier English versions, also lost, showed the same variations. But a few general points may be mentioned, illustrating with fair accuracy the contrast both in spirit and form between French romance written for the higher classes and English romance written for the lower. Narration of adventures was usually reproduced in a full and comprehensible manner, but where French sentiment was not clearly understood or fully appreciated poets frequently bungled. Detailed analysis of courtly love sentiments was neither understood nor appreciated by the English romancers. Even when a poet attempted to reproduce the love theme in full, as in "William of Palerne," he did it very badly, simply from lack of understanding. He was not attempting to adapt it to suit an audience with different tastes, because he wrote his poem for the Earl of Hereford, nor did he lack ability, because in most other respects he improved upon his French original, especially in humour and description. But when poets attempted to change the love-theme to suit their audience, they frequently presented it in a very garbled form. The poets and the audience desired a love-theme, but were not attracted by that delicate sentiment and detailed analysis of emotion which have always been an outstanding feature of French literature. The English poets, therefore, attempted to omit such passages, but had not sufficient skill to abridge artistically.

The French romances usually consisted of a medley of ideas, borrowed from various sources, but welded together harmoniously. Even an accomplished poet would therefore experience great difficulty in making drastic abbreviations and alterations without bungling, unless he recast the whole theme. The average English romancer was not an accomplished poet, rarely attempted any systematic recasting, and so, in attempting to reduce his original to half or less than half-size and eliminate such episodes as would not be attractive, he produced clumsy and inartistic work. Sometimes features of vital significance were omitted, and sometimes explanations essential to the full understanding of the theme or of an individual episode. In the English "Lay le Freine" the foundling child who becomes the heroine is given to the porter's daughter to be suckled, but the explanation offered in the original lay of Marie de France that this daughter was a widow with a new-born child is omitted. This omission, though trivial in itself, serves to show the carelessness and lack of attention to artistic detail so common in English romance. "Sir Tristrem" is an extreme example of clumsy adaptation, because dealing with one of the least attractive of all themes to an English audience and written by a poet of no merit. The French versions describe how Tristram kills a kinsman of Queen Iseult of Ireland, and that when the queen learns of this she and her daughter refrain from killing him only because they had sworn to produce him to fight against the steward who had claimed to be the slayer of the dragon killed by Tristram. Iseult, the daughter, had been promised in marriage to the slayer of this dragon, and she loathed the steward. In other words, they spare Tristram purely for politic reasons. In the English romance a very stupid reason is offered; the two Iseults are described as desirous of killing him, but each wishing to be the avenger; Tristram's life is spared only because they continue wrangling and fighting each other until the king comes to investigate the disturbance and so prevents the murder. When Iseult arrives in Ireland she naturally wishes to conceal from King Mark her loss of virginity; she therefore persuades her maid to take her place in the bridal bed on the wedding night. In French romance the details are so arranged that this deception is possible, and the maid's action is portrayed as a loyal sacrifice to save her mistress from disgrace. The sacrifice of virtue by a loyal maid was a common theme in legend, but apparently made little impression on the English poet, who describes the episode as a vulgar intrigue, offering no reason why the husband sleeps with the maid instead of with his wife. The episode of the love potion is similarly bungled. In French romance Iseult refuses to drink it with King Mark because she has already given her love to Tristram; the English poet merely states that she had no need of it. In French romance, also, Tristram rescues Iseult from an abductor and takes the risk of spending a night with her in a forest before escorting her back to Mark; the English poet magnified the one night into seven, obviously with the intention of impressing upon his audience the intensity of their love. One night's absence would not necessarily arouse suspicion, but no man could pretend that darkness had prevented his return with the wife for a whole week; this exaggeration was therefore entirely out of place.

"Floris and Blauncheflour" offers similar but less serious

omissions which mar the beauty of the work. In the French aristocratic version the hero travels to Babylon disguised as a merchant and avoids arousing suspicion by continually purchasing goods and talking on business matters with the innkeepers; in the English version he adopts the same disguise, but the poet was not sufficiently interested to make the disguise thoroughly realistic, and allows him to act too much like a prince; in the French popular version no disguise at all is used, the hero travelling all the way frankly as a prince and depending for his safety merely on his skill and strength. The English poet also failed to realise the significance of the most dramatic and most charming love episode in the whole story. Floris has been admitted secretly into the harem, but is discovered by the Emir's chamberlain owing to his and Blauncheflour's lack of precaution. Each morning two maidens had to attend the Emir at his toilet, and on this particular morning it is the turn of Blauncheflour. Her partner, Clarice, calls her, but, receiving no answer, concludes that she has already gone. The chamberlain is later sent by the Emir to look for her, and finds her asleep in Floris' arms. In the English version he at once discovers Floris to be a man, and reports to the Emir; in the French he mistakes Floris for Clarice, and tells the Emir a touching story of the great love between Blauncheflour and Clarice which makes them even sleep together; then he suddenly perceives Clarice standing in the Emir's room. The English poet, by omitting this episode in his anxiety to abridge, robbed this portion of the story of nearly all its beauty. The English romancers, on the whole, seem to have been inappreciative of artistic detail; they retained the most important facts and abbreviated by omitting those deft artistic touches which the cultured reader desires, but which an illiterate audience would consider unnecessary.

But the commonest feature of crude workmanship is over-emphasis, and over-emphasis is the vice of no one country and no one period. The modern novel, drama, and cinema film offer numberless illustrations of that excess of pathos which yields sickly sentimentalism and that excess of sensational incident which yields crude melodrama. Medieval English romance cannot be accused of sentimentalism—that vice was reserved for modern enlightened generations—but is certainly saturated with sensational melodrama. The distinction here between French and English romance is not one of kind, but merely one of degree; both aimed at sensationalism, but where French romancers usually restrained their fancy sufficiently to make the significance of their themes reasonably clear, the English poets exercised no restraint at all; they catered for an illiterate audience which generally judges importance by quantity and size, not by quality and proportion. Since many French romances must have been lost, it is unsafe to assume that all distortions in English versions have been entirely due to English writers, but a comparison between the existing English and Anglo-Norman versions of "Beves of Hamtoun," even though the latter may not be the direct original of the former, will serve to show what were probably characteristic distortions of English romance.

Ignorance of or lack of interest in feudal custom led the authors of this and other English poems to regard the honour of knighthood as lightly as many people to-day regard the Orders of the British Empire. The mother of Bevis and her lover, the Emperor of Almaine, both, on different occasions, promise to knight messengers as a reward for bringing good news. The Anglo-Norman poet makes no such statement, and even to-day, in spite of the lavish profusion of honours, couriers and other such temporarily distinguished citizens have usually to be content with minor decorations or even with gold watches. Feudal princes were jealous of their privileges, and careful romancers did not degrade knighthood in this careless manner. Reinbrun, son of Guy of Warwick, shows even less regard for convention, and dubs himself knight instead of waiting for some superior to recognise his merit.

Ignorance again led the English poet to call the Saracen god Apolyn,[1] where the Anglo-Norman offers the more correct Mahoun.[2] Most of the alterations and distortions, however, arose from crude and desperate attempts to enhance the hero's prowess, and were probably due to some English poet, even if not to the author of the existing version. A river in the Anglo-Norman becomes in the English romance a sea, which is crossed by Bevis only after swimming for twenty-four hours. His son Miles rides to London on a dromedary, where not only the Anglo-Norman, but even another English MS. give him that humdrum mount, a horse. Bevis also spends three days in prison and a fourth day escaping, entirely without food, but in spite of this prolonged fast kills a giant thirty feet high by striking him on the neck. The Anglo-Norman poet describes the giant as only nine feet in height. In his first combat the 700 enemies of the Anglo-Norman become 10,000 in the English, and later fifteen Saracens become fifty, all of whom he kills single-handed. An ambush of foresters is augmented by twenty-four knights, all of whom he again fights single-handed, and this time with the stump of his broken spear. Still later 400 Saracens become 60,000, and, not satisfied with these exaggerations, the English poet offers two further adventures, unmentioned in the Anglo-Norman poem. Bevis kills a dragon whose breath had infected Rome with malaria, and finally fights against a dense host in the streets of London with only a few supporters; 32,000 are killed, 5,000 by Bevis alone. It was a fitting conclusion that this Hercules amongst warriors, his wife, and his remarkable horse should all die on the same day.

The significance of this strong contrast lies not in the difference between English and French poets, but between unskilled poets writing for an illiterate audience and artistic poets writing for a cultured one. Nor was there

[1] Apollo.
[2] Mahomet, usually regarded by romancers as a god, not as a mere prophet.

any sharp line of division. Between poets like Marie de France or Chrétien de Troyes and the crudest English poets all grades existed both in French and English. And the same contrast still remains—between the penny dreadful and the romances of a Scott or a Stevenson. In each case the aim of the cruder work is the same—to arouse admiration for a hero in the minds of an audience devoid of critical judgment. The result is likewise similar—lack of all human appeal because the hero is unconquerable. A story that presents conflict must make it real conflict, which is impossible if one party is invincible no matter what odds oppose him. Not even Milton in "Paradise Lost" could make the war in Heaven a dramatic conflict, simply because God was invincible.

English romances were usually written in the couplet of four stresses, and occasionally in stanza forms. This short-lined couplet was not sufficiently weighty or impressive for most themes, but could be used with good effect in a fairy type of romance like "Sir Orfeo." Sometimes the English poet chose a particularly unsuitable measure, as in "Sir Tristrem," the doggerel verse of which was hopeless for a story of tragic love. The alliterative verse of "William of Palerne," though well handled by the poet and excellently suiting descriptive passages, was too vigorous and forcible for an appropriate expression of sentimental love. In "Sir Thopas" Chaucer adopted the worst and most monotonous verse-form of the period, and so parodied not only the spirit, but also the form of crude romance. His satire was not, of course, directed against all romance—he wrote romance himself—but only against the crudest examples.

In most of the romances written for the lower classes little attempt at artistic diction was made; the authors, like those of modern popular novels, catered for people who could not appreciate artistic refinement and cared only for the sensational incidents of the story. They were more hampered than the modern popular novelist in that they wrote in verse and had to find rhymes. To make their labours easier, poets, in the course of time, coined a large number of rhyming tags which could be introduced wherever rhyming difficulties arose; these delay the progress of the action, but make composition easier. When the author of "King Horn," for example, stated that Horn was

> "Fairer by a rib
> than any man that libbe."[1]

he was not attempting to found a futurist or any other new school of art, he simply was either too lazy or in too great a hurry to look for suitable rhymes. Similarly, when the author of "Ywain and Gawain" attempted to emphasise a lady's beauty by writing

> "Folk came far and wide
> To see her back and side."

it was not his desire to offer to his audience a similar attraction to that offered by a modern beauty chorus; he was simply restricted in his anatomical delineation by the difficulty of rhyming. A knightly audience would demand and receive a full description of her charms, a popular audience would insist that she be beautiful, but would not desire to have the story interrupted in order to hear the details. Such romances were designed for oral recitation, and may even at times have been chanted to the accompaniment of a harp. The romances composed for knightly patrons in the fourteenth century were probably intended for reading, and closely followed French models in their emphasis upon artistic ornament and design.

Although presumably all English romances were based on French versions, not all existing English versions derive directly from the French; some are copies or adaptations of earlier English versions, now lost, and of others the direct original is unknown. Where two or more MSS. of the same romance are still preserved, the variations are often so great that mechanical copying from a written version cannot be assumed. There are at least three possible reasons allowing for almost indefinite variation : (1) deliberate incorporation of new episodes to suit new or

[1] lives.

local interests; (2) transference from one dialect to another, in which poets would not always trouble to give an exact rendering; (3) the copying of a romance from memory.

Not only would an enterprising adapter of a French romance be sometimes inspired to incorporate elements of local interest—local anecdotes and traditions—but later English poets of other districts might similarly alter passages in copying an English version. Just as oral legends change to suit new conditions, and just as musical comedy to-day in moving from London to Brighton or Blackpool will vary its incidents to include topical allusions, so possibly medieval romance was deliberately varied to suit different generations or localities. In "Havelok the Dane" all the characters except Grim and Havelok bear names different from those of the French versions, and a possible explanation is that the English poet knew of a similar local story which he incorporated to arouse greater interest. Although the fisherman bears the same name, Grim, in all versions, he may have had a different name and even a different vocation in oral legend. The Anglo-Norman Gaimar, author of the earliest existing version, had for patroness a Lincolnshire lady, and may therefore have invented either or both name and vocation to localise the story in Grimsby. Any changes from oral legend to written romance must remain uncertain for lack of evidence, but some of the variations between French and English, or between two English versions of the same romance may possibly be attributable to this reason.

The copying of a romance from one dialect to another would not necessarily involve wide variations in subject matter, but in some cases changes of rhyme would be necessary, and these in the hands of a lazy poet might easily lead to substantial variations in individual episodes. This cannot, however, be regarded as the origin of any serious departures from the original.

Whether copying of romances was ever done from memory it is impossible to discover; most English romances would be recited to an audience, but not necessarily from memory. From a misplacement in the text it has been conjectured that the existing MS. of "Havelok the Dane" was copied from a MS. which had only twenty lines to the page,[1] and would therefore be small and easily carried. A MS. with such small pages would be of great convenience to a travelling minstrel, but of no especial benefit to a reader. In the romances themselves there is plenty of evidence for oral recitation, though not necessarily from memory. Many passages are nothing more than personal remarks of the minstrel addressed to the audience,

"Therefore listen a little stound."[2]

"Herkneth to me good men,
Wives, maidens, and all men."[3]

"At the beginning of our tale
Fill me a cup of good ale."[3]

The length of many romances makes it difficult to believe that minstrels regularly or even frequently recited from memory, although constant practice and constant attention to one single pursuit would enable them to memorise more easily and to retain memorised knowledge much longer than people who pursue a variety of interests and are unaccustomed to memorising. The copying of MSS. would be a laborious task, and some minstrels, who had ready to hand a large number of rhyming tags, would perhaps find it easier to memorise than to copy. A few readings would be sufficient, because the rhyming tags would make lapses of memory of comparatively little importance and each recital would lessen the strain upon their memory. If this practice was ever followed, some romances may be copies made only after several recitations; where memory failed, the minstrel would have to improvise, and each successive improvisation would cause variation from the original. Different MSS. of the same romance often show discrepancies not wide enough to

[1] The existing MS. has ninety lines to the page—in double columns.
[2] "Ywain and Gawain."   [3] "Havelok the Dane."

M

suggest deliberate alterations of the theme, not necessary because of any change in dialect, but yet too wide to be mere negligent miscopies from a written text. Of the three MSS. of "King Horn" two offer these variants of the same line:[1]

> "That his head fell to his toe."
> "His head off gan went."

Of another line all three MSS. offer variants:[2]

> "And Fykenyld by his side."
> "With him rode Fokenild."
> "At home (he) left Fikenhild."

In "Guy of Warwick" the first line of one couplet of two MSS. is the same: "The fields soon they have through gone." But the second line in one is, "That were the towns beside on," and in the other, "Downs and valleys they spared none." In one MS. of "Beves of Hamtoun" the hero's mother has for her lover the Emperor of Almaine, in another MS. his brother. None of these variations can be regarded as deliberate alterations of the story, nor yet as miscopies from a written text. The most natural explanation seems to be that at least one of the versions—possibly all—was written from memory, the discrepancies representing improvisations due to lapses of memory. In both examples cited from "King Horn" the variations include different rhyming words; this necessitated a change in the next line, even though the minstrel may have memorised it perfectly. Also in "King Horn" the name assumed by Horn when he wishes to conceal his identity is Godmod in one MS., Cuberd in the second, and Cutberd in the third. The difference between the first and the remaining two can hardly have arisen from miscopying, because only one letter remains the same. But there is sufficient similarity in sound to make false hearing possible. This would imply copying or memorising from dictation.[3] Similar evidence, of both kinds,

---

[1] l. 606.   [2] l. 644.

[3] In one passage of "Sir Eglamour of Artois" is a line "Thus *heard* I a clerk read." This may imply that the minstrel may have memorised or copied from an oral recital.

abounds in English romance, but cannot be regarded as certain proof of memorising. It is, however, possible that minstrels may sometimes have memorised romances, sometimes from written copies, sometimes even from the recitations of other minstrels. This would not only explain many of the variations between different English versions, and between English and French versions of the same romance, but also would account for many passages which are stupid and clumsy and vindicate the original adapters of French romance from some of the charges of crudity and bungling which would otherwise have to be laid against them.

Oral recitation, in allowing the minstrel to address personal remarks to his audience, also permitted him to incorporate episodes which would advertise his profession. In most romances minstrels are portrayed as honoured guests at festivals and as recipients of rich gifts. In the romance of "Ipomydon" the hero is alleged to have given the minstrels £500, but this must be regarded less as a serious estimate of self-worth than as a type of that pious hope which in a modern materialistic age impels people to claim excessive compensation from insurance firms and in breach of promise suits.

In spite of all their distortions and exaggerations, the English romances are frequently more direct and sincere than the French, even though less attractive to an educated reader by reason of their crudity. They lack the deep significance of the best French versions, but they also refrain from lingering over the details of love-making and social etiquette. Their constant aim was to record the deeds of a brave man, to relate how he served the State, or won his wife by daring exploits, and in spite of their crude exaggerations and misplaced emphasis, they are almost invariably wholesome. They rarely have as subject any theme which idealised or even countenanced a code of conduct which was opposed to generally recognised moral conventions. The best of these popular romances, such as "Havelok the Dane" and "King Horn," lack artistic finish, but have the merits of good ballads; they relate exciting stories in a vigorous racy style and pay enthusiastic reverence to valour and honesty, to all those characteristics which the English race regards as essentially manly.

The same wholesome atmosphere, but in a far more artistic setting, pervades the few romances written in English for the knightly classes—romances such as "William of Palerne," "Morte Arthure," and "Sir Gawain and the Green Knight." "William of Palerne," though marred by an unsuccessful attempt to reproduce the detailed love sentiment of the French original, deserves high praise for its descriptions and its humour. The humour particularly serves not only to vary the monotony, but also to lessen the sentimentalism of the love scenes. In the middle of a long description of the Emperor's daughter's wedding we are shown the irate old father, fuming with impatience and finally bursting into his daughter's room to ask why she delays so long. The "Morte Arthure" is also made attractive by a highly spirited diction and by beautiful descriptions of external nature. But "Sir Gawain and the Green Knight" best represents the highest ideals of English romance. Surpassed only by the two great German romances, "Tristan" and "Parzifal," and equalled by very few French romances, it combines the best qualities of courtliness and refinement with an intense human appeal. The simplicity of design and the avoidance of exaggeration allow the reader to concentrate upon Gawain's character and to see in him a vivid symbol of chastity and truth. No other romance is more worthy of the name, "romance of chivalry," in the widest acceptance of the term. Not all the skill of French poets could make Lancelot, or even Percival and Galahad, so truly representative of chivalry as this anonymous poet has made Gawain. The externals of refinement are lightly sketched, but the essentials deeply emphasised. In a few brief words we are told that Gawain met with many a strange adventure in his search for the

Chapel of the Green Knight, but our attention is not distracted by any account of them. The poet concentrates upon three episodes, the two encounters with the Green Knight and the chastity test, and these are used to show the hero's valour, loyalty and purity. The interest is heightened by vivid descriptions of scenery and of the three hunting episodes, but all are subordinated to the portrayal of character. And the poet's consummate skill is shown at its best in his contrast of the three hunting scenes with the three chastity tests, the regular transition from the hunting-field to the bedchamber, thrice repeated, accentuating the courtliness of the latter episodes and the constancy of Gawain. The alliterative verse admirably fits the descriptions of rugged scenery and of Gawain's strange adventures. Even the love passages, being very brief and embracing no analysis of sentiment or emotion, are not spoiled by this vigorous metre. Unfortunately the North-Western dialect, in which it is written, is as foreign to the modern reader as Anglo-Saxon, and therefore has caused to be neglected a romance which would offer as great an interest as almost any work of Chaucer.

CHAPTER X

THE INFLUENCE OF RELIGION ON ROMANCE

WITH THE DOWNFALL OF THE RO-
man Empire the whole fabric of classical
learning and Latin civilisation dissolved,
leaving the nations of medieval Europe
immersed in a bewildering medley of popular superstitions and confusedly mingled mythologies. The races
of Western Europe were very diverse, and Roman
conquest, followed by frequent Teutonic raids into the
Celtic countries of the South, led to an intermingling
of incongruous Latin, Celtic, and Germanic elements,
devoid of that strong unifying force which might have
co-ordinated them into one harmonious whole—Roman
Government and classical learning. The confusion resulting from this haphazard mingling of different racial sentiments, different religions and different historical traditions, was still further increased by the introduction of
Christianity, a new, strange, and undeveloped religion
which, in spite of its inherent value, only added at first
a host of new symbolical figures—angels, devils and saints
—and an elaborate ritual which fostered rather than
checked blind superstition. The philosophy at the base of
this ritual and symbolism was destined to exert a beneficial
influence later, but for many centuries it remained but
one more mythology making confusion worse confounded.

The bewilderment resulting from this medley of crude
and ill-assorted superstitions is well exemplified in the
engravings on the Franks Casket which present characters
from five distinct traditions—Weland the Smith of Germanic legend, Egil the Bowman of Norse mythology,
Romulus and Remus of Roman legend, Titus at Jerusalem
from Roman and Jewish history, and the Adoration of the
Magi from the New Testament. An oriel window in the
library of Merton College, Oxford, offers an even more

striking illustration—a picture of the Crucifixion as the centre-piece, with Venus on one side and Lucretia on the other. History, legend, and mythology were inseparable in the medieval mind, and, although it need not be assumed that every detail in romance was accepted as literally true, it is certain that critical judgment was entirely lacking until the Renaissance of the fifteenth and sixteenth centuries again revived classical learning.

Roman domination had naturally inspired a wholesome respect among the subject races for all things Latin; especially were the unlettered barbarians of Gaul and neighbouring provinces inspired with a blind reverence for Latin learning, and with the downfall of the Roman Empire this reverence was transferred to the teachings of the Church, which also had its headquarters at Rome. For a time the Church was worthy of this respect, for the early Christian Fathers had been scholars well versed in classical literature and philosophy and able to establish ecclesiastical doctrine on a sound basis. But by the time that Western Europe had been fully Christianised the Church had come to be governed by unlearned men, some of whom governed badly because of ignorance, others because they saw how easily absolute ascendancy could be gained over an illiterate and blindly trusting people. A rigid dogma had arisen because the people could not comprehend the philosophy of Christ's teaching, but could appreciate ritual and symbolism which had formed a large part of their own earlier heathen faiths. Able leaders could have gradually guided the people to a deeper understanding of religion and morality, but the Church was content to rely indefinitely on rigid dogma and elaborate ritual, with the result that both learning and religion became a mere mechanical process of slavish repetition from century to century, with distortions gradually accumulating. This blending of races and traditions, the further imposition of a new and non-national religion, and the deadweight of conservative ecclesiasticism eventually made epic and national literature impossible; but this same mingling of alien elements fostered the growth of romance.[1]

The gradual substitution of mechanical ritual and rigid dogma in place of Christ's moral and ethical teaching could only lead to men regarding religion as a mechanism —religion became rather a law to be upheld than a guide to moral conduct. The Church to a large extent perpetuated the tradition of that Roman rule which had crumbled before the invasions of Goths and Vandals, and both demanded and received the same implicit obedience to its laws. The only concrete remnant of Roman influence that existed in a reasonably developed form was Roman jurisprudence, which, therefore, became infused into medieval religious thought, and the more easily because it harmonised to some extent with the teaching of the Old Testament. This aspect is most clearly reflected in the chansons de gestes, which have as their main theme national and religious warfare. In them the Christian religion is portrayed as a law to be obeyed and defended; Saracens are given the option of death or baptism because they are enemies of God and the Church. The medieval baron, both in life and in romance, did not seek to convert the infidel to a better way of life, but to bring him under the sway of the Christian Church and therefore under God's dominion. God was the supreme judge, jealously watching over His people and punishing all rebellion against His laws unmercifully; the Church was the interpreter of His law, and its rules were therefore binding on all peoples. All disasters were regarded as the consequence of disobedience to God's commands, and the people lived a precarious life between tempting fiends on the one hand and a rigorous, all-powerful judge on the other.

The romances of chivalry concentrated more on the philosophical and moral aspects of Christianity, but could only adopt the mechanical conceptions of the Church.

[1] The excessive mingling of incongruous elements in romance is illustrated in Chapter XII.

The external phases of religious duty were constantly stressed—attendance at Mass, confession, penance, pilgrimages—and, although not the most ideal guides of human conduct, they must have had a beneficial influence upon the audience, who were thus constantly reminded that the ideal hero was not only a good fighter and a devoted lover, but a loyal Christian as well. In most romances stress is laid on the need of reliance on God's help if success is to be achieved. In nothing is this reliance on God's direct intervention shown so clearly, both in life and in romance, as in the conviction that trial by combat was an infallible test of justice; not until long after the Middle Ages was this test abolished. Romancers were especially fond of presenting trials by combat as a test of superiority between rival religions; Richard Lion-heart is challenged to a duel by a Sultan to test whether Jesus or Jupiter is the greater God.

The romances also, in accord with contemporary belief, presented all men as sinners, even the heroes and heroines, and all must expiate their sins before regeneration was possible. Lancelot and Guenivere retire to monasteries, and many a hero of romance undertakes a pilgrimage to atone for the deaths he has caused, even though in fair fight and for good reasons; Guy of Warwick undertakes such a pilgrimage, and his wife, Felice, devotes herself to charity during his absence—feeding the poor, endowing abbeys, and repairing roads and bridges.[1] The penances performed by knights were frequently fantastic; in "Sir Gowghter" the devil child, half-brother to Merlin, eats food only from dogs' mouths by way of penance. Penance and pilgrimages may appear a crude method of regeneration, but the magician's wand of many modern authors is still more crude; in many a modern novel sinners far worse than the most sinful heroes of romance become saints without any outward and visible sign to mark their new

[1] The last item was a common aspect of charity. There were no local councils to collect rates and maintain roads with the money. The barons maintained roads and bridges sometimes as charity, and sometimes recouping themselves by collecting tolls.

inward and spiritual grace, and the heroes and heroines of the average film story undergo vital changes of character in a few hours. The dawn of a new day did not bring the dawn of a new character in medieval romance without some definite expiation of sin. The morality was often mere ritual, but a ritual which did impose some hardship upon the sinner; the ritual of modern fiction is too often but a rapid change of thought rewarded by an eternity of pleasure; a worthless profligate will become a noble character by marrying a pure and innocent woman. The medieval mind would not consider that a satisfactory penance, and although it invested the Church with abnormal powers of conversion, it did not consider that sin could be discarded like an old suit of clothes, in spite of all its belief in magic.

The prevailing faith in the unlimited powers of Church ritual is well exemplified in the Charlemagne romances; Saracens became pure and chaste immediately after baptism. But this profound belief in the power of symbolical rites, though tinged with superstition, rarely led to any decisive distortion of moral values. The converted Saracens had been evil only because infidels; their sins arose not from moral perversion or from inherently evil character, but merely from ignorance of the true faith and lack of God's support. Saracens portrayed as fundamentally evil were rarely portrayed as converted; their punishment was death. This same emphasis upon the value of religion made romancers represent their heroes as unwilling to marry Saracen maidens until they had rejected their false faith, and in "The Sowdone of Babylon" Roland refuses to accept even a Saracen concubine. In real life crusaders would rarely have been afflicted with such scruples, and in "Sir Ferumbras," which relates the same episode, Roland accepts the concubine without demanding conversion. In "Huon of Bordeaux," Esclaramond, the Saracen Emir's daughter, asks Huon to kill her father and elope with her; but he, too, refuses to marry her until she is baptised.

A prominent feature of the religious emotionalism of the Middle Ages was the great number of visions and prophetic dreams claimed by both men and women—visions of God, Christ, the Virgin Mary, Saints and Apostles. "The primitive mind thinks in pictures, and in pictures it reasons and resolves."[1] These visions and dreams were the result of this habit and of psychoneurosis, caused by excessive fasting and penance allied with intense introspection of sensitive minds. The secluded lives of monks and nuns and the austerities they daily practised fostered neurotic tendencies which led not only to spurious visions, but even to almost incredible phenomena. There seems every reason to believe the statement that St. Francis of Assisi, after pondering intensely on the Passion of Christ, developed on his hands and feet marks which corresponded to the wounds on Christ's. All such visions and dreams were accepted by the people as direct and sacred messages from God, and the romances present numberless examples. Charlemagne and Arthur are portrayed as constantly warned through such agencies of the disasters that would follow certain actions and as similarly guided to the right way. In "The Siege of Melayne" Charlemagne is advised by an angel in a vision to help the people of Milan. He is similarly portrayed in romances relating his expedition to Spain as guided by St. James, and in the receptacle which holds his body at Aix-la-Chapelle are scenes of St. James appearing to him in a dream, and of a line of stars guiding him through the Pyrenees. Few heroes of romance failed to experience at least one vision or dream of a prophetic nature.

Miracles also, which held so conspicuous a place in Church history, naturally were frequent in romance. Their extremely limited knowledge of science and of natural laws led people to regard as miraculous many phenomena now generally understood and fostered a tendency to distort the most natural occurrences into miracles. In Geoffrey de Vinsauf's chronicle of King Richard's Crusade

[1] Canon Streeter, "Reality."

it is recorded that a soldier's life was miraculously preserved because a piece of paper bearing God's name
deflected a dart; even during the Great War many people
were inclined to regard as miraculous the deflection of a
bullet by a Prayer Book or Bible, forgetting that a volume
of Restoration Comedy would have been equally effective.
In "The Siege of Melayne" it is recorded that a Sultan
who attempted to burn a Crucifix was blinded by the
flames, and in "The History of the Holy Grail" Celidoyne,
when thrown over the battlements of a castle, is caught in
mid-air by nine snow-white hands and brought gently to
the ground. Amongst illiterate or shallow-minded people,
whether of the Middle Ages or to-day, the supernatural
elements of religion—its visions and miracles—appeal far
more than the ethics.

The romances also present many examples of that crude
religious symbolism which reflects the desire in all ages
of illiterate people to symbolise abstract philosophical
conceptions in simple concrete terms. The spirit animating
this desire is fundamentally sound, and has given rise not
only to Church ritual, but to every form of art. Yet
attempts to symbolise highly complex conceptions in
simple forms inevitably lead to drastic distortion. "The
History of the Holy Grail" presents an extreme example
of crude symbolism—a Phœnix typifying Christ, whose
manifold and marvellous powers could only be represented
by giving it a dragon's head, two horns, a long neck, a
lion's breast, and an eagle's feet. Relics, which were
supposed to retain the powers of their original possessors,
were also highly valued, and heroes of romance safe-
guarded themselves by wearing some wherever possible;
Roland's sword, Durendal, is described in "La Chanson
de Roland" as decorated with a tooth of St. Peter, the
hair of St. Denis, and part of the Virgin Mary's apparel.
Since men received all their religious teaching through
symbolism, heroes of romance naturally adopted the same
plan when attempting to convert Saracens. And their
crude attempts again illustrate how the medieval mind was

attracted by the mysteries rather than by the ethical teaching of Christianity. Roland, when attempting to convert Vernagu, a Saracen Prince, completely ignored the simple doctrines of Christ and rushed in where even theologians often fear to tread, boldly essaying an elucidation of the Trinity, which he likened to a harp composed of three elements, wood, strings, and sound.[1] Vernagu cheerfully accepted his explanation, but insisted on fighting to decide whether Christianity or Mohammedanism was the better religion.

In spite of the blind reverence paid to the authority of the Church, men were not always blind to the unconscious humour latent in its dogmas, although it is to be suspected that the generator of any deliberate humour on ecclesiastical matters was usually a cleric—the average layman believed in the infallibility of the priest, the average priest would realise the shortcomings of his profession and the doubtful value of many of its institutions. Salimbene tells a story of some Frenchmen who, becoming blear-eyed after heavy bouts of drinking, were accustomed to ask the priest to drop a little Holy Water in their eyes, until a monk named Bartholomew suggested that it would be more efficacious to put the water in their wine instead.[2] In some romances humorous gibes are made at men and objects usually revered. Priests must have been held in contempt by many of the rough soldiers and barons of the time, and in "Guy of Warwick" many jests are made about the tonsured heads of ecclesiastics. Men whose scalps had been cut off in battle are mockingly called priests, and all those who were afraid to accept the challenge of the Danish warrior, Colbrand, are likened to the men with shaved heads, *i.e.* priests. Similarly Sir Ferumbras, leader of the Saracens besieging Rome, on discovering that a sortie of Roman soldiers is headed by the Pope, whom he

[1] "Roland and Vernagu."
[2] Recorded in H. O. Taylor's "Medieval Mind." Salimbene was an Italian Minorite Friar of the thirteenth century and author of a chronicle which gives a vivid picture of life in Italy and France during the twelfth and thirteenth centuries.

recognises by his tonsured head, tells him to run away home out of harm's way, and the author remarks that he was only too glad to reach safety again. It is very probable that the scepticism which was so evident in the fourteenth and fifteenth centuries had been growing steadily ever since the revived activity in scholarship in the twelfth. The Church had pushed its claims to infallibility too far and exercised its jurisdiction too rigidly, and so encouraged doubt and cynicism amongst intelligent and thinking men.

In an age when all learning centred in the Church it is only to be expected that literature should be regarded chiefly as a medium of instruction. Artistic beauty was not despised or neglected in the Middle Ages, but regarded as an adornment in God's service; artistry that did not serve this purpose was discouraged by the Church. For this reason, although conscious artistry both in structure and in diction are by no means absent from medieval literature, poets cannot be said to have regarded their work as an art in the sense that modern writers have done. The ostensible object of romance was to instruct, even though the real aim of many romancers may have been to entertain. Theories change frequently and greatly, but human nature very little. And so, in spite of the prevailing theory as to the duty of literature, the audience of romance was no doubt similar to that at a modern public lecture; it demanded truth, but would not stomach unpalatable truth or truth undecorated with pleasing ornament. The romancer, therefore, depending on the favour of his patrons, had to tickle their fancy, even though his ostensible purpose was to teach.

The primary claim was, of course, the recording of historical facts, but many also claimed a moral purpose as well, stating that they related the deeds of brave men of old as an incentive to their audience, who would, no doubt, appreciate this claim, provided that the moral instruction was not too prominent.[1] Many romancers

[1] This claim was made by the authors of "Richard Cœur de Lion," "Morte Arthure," and "Guy of Warwick."

frequently interrupted their narrative to point a direct moral, sometimes relevant, often irrelevant. In "The Life of Alisaunder" there are frequent passages which show the poet's anxiety to impress upon his audience the value of the Church and of Christian doctrine: "There is not so fair a thing as a knight except the priest in God's service;" "Love is sweet, but the best love is Mary." And the poet concludes by expressing his grief that Alexander died a heathen. In "The Destruction of Troy" the poet reproved Homer for extolling Achilles, who had treated Hector and Troilus so shamefully, and illustrates from Helen's love for Paris and the desertion of Troilus by Briseis the wantonness and fickleness of women. In crusading chronicles and romances the conquest of Palestine by the Turks is attributed to the sins of Christians, and in "The Sowdone of Babylon" the same reason is alleged for the capture of Rome by Saracens, and its recapture by Charlemagne ascribed to his faith in God. Many romances also begin and end with brief prayers for the audience and the expression of a hope that the hearers will follow the good examples offered to them.

Apart from these isolated moral passages, many romances present a fairly consistent moral ideal, which is never completely submerged even when they are filled with sensational episodes. Even "Huon of Bordeaux" which presents perhaps the best illustration in all romance of sheer sensationalism, still reflects the general axiom that conduct can have no moral quality unless based on the law that every action has its inevitable consequence. His misfortunes are represented as arising from rashness and libertinism—he is shipwrecked because, in spite of warnings, he insists on having sexual intercourse with his betrothed before marriage. This is typical of the crude manner in which moral laws were inculcated, but crudity is to be expected at a time of mechanical dogma and lack of education. The best romances, written by men of intellectual ability, presented ideals of conduct in a more worthy manner; the German "Parzifal" stresses how nobility of character is attained only by constant striving against hardship and temptation—a theme so nobly championed later by Milton in his "Areopagitica"; similarly, the English romance "Sir Gawain and the Green Knight" stresses the nobility of chastity and faith. The frequent introduction of chastity tests—cups from which only the pure may drink, mantles which only the pure may wear, and fountains in which only the pure may bathe—shows that great emphasis must have been laid upon purity, and that audiences never tired of listening to these tests of moral worth. The actual tests selected[1] would serve as a novelty, but the consistency of the moral aspect selected must reflect the sentiment of the time.

One of the most prominent features of the religious teaching of the time, and a feature largely reflected in romance, was a widely prevalent emotionalism and sentimentalism —the tendency to foster ecstasies in devotion and extreme fanaticism in doctrine. The ancient Greeks had pondered over the question of good and evil sanely and rationally; they were neither mystics nor ascetics. In a later decadent period their philosophy was degraded by the introduction of fantasy and superstition and encrusted with superstitions incorporated from Eastern religions. The Romans, largely aided by Greek learning, had also built up a rational philosophy of life which decayed with the downfall of their Empire. As learning decayed, the people of Europe, having sunk back into ignorance, ceased to be influenced by earlier Greek and Roman philosophy, became more and more fascinated by the superstitions which had invaded it, and were prepared to accept any exaggeration and to respect ideas in proportion as they were removed from an actual human basis. Christianity was the one great power which could have supplied the place of earlier Greek and Roman philosophy and carried them to greater heights. The teaching of Christ, as far as it is recorded, was built on a broad, sane, and practical

[1] For a fuller account of these tests see Chapter XII.

basis; He was no mystic nor was He even an ascetic, as was His forerunner, John the Baptist. "He came eating and drinking—He enjoyed life to an extent that scandalised His critics. He was inclined to laugh at the grave and solemn Pharisees; and they did not like it."[1] He lent no encouragement to either mysticism or fanaticism. But the incorporation into Christian doctrine of elements from the degraded Greek and Eastern philosophies, the ignorance of the Church leaders, and the influence of superstitions with which the peoples of Europe remained saturated in spite of Christ's teaching increasingly fostered mysticism, fanaticism, and asceticism. As a counterblast to the vices and corruption which reigned rampant under the later Roman Emperors, the Christian devotees practised rigid austerities, which, though wholesome enough at first, soon became an obsession, and, as Canon Streeter has stated,[1] "History shows that austerities, studiously devised as a means to spiritual self-culture, tend to produce a capacity for self-sacrifice only at the price of a fanatic limitation of the moral vision. The power of the ascetic ideal to make minds indifferent or even hostile to the highest moral and intellectual movements of their day has been the tragedy of religion in East and West alike." This then was the great flaw in the medieval Christian faith; instead of moral and intellectual progress—the ideal of Christ—were fostered mystical ecstasies, elaborate ritual, and physical mortifications—the older ideals which Christ so strenuously opposed. Medieval religious thought became a great well of emotion, an absorption in mysticism and ritual instead of in human character; ideals were fostered which were so divorced from nature as to be neither possible nor wholesome. Even the greatest figures of medieval Church history, like St. Francis of Assisi, were of a predominantly emotional type and encouraged excessive emotionalism and sentimentalism in others.

Such was the field from which the harvest of romance was gleaned, for the period of romance was one of great

[1] Canon Streeter, "Reality."

N

emotional yearning similar to, but much more crude than that of the early nineteenth century. That of the later Middle Ages was blinder and more passionate because religious, that of the nineteenth century more restrained and reasonable because political, social, and economic and because it arose in a more enlightened age. It is not surprising, therefore, that the dominant features of romance are a craving for marvels, mysteries, and sensation, for intense emotionalism yielding both intense love and fanatic hatred—the willingness of heroines to abandon themselves to handsome and doughty lovers, blind to all the hazards of illicit love, and the fanatic hatred towards religious foes, a fanaticism so strongly fostered by the Crusades and by a militant Church that God became crystallised in men's minds less as a God of love than as a Grand High Executioner of infidels.

Emotionalism and sentimentalism in love largely arose from the increasing adoration of the Virgin Mary so zealously fostered by the Church during the Middle Ages. Although at first Mary had no place in the Divine Hierarchy, it was only natural that the mother of Christ should in time come to be regarded almost as a Divinity and as a natural intermediary between men and God. In the fourth century St. Chrysostom not only denied her divinity, but even reproached her as having been too proud of her position. Gradually, however, arose the doctrine of immaculate conception, which both raised Mary on to a level higher than other women and made the Church regard virginity as the great ideal. During the fourth and fifth centuries orthodox bishops objected to her deification, but the people had been so accustomed to goddesses—especially goddesses of production—in their old religions that they were powerless to check the tendency to elevate her to divine rank.[1] At the Synod of Alexandria in 430 and at the Council at Ephesus in 431 Mary was

---

[1] It has been suggested by Flinders Petrie, the famous Egyptologist, that the Egyptian worship of Isis may have materially assisted this deification.

officially proclaimed as the "Mother of God." During the
eighth and ninth centuries she came to be called the
"Saviour of the World" and regarded as an independent
saviour, not merely as the mother of a saviour. Thus arose
an independent cult of Mary which fostered an emotionalism that could never have become so intense merely from
the worship of Christ. With the composition in the
twelfth century of the "Ave Maria" and its introduction
into Church services the movement was completed. Mary
became a sort of goddess of beauty, love, and humanity,
inspiring men with these ideals and so helping to free men
from sterile dogmas even while fostering a tendency
towards sentimentalism in devotional exercises. An order
of secular knights, La Chevalerie de Sainte Marie, proclaimed her as its patron, and poets composed songs in
her honour, frequently using conventional terms of secular
love lyrics—cf. one of Gottfried von Strasbourg,

> "Thou art a potion sweet of love,
> Sweetly pervading Heaven above."[1]

This cult, mingling with other influences of the time,
helped to foster the sentimentalism so prevalent in love
romances.[2]

The intense emotionalism of medieval religious thought
is most clearly seen in its fanaticism, rigid adherence to
all the minutiæ of dogma, and intense hatred of all alien
doctrines, whether of other religions or within the Church
itself. The medieval mind was incapable of understanding
alien religions, and so grouped them all together as devil
worship. Not only did romancers, in their ignorance,
believe that the prophet Mahomet was a god worshipped
by the Saracens, but also accredited them with other and
quite incongruous gods, such as Apollo and Jupiter. In
"The Sowdone of Babylon" they are even afflicted with a
god called Alcaron,[3] although the poet shows a better

[1] Taken from "The Evolution of Love," by Emil Lucka.
[2] The characteristics and various origins of the love element in
romance are discussed in Chapter XIII.
[3] =The Koran.

understanding in another passage where he portrays the
Saracens singing "The dirge of Alcoran, which is the
Bible of their faith." The misconceptions of romancers
were largely excusable, since the Saracen foes of the
crusaders included not only the monotheistic disciples of
Mahomet, but also polytheistic Persians and idolatrous
Bedouins. All heathen gods were quite naturally regarded
as devils in Satan's service, a belief which was later turned
to magnificent account by Milton in his "Paradise Lost."

Under such circumstances it is not difficult to understand
the intense enthusiasm that was roused at the proclama-
tion of a Holy War to wrest Palestine from the Turks, and
since the Crusades became the most conspicuous feature of
medieval religious activity, many romances were permeated through and through with this crusading spirit.
Romances were written to celebrate the leaders of the
First Crusade, Charlemagne and his peers were presented
simply as crusaders of an earlier date, and most heroes of
romance, whatever the theme, came into conflict with
Saracens on one or more occasions.

In the early centuries of the Christian era not only all
ecclesiastics, but even all lay Christians were forbidden
by Church law to fight; warfare of any kind or for any
purpose was viewed as heinous sin. But the repeated invasions of Southern Europe by pagan barbarians from
the North made this an impossible ideal, and the self-
defence of the fifth and sixth centuries became open
militarism in the eleventh. By the eighth century the
Church no longer forbade even its officials the exercise
of arms, and before the end of the ninth century two arch-
bishops and eight bishops had died on the field of battle.
Religious warfare came to be regarded as man's chief duty
to God, and the Church became a militant and temporal
power, urging men to war and openly seeking worldly
wealth, which in time became so vast as to attract a host
of greedy adventurers who sought only personal aggrandisement and not the service of God.

During the eleventh century pilgrims returning from

Palestine continually complained of ill-treatment from the Turks, and so fostered an ever-increasing rancour against the infidel rulers of Jerusalem. Many of their tales must have been gross exaggerations encouraged by the credulity of an illiterate and superstitious people. Men in all ages have been only too willing to credit any evil of a foe, and during the Great War returned prisoners were not only encouraged, but even expected to charge the Germans with cruelty. Not only did such accounts yield sympathy and lavish hospitality, but any prisoner who dared to say he had been well treated was openly regarded with suspicion. Just so the medieval pilgrim soon found that tales of persecution were a passport in every European country and brought him rich gifts from a sympathetic audience. We of to-day can sympathise with the Turks, at least to some extent. The experienced traveller may easily visualise the feelings of the average Swiss or Italian who sees his country transformed into a playground or museum for endless hordes of foreign tourists, who too often regard the natives as provided by a thoughtful Providence for their amusement. The Turks of Palestine were plagued with a never-ending stream of sanctimonious pilgrims, many of them notorious rascals who would shrink from no fraud or crime, and nearly all of them despising the Turks as vile infidels, accursed of God. It was to be expected, therefore, that these same Turks, who also viewed the Christian pilgrims as infidel dogs, would often vent their scorn in a direct and drastic manner. At a later stage the crusading princes who governed many parts of Palestine had to take severe measures against pilgrims who too openly showed their contempt and who often fomented discord without a vestige of reason.

The warfare between civilised Christians and barbarian Turks—to adopt the medieval view—seems to have arisen chiefly as a result of pilgrims' complaints and the desire of a militant Church to extend its authority. It opened with the advance of motley, undisciplined hordes which committed so many outrages in Christian countries that very few survived to reach Palestine, where they were quickly exterminated by the far more highly disciplined Turks. The first band, led by Walter the Penniless, ravaged Hungary as it passed through on its way to Byzantium, and the second, under Peter the Hermit, who claimed to have been ordained to this task in a vision from God, massacred a large number of Hungarians and was almost exterminated in revenge. A third army of Dutch crusaders also ill-treated the Hungarians, and was similarly exterminated. Other bodies amused themselves by massacring all the Jews they met. So began this Holy War, blessed by the Church and ordained as a service to God. The main body of Crusaders, better disciplined and led by responsible barons, carefully avoided these excesses, but were unable to enlist the support of the Byzantines, who had hitherto avoided open conflict with the Turks and suspected that this crusading fervour would soon cool and that the intense religious fanaticism engendered would recoil on themselves. Later events proved their wisdom, for this fierce ardour was quickly quenched, and the Byzantines were left to bear the brunt of the religious hatred which had been roused; after suffering constant invasions they were finally overwhelmed with the fall of Constantinople in 1453.

Shortly after the First Crusade, William, Archbishop of Tyre, wrote a chronicle which relates in detail the whole campaign and vividly portrays the quarrels with the Byzantines and the haughty, undisciplined temper of the crusading barons. They suffered disaster after disaster from the superior strategy of the Turks, and so reduced their efficiency by lack of disciplinary methods, which allowed their camps to swarm with spies, prostitutes, and rascals of every description, that even their victories were truly Pyrrhic victories and their defeats wholesale massacres.

A famous French critic, Gaston Paris, remarked that it is a French habit to believe that it is their duty to make other people happy and blessed, even if force is necessary to accomplish this aim, and perhaps that was the main reason why most of the crusaders were French. Although the only official leader was the Bishop of Ruy, Papal legate, a French baron, Godfrey of Bouillon,[1] seems to have been regarded as the most inspiring figure, and was depicted as the official leader in both chronicles and romances. The two existing romances, which make this crusade their theme—the "Chanson d'Antioch" and the "Chanson de Jérusalem"—were designed solely to extol Godfrey and to portray him as a saintly warrior ordained by God to this task. This conception became so wide-spread that he was eventually ranked as one of the nine Worthies, along with Charlemagne and Arthur. Even the haughty barons seem to have found only one fault with him—that he attended Church services too frequently—and therefore raised little objection to his appointment as King of Jerusalem when the crusade had ended. These romances, written during the twelfth century, and possibly composed very shortly after the events, reflect history far more accurately than do the Charlemagne romances. They present vivid pictures of the coarse and brutal barons fighting partly for their Faith and partly for personal glory and gain. They stress the militant aspect of the Church, where the Grail romances stress the ethical and mystical; the crusading barons were the heroes loved of men, Percival and Galahad appealed mainly to women.

England took no part in this First Crusade, and there are extant no English romances dealing with it. One English romance, "The Chevalier Assigne,"[2] is remotely related to Godfrey of Bouillon, but mentions neither the crusade nor Godfrey. It presents an old legend—the transformation of children into swans by black magic and their eventual restoration to human shape. Godfrey was reputed to be descended from a swan-maiden and called the Knight of the Swan. This type of legend has been immortalised in Wagner's opera "Lohengrin," which also has no direct relationship with Godfrey. Caxton translated the chronicle

[1] Often called "Godfrey of Boulogne" because Boulogne was his father's seat.   [2] The Knight of the Swan (Chevalier à Cygne).

of William of Tyre into English and named his work
"Godfrey of Boloyne" simply because Godfrey had been
portrayed in the original as the chief crusader. The only
extant English crusading romance is "Richard Cœur de
Lion," which relates, with a good deal of exaggeration,
Richard's exploits in the Third Crusade of 1190, an
expedition undertaken to wrest Jerusalem from the Turks,
who had recaptured it in 1187.

All three of the above-mentioned romances, as well as
those on Charlemagne's expeditions to Italy and Spain,[1]
clearly reflect the religious fanaticism of the later Middle
Ages, a fanaticism which led, on the capture of Jerusalem,
to a barbarous massacre of Turkish men, women, and
children, even in the very temple, and which was destined
to bathe all Europe in blood in an attempt to suppress
heresy within the Church itself. There is a vast difference
between deep religious thought and fanaticism. Fanaticism is pure emotionalism, and is often caused merely by a
diseased nervous system. Deep religious thought breeds
moral health and progress, fanaticism only moral disease
and chaos. Canon Streeter[2] made the distinction very vivid
when he wrote, "In almost every asylum there is someone
who is quite convinced that he is the Messiah; so was
Jesus Christ—but that is the end of the resemblance between
them." The acceptance of the Old Testament as a sacred
and divinely inspired work instead of Jewish history,
legend, and literature made men believe that the ruthless
extermination of the Canaanites, regardless of age or sex,
was really commanded by Jehovah and that the slaughter
of Saracens and Jews was a sacred duty. The coronation
of Richard I in 1189 was celebrated in many English
towns by a wholesale massacre of Jews, since infidels
were regarded simply as poisonous vermin that must be
destroyed. The usefulness of Jews as moneylenders alone
preserved them from complete extermination. Warfare of
any kind breeds fanaticism because people cease to use
their reasoning faculties and become saturated with

[1] See Chapter II.   [2] In "Reality."

emotionalism. Intensive propaganda during the Great War roused men's passions to such a pitch that even the mildest of men and women regarded the whole German nation as vile, and regretted that the Allied armies did not wreak vengeance for the destruction of French towns. So in the Crusades, hatred engendered by real and supposed brutalities of Turkish officials roused men to a massacre of women and children who were entirely guiltless. If it may be assumed that the sentiments expressed in romance reflect the sentiments of the audiences for whom they were composed, it is clear that the rights of infidels were utterly disregarded; the killing of Christian ambassadors by infidels was regarded as an outrage to both decency and honour, but to infidel ambassadors was accorded no respect. The exultant tone in which the author of "Richard Cœur de Lion" holds up for admiration the killing and eating of Saracens by Richard and the serving of prisoners' heads as food to Saracen ambassadors testifies to a blood-lust and religious fanaticism verging on madness. The killing, by Roland and Oliver, of Saracen ambassadors journeying to Charlemagne's Court, and the killing of a Roman councillor by Gawain when ambassador to Rome, are simply recorded as praiseworthy deeds.[1]

In many romances God is portrayed as being chiefly occupied with killing infidels and exhorting knights to do so for him. In "The History of the Holy Grail" a heathen named Lucien is struck dead by God for denying the virginity of Mary, and 150 other heathens are similarly killed for refusing conversion. In the same romance another heathen king, after conversion, kills all his followers who refuse to be converted, so that "by God's grace the realm becomes Christian." Crusading service seems to have been considered almost as essential as service during the Great War; to shirk it was to be branded as a coward, and Geoffrey de Vinsauf in his chronicle of

[1] This fanaticism must not be confused with foul play; ambassadors were killed or insulted only because the discomfiture of an infidel was regarded as a more sacred duty than the honouring of an envoy. The taking of an unfair advantage was never held up for praise.

King Richard's crusade records that distaffs and wool were sent to men who refused to enlist—an early precedent for the white feather of 1914 and 1915. Songs were composed exhorting knights to enlist and describing the sorrow of crusaders who had to leave their loved ones behind; the most famous is the German "Crusader's Song" by Hartmann von Ave.

The worst result of this long-protracted religious warfare was the establishment of an enduring fanaticism towards all who opposed not merely Christianity, but even those doctrines authorised by the Church. Early in the thirteenth century the Inquisition was founded by Pope Innocent III, and this, beginning with the massacre in 1216 of 27,000 heretics at Beziers, led to centuries of persecution of all who would not conform to Church dogma. Disobedience to the Church was considered as tantamount to disobedience to God, and in many romances God is portrayed as jealously watching for the least signs of heresy and ever ready to launch His bolts against those who displease Him. When Nasciens, an important character in "The History of the Holy Grail," leaves home on God's service, his servant is struck dead merely for requesting him to return home to his wife, and when a passer-by asks how the servant has met his death, and, on being told the reason, exclaims that he deserved his fate, he is also struck down by God. Thus arose a religion of fear, men not daring to disobey the slightest commands or reject the most minute doctrines of the Church. Even to-day in places religious hostility remains stronger than racial, and the romances strongly reflect the extreme fanaticism of the later Middle Ages. Religious persecutors are usually sincere in their beliefs; so are madmen; but the latter are segregated out of harm's way.

During the latter half of the twelfth century Arthurian romance became far more prominent than Charlemagne or any crusading romances, and although the Arthurian legend itself began as a theme of organised and partly religious warfare, the almost exclusive emphasis on the love element seems to indicate that religious warfare, and perhaps organised strife of any kind, made little appeal to women. The chansons de gestes no doubt continued to interest men strongly, for new versions were made from time to time, and even the composite Arthurian romances, such as the prose "Lancelot," deal largely with national warfare. However this may be, there can be no doubt that this conflict with Saracens had gripped men's imaginations to the exclusion of all other themes of war, even in England, which supported only one crusade, the third. All enemies in romance became not only religious foes, but almost exclusively Saracens, and Saracen warfare became a stock episode in stories of every kind. The theme of "The Four Sons of Aymon" is Charlemagne's conflict with rebel vassals, but even here a messenger arrives during a siege to report that Saracens are besieging Cologne, and Roland is sent to drive them away. In legend and in chronicles Arthur is presented as the British leader against the Saxons, but in the romances they are frequently called Saracens. Likewise in "King Horn" the Viking raiders are called Saracens. Crusading influence is seen most strongly in the composite prose romances of Arthur, in which the main theme is his warfare against the Saxon invaders of Britain; in the prose "Merlin" the allied armies under Arthur's command carry the crusaders' banners—a red cross on a white ground. The romancer, to retain interest, must seize on those factors which will arouse popular zeal; the conflict between Britons and Saxons or between Saxons and Vikings was buried in the past, and no description, however vivid, could stir up fervid patriotism, while religious hatred had been roused to such a pitch that any mention of Saracens would attract keen interest. Just as the Anglo-Saxon word "Wealas," which gave the modern name Welsh and probably was a tribal name in origin, became a general term for foes of any kind, so did the term "Saracen" during the twelfth and thirteenth centuries. The crusading romances culminated in an Italian poem by Tasso, "Jerusalem Delivered," which was later translated into English verse by Fairfax. Thus the beginning of the Renaissance saw the three great themes of European historical and legendary warfare celebrated in artistic poems, a fitting conclusion to the long series of romances.[1]

In the early days of the Church warfare against pagan barbarians was vitally necessary to preserve the remnants of civilisation in the Roman provinces from extermination; then the Church had been content to let others fight for it and was loth to take any part itself. Centuries of defensive warfare had made the Church a militant body anxious to extend its authority and welcoming the Crusades as a means to this end. But, although the Churches of Western Europe preached Holy Wars for over two centuries, hounding men on to sacrifice their wealth and their lives for a purpose largely vain, the crusading princes and barons slowly came to realise that the Saracens were not monsters, that in many respects they were more highly civilised than themselves, that they were more advanced in scholarship, science, and medicine and at least equally versed in chivalrous conduct. Even the romancers whose definite object was to magnify the deeds and chivalry of Christian knights were not too bigoted to accredit Saracens with chivalrous motives. In "Duke Rowlande and Sir Otuell of Spayne" a Saracen king Clariel, after defeating and capturing Ogier, one of Charlemagne's peers, sends him to his betrothed to have his wounds healed and be kept secure from harm.

But although the real purpose of the Crusades is hardly worthy of praise and caused much misery and evil, this long-protracted struggle was not devoid of beneficial results. By weakening Mohammedan power through the continual drain of man-power and wealth, it effectually prevented a Mohammedan conquest of Western Europe, a danger which had been threatening for centuries and had almost been accomplished before the days of Charlemagne. The Crusades, by banding together the whole of Southern Europe in one single purpose and by carrying the warfare

[1] Ariosto's "Orlando Furioso" of the Charlemagne legend, and Spenser's "Faerie Queene" of the Arthurian.

into Saracen territory, prevented the subjugation of each
European country in turn, a task which would have been
comparatively easy. Also by weakening the power of the
great French barons the crusades enabled kings to attain
effectual power and so introduce stable government.
Their influence upon learning and literature, the result
most pertinent to this work, was equally great; the consequent interchange of ideas between East and West and
the introduction of Eastern learning were the chief factors
in the temporary renaissance of the twelfth century which
in its turn prepared the way for the much more active
renaissance of the fifteenth. A new and stimulating realm
of ideas was opened up to literature, and romancers
thoroughly exploited the luxury, magic, and mystery of
the East.[1]

Even the fanaticism and fantastic features of the
Crusades, as reflected in romance, though unworthy of
praise, deserve neither the derision nor the contempt that
are frequently lavished on them. The ostensible purpose
of both the Crusades and modern efforts to carry civilisation into native territories has been the improvement of
the peoples concerned. It is at least open to question
whether the superficial conversion of Saracens by brute
force is less ludicrous or less praiseworthy than the conversion of natives in tropical lands from a healthy open-
air life to unhealthy and unsuitable factory work, which
is the chief aspect of our boasted extension of civilisation.
Many crusaders may have been more intent upon personal
glory and gain than upon the extension of Christianity,
but it may safely be assumed that a larger proportion of
crusaders had lofty motives than of modern empire-
builders, the great majority of whom have as their sole
purpose the increase of their own personal wealth. There
seems no reason to believe that the exploitation of natives
by modern industrialists is either worthier or more beneficial than the pursuit of wealth and fame by the earlier
churchmen and crusaders.

[1] A detailed discussion of Eastern influence upon romance will be
found in Chapter XII.

CHAPTER XI

CHIVALRY

MEDIEVAL ROMANCE HAS OFTEN IN modern times been called the Romance of Chivalry. No more appropriate title could be given, because, in spite of all its faults of exaggeration and distortion, it does strongly reflect the ideals of chivalrous conduct which inspired men of the twelfth and thirteenth centuries. Not all the sensationalism and supernaturalism of the adventures undergone prevent the ideals of knightly character from standing out clearly and impressively, for the deeds of knights-errant, however fantastic or unreal, were performed not for personal gain or glory, but to right wrongs and succour the oppressed.

In origin the terms chivalry and cavalry were but different dialectal forms of the same French word designating mounted troops. Both were borrowed into English; the latter has been restricted to its original meaning and the former almost entirely restricted to the secondary application, a code of conduct. Since the higher ranks of men in the later Middle Ages always fought on horseback, the term chivalry came to mean the knightly class, and then the ideals of character of that class. The ideals of chivalry— courtesy, loyalty to duty, and service to the oppressed— were the combined product of social customs and religious teaching. The dominant practical basis was the organisation evolved to assure unity within the State against hostile alien aggression. When the downfall of the Roman Empire had left Italy and the Provinces at the mercy of invading Goths and Vandals, many of the smaller land-holders sought protection from those more powerful, and leagues of defence were formed to resist barbarian invaders. Since the organisation and expense mainly devolved on the most powerful, the weaker members of each league surrendered their estates to the head of the league and received them back as tenants. They also pledged themselves to render service whenever demanded, and in return received the assistance and protection of all members of the league. By the tenth and eleventh centuries this system of vassalage had become rigid and minutely defined, and, from the word "feudum," which signified this holding of land in return for service, was coined the word "feudalism," to designate the whole system with all its rights and privileges.

A host of separate leagues offered inadequate resistance to organised invasion, and so, in the course of time, the whole of a nation came to form one league, with the king as overlord and all other men vassals in some degree. The more powerful the baron the greater his independence and the greater his reluctance to pay feudal homage; the weaker the king the more did the powerful barons refuse to perform their obligations, though demanding implicit obedience from their own vassals, even against the king. All ranks from king to the most petty knight formed one large class, which formed the nobility or "chivalry" of France. In the feudal system all lower ranks were regarded as mere servants or hirelings, and therefore beyond the pale of society. It is important to remember that men firmly believed that these two classes had been distinct from the beginning, and, as stated in the "Book of St. Albans," that gentlemen descended from Seth, and churls from Cain, the latter class including all below the knightly families. In theory chivalrous conduct was confined to the knightly class, because the churls were regarded as a distinct order of beings, just as women in Eastern countries were considered to have no souls. Therefore harsh treatment of a vassal knight or churlishness to a lady was an offence against chivalry, but not so the same treatment to a citizen or peasant, although common decency forbade men to condone excessive cruelty to churls.

Feudalism thus inaugurated a well-disciplined organisation essential to the safety of the State. But to this practical aspect of vassalage was linked a more idealistic

feature which originated in Teutonic custom. Amongst
the Germanic tribes no system of land tenure operated,
because land was held in common, but the supreme importance of the king or chieftain to the tribe led to the practice
of forming a royal bodyguard which Tacitus in his
"Germania" called the "comitatus." The king was the
only unifying link, and his death without leaving an heir
would almost inevitably lead to disintegration, because no
other one man would be acceptable to the whole tribe.
Disintegration means weakness, and often led to the servi-
tude of a kingless tribe to alien rulers. The bodyguard
organised to protect him in battle consisted of carefully
chosen warriors pledged to cover his retreat or die by his
side if the battle should be lost. The disadvantage of this
system was that one defeat in which the king was killed
frequently led to a complete annihilation of the tribe,
since the men who could have retreated and raised fresh
forces to renew the strife were vowed to die on the field of
battle. The Norman invasion of England might have
come to an inglorious end if it had not been the sacred
duty of Harold's chief supporters to die with him. The
great advantage of it was that it did ensure material
protection for the king and courageous fighting by his
followers.

This system of "comitatus" combined with that of land
tenure to form the broad basis of feudalism. The oath of
service was a sacred rite, in which the vassal removed his
sword and spurs, knelt, put his hand in that of his overlord, and swore to be his "man." The sacredness of this
"hommage-lige," as it was called, is well exemplified in
"Floris and Blaunchflour," where Floris is advised that
he can gain entrance to the Emir's harem where his
beloved lies captive only with the porter's assistance.
Pretending to be a builder seeking inspiration in Babylon,
he gives the porter a rich gift on condition that he becomes
his "man." The porter, having given his pledge, dare not
break it, even though he knows he has been tricked and
that to admit any man into the harem will mean almost

certain death to himself. It is not a question of whether
in real life a porter would or would not risk his life in
performance of his pledge; he is but a symbol illustrating
the sacredness of fealty in the eyes of the poet and his
audience. The great value set on oaths and pledges is well
illustrated in the Arthurian romances, in which any
defeated foe is usually required to swear that he will
deliver himself to the king. This picture of unescorted
knights wandering along the road to Camelot and to
imprisonment is not so fantastic as it may seem, for not
only would the average knight shrink from breaking a
solemn pledge, but even in modern times few prisoners of
war, released upon parole, would be mean enough to
break their contract. The medieval knight could be
absolved from an oath only by a priest, and although this
was a sane and useful practice where pledges had been
extorted by force, such as Harold's vow to surrender the
English throne to William of Normandy, it is one of the
most inglorious aspects of the Crusades that prisoners
released by Turks on condition that they took no further
part in the fighting were absolved from their oaths by
the Church. Harold could have kept his pledge only by
betraying his countrymen, and, moreover, was not a
prisoner of war, but a guest detained by fraud. The
crusader had to face no such dilemma; by his capture his
services were ended; he had the choice of remaining a
prisoner or returning home. The Church in absolving him
from his oath was guilty of deliberate fraud unworthy of an
institution which professed to teach morality.

The ideal fostered by this dual service was, therefore,
similar to that of the ancient Greeks, that service to the
State was man's supreme duty, to which all personal
aims must be subordinated. The complexities of modern
life and the domination of commercial interests have
almost entirely killed this ideal of general service, which
can only be aroused in times of national danger. The
earlier simplicity is no longer possible; we cannot thrive
upon a few clear-cut and rigid codes of conduct; and com-

o

mercial rivalry can only foster absorption in private interests. The mass of people, therefore, make little or no attempt to serve the State, but expect constant service from the State; some people desire to serve the State, but attempt duties entirely divorced from their daily work, and, therefore, through ignorance, as often hinder as assist; and others exploit the State and the trust and generosity of the people to further their own ends. The rising tide of materialism has made ambition too personal, and the average boy is encouraged to regard as his goal in life personal gain rather than disinterested service. Whether there has been any great difference in actual practice between the two periods it would be difficult to estimate, but the national ideal has fundamentally changed from that of serving the State to that of expecting and demanding assistance from the State. The fascination of medieval romance largely, if not wholly, lies in this picture of disinterested service. The knightly heroes embarked upon their perilous voyages literally to carry out the age-old precept "to aid the widow and orphan and all such as are oppressed."

Not all the ideals of chivalry arose from feudalism. This gave only the practical basis of unity, the need for men to consider the State as a whole and to sink their own interests in the furtherance of a common aim, and the consequent necessity for implicit obedience to orders and for unswerving faith to their overlord. The more refined and exalted aspects originated partly in the teaching of the Church and partly in the influence of women. At this early period few could read the Gospels, even when translated, and men were surrounded by pictures on stone and glass of Christ sitting on the Judgment throne; the usual conception of divinity was therefore one of stern justice rather than of mercy. The ever-increasing devotion paid to the Virgin Mary as supreme intercessor must have had a refining influence upon men, taught them to be more gentle and merciful in their attitude towards inferiors, and led to a more exalted and idealised conception of women as a whole, so paving the way to greater courtesy towards and consideration of women and children.

When women also became the patrons of literature, romancers had to portray them as supreme and fashion the character and conduct of their heroes to suit female tastes, and so the romances in their turn would exercise a refining influence upon knights. Men therefore owed service to their lord as a practical duty, to women as a matter of courtesy and because of their helplessness and need for protection. To these two ideals was added yet a third, service to the Church and to the Christian Faith, which in its turn led to the emphasising of Christian virtues—humility, purity, and godliness. These three influences led to that code of chivalry which was a guiding star to the whole nation and which was faithfully mirrored by nearly every romancer.

The Church and Feudalism had for long been closely linked, for bishops not only were feudal lords, but also during crusades commanded armies. It was therefore an easy and a natural step to make the initiation ceremony of knighthood a sacred religious rite. In addition to receiving the customary sword tap on his neck from a feudal superior, the knight had his sword blessed by a priest and spent the following night in church praying for God's guidance in his knightly duties. The Christian knight, therefore, could not restrict himself to the two duties of loyalty and courtesy; he had also to avoid pride and debauchery. The Church ordained humility and purity, but not celibacy. Yet although the knight could marry, chastity was regarded by the Church as the supreme ideal, and therefore in the Grail romances, fostered if not inspired by the Church, those knights, like Galahad, who symbolised chastity were ranked as the greatest of all. Even in actual life the most famous knights were those of the two celibate Orders, the Templars and the Hospitallers, founded early in the twelfth century to protect pilgrims to Jerusalem and to fight the Saracens. The iron discipline and severe training of these knights made them very useful in crusades and inspired the Turks with such great fear that none captured was ever ransomed. All were put to death, because the Turks knew that any that they freed for ransom would sooner or later exact a bloody vengeance. Their discipline, however, was too strict to ensure permanence, and they became such a menace in Europe that they had to be disbanded. The Church forbade not only marriage, but even the normal recreations of their class, hunting and hawking. The sole occupation allowed to them was fighting, and so in the intervals between crusades their only possible exercise was warfare with other Christians. Men who combined great physical strength and ferocity and who were deprived of all exercise in times of peace could not be expected either to remain chaste or to suffer restraint during war. Even marriage has never been sufficient to check all illicit lust, and in the absence of this check and of physical recreations to keep their minds and bodies employed it is not surprising that they became, as Buckle called them, "establishments that inflicted the greatest evils on society, whose members, combining analogous vices, enlivened the superstitions of monks with the debauchery of soldiers."[1] Gawain for a time had been the symbol of chaste knighthood, but this conception could not endure, because in life celibacy is too unhuman to attract and sustain interest. It may possibly have been the influence of these celibate Orders that inspired some poet to portray a hero whose chief feature should be chastity, but in the absence of some very definite objective this conception could not possibly rival with success the conceptions of courtly and of sentimental love that a female audience desired. The Templars and Hospitallers were celibate because their mission was a sacred one; they were in effect the defenders of the Holy Land. So in romance it was possible to arouse interest in celibate heroes if they were aiming at a suitable objective, and this the Grail Quest supplied. To present as finder of the Grail containing Christ's blood any knight who was

[1] Buckle, "History of Civilisation."

not absolutely chaste would have been to defy the most vital principle of the medieval Church. The chastity of Gawain endangered the whole fabric of Arthurian romance; that of Galahad, designed only for one especial quest, offered no real clash of interests, and was also thoroughly in harmony with contemporary sentiment.

It must not be assumed that the ideals of chivalry mirrored in romance reflect the actual practice of the times. Actuality always falls short of ideals if the ideals are worth having, and the divergence between ideal and actual was perhaps greater in the Middle Ages than at any other time in European history, because then ideals were more removed from human scope. The ideals of ancient Greece and Rome were sound and good, but largely practical; a well-trained and well-disciplined man could hope to achieve almost all of them. Those of modern times are also based on more practical grounds than those of the Middle Ages, although medieval religious thought still maintains a strong influence over large sections of the people. Many people and even many clergymen still formulate rigid principles of conduct which neither have a broad or deep foundation nor are necessary to most. The medieval Church exaggerated and refined its principles of conduct until practically no human base was left at all. The early Christian Fathers like Ambrose and Augustine were well versed in Greek philosophy and reflect its restraint and sanity in their writings. But with Jerome and Gregory began a period in which all pagan learning was condemned, and as no real Christian scholarship had begun, the Church was left stranded without a guide. To understand Christ's teaching a well-trained mind and a sound philosophical teaching were essential. Except for a few men of rare natural ability who were usually suppressed as heretics, the medieval Churchmen were necessarily devoid of both, and so distorted Christ's teaching and formulated ethical codes divorced from natural law. Natural impulses, which, if well directed, were not only wholesome and healthy, but even essential to the well-being of man, were condemned by the Church as sin. The distorted minds of monks could not realise that in a beautiful world man will naturally have an instinctive liking for what is beautiful, and so pleasure in any beauty not designed directly for the service of the Church was sternly repressed. Instead of guiding wholesome recreations like miracle plays, communal singing and communal dancing, the Church attempted to suppress them, and so fostered greater excesses, because the people continued to indulge in them, but in defiance of the Church instead of under its guidance. Furthermore, the great natural law of sexual impulse was regarded as unnatural and sexual intercourse viewed as sin even in marriage. The teaching of the Church had become so distorted that it did not clearly realise that this impulse was given to man to ensure propagation of the race. It only realised that prevention was impossible, and so regarded married love as a minor sin, but still a blemish on man's purity.

Chivalrous ideals, therefore, became impossible of attainment, partly because of incessant warfare, which brutalises man, and partly because the ideals became too exaggerated. A literal acceptation of medieval Church beliefs could only produce a freakish character or lead to disaster, and the outstanding example in history of such literal acceptation is Louis the Pious, King of France. He believed implicitly that prayer and fasting would ensure God's aid and yield victory over the Saracens. Stubbornly refusing all material advice, he persisted in this monkish behaviour until the Crusade was lost and he and all his army were prisoners of the Turks. The ransom necessary to free them nearly ruined France, and Church teaching was to blame. Prayer and fasting, penance and confession are not ideals of conduct, they are but symbolic means to an end. To attain material ends material means must be used; the Saracens could be defeated only by weapons, organisation and physical strength; a campaign is not the time to mortify the flesh by fasting, it must be strengthened by feeding; and these material means can still be inspired by lofty ideals. The romances naturally reflect distorted ideals, but still serve to show that the people were inspired by noble motives.

As time went on the exaggerated and distorted teaching of the Church became productive not of moral progress, but of apathy; people realised the utter impossibility of fashioning their daily life upon such ideals as celibacy, monastic life, continual fasting, absolute poverty and avoidance of healthy recreation; they were willing to believe that their natural desires were sinful, and so followed the mechanical process of committing sins and expiating them by penance. The underlying basis of most of these ideals was very sound, but ignorance had converted them to formulas, and active life cannot be based on a formula. Distortion in one direction inevitably leads to distortion in another, and the blind following of many medieval tenets in the Churches of to-day is largely responsible for the many perversities of moral truth in modern literature by men who have become impatient of rigid dogma.

With the decay of feudalism which had provided a practical basis for many wholesome ideals, and with this distorted teaching of the Church, chivalry ceased to be a driving force and became degraded to preciosity. In the fifteenth and later centuries spiritual ideals were replaced by mere conventions of behaviour, courtly conversation, and punctilios of conduct in the drawing-room, until the terms chivalry and gentlemanliness came to imply only an observance of elaborate etiquette. The Church had never offered a practical basis for knightly conduct, feudalism had; while feudalism remained, Church teaching was a useful support; when feudalism decayed, Church teaching was too unpractical to be a guide. Honour, the foundation of feudalism, came to be mere vanity, and gambling debts became debts of honour because payment was not legally compulsory, while to ruin a tradesman by refusing to pay for actual goods delivered was not in any way dishonourable. Disinterested service to others was replaced by personal vanity, so that it became more dishonourable to receive a trifling insult without fighting the calumniator, than to offer the grossest insults to an unprotected female. How different was this spirit from that of medieval romance, where Gawain, whose brothers have been killed by Lancelot's knights, refuses to seek vengeance because to do so would wreck the unity of the Round Table, and refuses to dishonour his host by accepting his wife's love though offered thrice in the most alluring manner! In seventeenth-century romance either of Gawain's actions would have appeared quixotic, because the spirit of real chivalry was dead. Even by the fifteenth century it had been sadly degraded, and it seems certain that Malory wrote his "Morte d'Arthur" primarily in the hope of reviving it by offering to the barons of his day the famous examples of earlier times. Spenser in two poems presents a contrast between the ideal and the actuality of knightly life. The "Faerie Queene" was written to illustrate the ideals of the perfect knight, "Mother Hubbard's Tale" to portray the actual corrupt and degraded life of contemporary courtiers.

Medieval romance must have been a great inspiring force, with its vivid presentment of moral virtue and of moral vice, even though the ideals presented were frequently removed so far from an actual human basis. It held up for all to admire men who performed their obligations and their pledges, no matter how great the sacrifice, men who were willing to suffer incredible hardship for the benefit of others and who maintained a constant respect towards women and children and deep reverence for the Christian faith. It consistently illustrates the essence of chivalry, the spirit of fair play, and the exaggeration of this aspect, though often making it appear ludicrous to modern readers, at least proves that this ideal was highly reverenced. Huon of Bordeaux expresses his willingness to elope with the Saracen maid, Esclaramond, but refuses her request to kill her father, who has held him prisoner, because to do so except in fair fight would be unchivalrous. Before his duel with the Saracen Fierabras, Oliver arms

his adversary, who has no squire, and during the combat
Fierabras offers his horse to Oliver, whose own had been
disabled. In "The Four Sons of Aymon," Renaud, after
unhorsing a Saracen opponent, dismounts to make the
fight more fair. This scrupulous regard for justice often
led to a fatuous sense of honour not only in France, but
also in real life. Roland refuses to sound his horn to recall
Charlemagne until his army has been almost entirely
destroyed, because to seek aid except in the last extremity
was regarded as cowardly.[1] King Richard scorns to attack
Saracens while they sleep, because to attack a helpless foe
was regarded not as strategy, but as treachery.[2] During a
long-protracted duel with Roland the Saracen chief
Vernagu wishes to have a rest, and Roland not only permits him to take a nap, but even places a stone beneath
his head to make him comfortable; when the duel is
resumed Vernagu in return informs Roland where he is
most vulnerable.[3] In the "Morte Arthure," Galiot, invading Arthur's territory, finds him with a very inferior force,
and so returns home again, granting him twelve months'
respite so that he may raise a sufficiently powerful army to
fight on equal terms. Such episodes are not the mere
exaggerations of fiction, but a true reflection of life and
the principles of the time. The crusaders lost many battles
because they scorned to use the stratagems employed by
the Turks, deeming ambushes and feigned retreats as a
cowardly method of warfare. Froissart's chronicles offer
similar examples from the Hundred Years' War. When
the Black Prince invaded Spain to assist Don Pedro to
regain his throne, Henry of Castille, his adversary, was
advised to hem him in among the mountains and starve
him into surrender. He rejected this counsel as unchivalrous and was utterly defeated. The medieval code of
chivalry was exaggerated and fantastic, but it was rigid;
every man knew what was considered right and what

[1] "Chanson de Roland."
[2] "Richard Cœur de Lion."
[3] "Roland and Vernagu."

wrong; Chaucer in his "Knight's Tale" and "Book of the
Duchess" and Malory in his "Morte d'Arthur" present
the spirit of chivalry in a nobler and more sober form, but
it is one of the problems of modern life that, having once
left the rigid principles of the Middle Ages, most men
have no clear idea of what is right and what wrong, or
what is chivalrous and what mean. The more that thinkers
come to understand human nature the more complicated
does life become and the more difficult it is for the average
man to scheme out a way of life for himself.

It must be remembered, of course, that this spirit of fair
play and chivalry was restricted, as all ideals were restricted, by feudal custom. Courtesy was not due to churls,
and even the most chivalrous knight was capable of permitting his followers to massacre unarmed peasants and
violate their wives and daughters. The Black Prince,
regarded as the mirror of chivalry, treated the captive
King John of France with perfect courtesy, even serving
him with his own hands, but calmly watched the sack of
Limoges, with its attendant massacre of innocent women
and children; they were churls.

Medieval romance, like all romance, usually mirrors only
the brightest aspects of life: the chivalry between knight
and knight, the loyal devotion of vassals, and warfare
which has some ostensibly good purpose. Rarely does it
mirror deliberately the darker phases of life, massacre
and violence, although the actual conditions of the time,
as well as its ideals, are clearly portrayed, even though
only in an incidental way. In spite of various attempts by
the Church to minimise warfare between Christian nations
and families, the period of romance was one of incessant
fighting, and most of the barons lived lawless lives in youth
and expiated their sins of violence by pilgrimages in old
age. In 1041 the Church ordained a "truce of God"
which threatened excommunication to any man who
fought between Wednesday evening and Monday morning
in any week, on any Church festivals, and throughout
Lent and Advent. In 1159 the Council of Latran, antici-

pating the later Hague Conventions, attempted to minimise the horrors of warfare by forbidding the use of bows
and arbalests in wars between Christians; but both edicts
were in vain. Modern warfare is too deadly for most men
to crave more than one experience; medieval warfare,
though deadly to the rank and file, held few terrors for
the knights. The crude weapons employed before the invention of gunpowder were of little avail against either
the armour of the knights or the defences of their castles;
it was also found more profitable to free a captured
knight in return for ransom than to kill him. The result
was that warfare was little more than an exciting pastime
in which the foot-soldiers might be killed in large numbers
and the peasants' farms destroyed, but with little prospect
of loss to the leaders. The Battle of Brémule of 1119 offers
a good illustration of the comparative immunity from death
of the knights; 900 were engaged in the conflict, 140 captured and three slain. It is not surprising, therefore, that
they took an inordinate pleasure in fighting, a pleasure
clearly mirrored in all the Charlemagne and many of the
Arthurian romances.

The Charlemagne romances naturally reflect this spirit
most clearly, because based on traditions of national and
religious war, but even the Arthurian legend began in
literature as a story of national warfare. Geoffrey of Monmouth presents Arthur as a warrior king, and in his invasion and conquest of Europe as very typical of Norman
princes; not only is he assisted by a Breton force, as was
William of Normandy in his invasion of England, but he
even follows the customary feudal practice of forbidding all
but his wife to hunt in the royal forests.[1] Both chronicles
and romances reflect the conditions familiar to their
authors, not those of the times which they profess to
portray; Charlemagne, ruler of the Franks, is presented
as king of France, England, and Denmark,[2] Arthur
frequently as king of all Europe. No greater compliment
could be paid by French and particularly Norman writers,

[1] "Morte Arthure."   [2] "Four Sons of Aymon."

for to them the supremely great man was he who was most successful in conquest. The constant warfare of the time, and the miseries it entailed are seen most clearly, not in the grandiose descriptions of great campaigns or the fierce combats of lusty and hot-blooded young heroes, but in simple little scenes of pathos, as in "The Four Sons of Aymon," where a baron begs Charlemagne to proclaim a truce so that they might all return home to visit their families, and in "La Chanson de Roland," where the barons are so overcome with emotion at the prospect of rejoining their wives and children after seven years' absence that they weep.

Many barons seized every opportunity of fighting because they knew that protracted peace would make their men effeminate. The castles were little more than military barracks in which lived a large number of men whose sole duty was to fight. In all periods barrack life in times of peace has a demoralising influence; soldiers even now are usually too illiterate to take pleasure in any intellectual recreations, their duties are too slight and too mechanical to keep their minds fully occupied, and the discomforts of barrack life drive them to seek recreation outside, which, in the absence of women's refining influence, frequently means drinking and debauchery. The medieval soldier could not read, had no places of public entertainment like the modern picture theatre in which to spend his leisure time, and was cooped up in confined quarters with little opportunity of healthy exercise or amusement, but with almost unlimited opportunities of drinking and sensual indulgence. So when Geoffrey of Monmouth describes Arthur as being urged to make war upon Rome because his men are becoming enfeebled with lack of occupation and indulgence in sensual pleasures, he is but reflecting the problem which confronted every medieval baron.

That warfare was man's chief occupation is also incidentally reflected in the affection which the heroes of romance lavished upon their horses and weapons. The names of the horses and swords of the most famous heroes have become household words,[1] and in "La Chanson de Roland" names are given to those of nearly every warrior mentioned.

The ignorance of and prejudice against alien customs displayed by nearly all men in this period are also clearly reflected in romance. This attitude is always intensified in periods of great hostility, whether in medieval or in modern times. During the Great War most people were easily persuaded by propaganda that the Germans were capable of any vile practice. The same fanatic emotionalism reigned during the period of crusades—"The Sowdone of Babylon" portrays Saracens as eating snakes fried in oil, which may have been true, and drinking the blood of wild beasts to increase their ferocity, which was probably nothing more than deliberate propaganda. Even in times of peace, both then and now, there is always an obstinate desire to credit foreigners with practising customs that are unnatural; Miss Matty of "Cranford" was not alone in thinking that Frenchmen largely subsisted on frogs. An extreme case of prejudice is seen in the chronicle of Geoffrey de Vinsauf, which praises the Emperor Frederick of Germany because, though knowing other languages, he respected his own so highly that he would use no other, and even conversed with ambassadors by means of interpreters; the author omits to state whether the unfortunate interpreters lost caste by speaking alien tongues.

The Charlemagne and crusading romances, which did not aim at offering examples of chivalry, as did Arthurian romance, clearly reflect the brutality and ungovernable temper of the average medieval baron. In "The Four Sons of Aymon," Charlemagne's nephew, after losing a game of chess, strikes his opponent, Renaud, who retaliates by killing him with the chess-board; choler must have indeed run high when even a game of chess could provoke such violence. In "The Sowdone of Babylon," Naymes, one of Charlemagne's peers, burns a Saracen captive alive and torments him with jests while he is

[1] Cf. Arthur's sword Excalibur and Renaud's horse Bayard.

dying; even Floripas, the Saracen heroine in whose room it is done, regards the incident as an amusing jest. Otuel, fighting another Saracen who refuses conversion, cuts off his cheek and then mocks him for showing his teeth.[1] In "Sir Ferumbras" Roland kills seven Saracen ambassadors who are travelling to Charlemagne's court, and takes their heads back to the Sultan, their master. Another peer advises the same Sultan to go meekly to Charlemagne in his shirt with a rope round his neck; yet the author expresses indignation because the Sultan orders the peers to be hanged. In "Richard Cœur de Lion" Richard is highly praised by the poet for killing the German Emperor's son with one blow of his fist, even though he had unfairly covered his fist with wax so as to tear the skin off his opponent's face. The serving of decapitated prisoners' heads as food to Saracen ambassadors is still another reflection of the brutal manners of the time. Whether such deeds were ever performed by the men to whom they are credited, or by anyone, matters little; they would not have been related as praiseworthy unless similar brutal deeds were regarded by the audience as natural and proper.

In times of incessant warfare man's safety largely depends upon his courage and physical strength. When warfare chiefly consists of hand-to-hand fighting, physical strength is often more useful than strategic ability. In the Middle Ages, therefore, bodily strength and physical courage commanded great respect, and fame in warfare gained in youth frequently preserved men and their families from molestation at a later period of life when their strength had decayed. The great importance attached to brute force and skill in arms is widely reflected in romance. Guy of Warwick states in defence of his continual fighting that a man must achieve fame in warfare when young so that his reputation will be a shield in old age. And most romances, especially those that deal with warfare, exemplify the importance attached to physical

[1] In "Otuel."

prowess clearly, even though often crudely. Charlemagne is frequently described as eight feet in height, and even, in one English romance,[1] as twenty feet. He is described as still powerful at the age of 100, or even 200 years.[2] Renaud, the rebel vassal in the "Four Sons of Aymon," is described as sixteen feet in height, and Vernagu, a Saracen prince,[1] forty feet in height, fifteen in breadth and possessing the strength of forty men. The romancer here seems to have realised that he had somewhat exceeded the limit, for he states that Vernagu was vulnerable only below the navel. If nature or the romancer had reversed the condition, Roland would have been compelled to copy David, and use a catapult. These exaggerations, especially when applied to foes, were intended to enhance the heroes' fame, and show that the chief stress was on physical strength, not on mental ability. Charlemagne is represented as having among his twelve peers one wise counsellor, Naymes, who corresponds to the Nestor of Homer's "Iliad," but none of them in any way corresponds to Ulysses, who combined great strength with great brain-power, and was therefore the ideal leader. Even that common test of legend, the drawing of a sword from a stone, probably originated in this reverence paid to physical strength, although presented in romance as an expression of Divine Will.

But of far greater significance in this respect is the frequent presentation in romance of marriage with an heiress as dependent on physical prowess; either a king offers his daughter or an heiress offers herself as wife to the knight who most successfully performs some difficult feat, which usually necessitates great strength and courage. The Earl of Artois[3] promises consent to his daughter's marriage with Sir Eglamour only if he first kills a famous wild boar, a hart which lives in a forest belonging to a giant, and a dragon which is harrying Rome. Felice

[1] "Roland and Vernagu."
[2] "Chanson de Roland."
[3] In "Sir Eglamour of Artois."

refuses to marry Guy of Warwick until he has won fame in foreign lands, and while obeying her request he has the misfortune to win a tournament, the prize of which he finds to be another heiress whose father demands a doughty son-in-law. Many knights of romance, and perhaps some in real life, were faced at times with similar awkward situations. The heiress of Calabria[1] proclaims that she will marry only that knight who, in a tournament she has arranged, overcomes all others. In the Dutch romance "Morien," an heiress dwelling in a land ravaged by a wild beast proclaims that she will marry only the slayer of the beast. Similarly, Tristram wins Iseult for King Mark by killing a dragon. And the best-known type of Arthurian romance, so ably used by Spenser, presents a lady seeking aid at Arthur's Court against foes who are ravaging her parents' lands, and eventually marrying the knight who undertakes the defence. Such episodes were, no doubt, included to add to the romantic spirit, but were taken straight from life. No woman could hope to maintain independence; if the heiress of an estate, she must find a husband capable of protecting her domains; if a widow destitute of sons, she must marry again for the same reason. The soldiers in her service required a leader to maintain discipline and organisation, and few if any women could fill such a position. Only the ruler of the estate could satisfactorily be leader, and therefore the woman who did not wish to risk losing her lands had to find a husband capable of defending her rights. In "Ywain and Gawain" this position is summed up in one significant couplet:

> "Women may maintain no stour,
> They must needs have a governour."

And the widow heroine of this romance immediately after her husband's death marries the knight[2] who had killed him. She did not love him, but had to take her maid's advice that if she did not marry soon, she would probably lose her lands.

---

[1] In "The Life of Ipomydon."   [2] Ywain.

Romancers made little if any deliberate attempt to reflect contemporary life in their work. In one sense their pictures are very remote from life, but wherever they added to the traditions on which their work was based they naturally portrayed episodes and features of life familiar to them, and therefore throw many interesting sidelights on contemporary history.

CHAPTER XII

THE SENSATIONAL AND SUPERNATURAL
IN ROMANCE

IN MODERN ENGLISH LITERATURE THE terms "romance" and "novel" still remain to some extent distinct, but the mingling of the best elements of both types by writers like Robert Louis Stevenson has made it impossible to retain a sharp distinction. The essence of medieval romance is most clearly exemplified, not by modern prototypes, but in the distinction we still retain in life between the terms "romance" and "reality." The latter implies actuality, the former baseless fancy divorced from life. And the world of medieval romance is remote from life, even though the best examples do present inspiring ideals and noble characters. Contemporary life and sentiment may be observed by the discerning eye, but it is only incidental; the romancer made no attempt to give a picture of life; he claimed to relate historical events of the past, and, in order to make them more pleasing, added every possible device to hold the attention of his audience. The average audience of every age and country demands from literature tales of adventure; the average female audience also asks for love. The outstanding features of medieval romance are, therefore, adventure and love, the love of a man for a woman being the pivot, and the adventures framed to enhance the portrayal of that love.

A highly educated and intellectual reader desires something more than romance; a flavouring of romance will please him, but the essence must be based on reality; the author must present great characters and great problems of life. The concentration in the Middle Ages upon what is exciting rather than what is inspiring was due to existing circumstances. The people were neither sufficiently intellectual nor sufficiently critical to appreciate literature like that of ancient Greece or to realise that the so-called history offered to them was almost entirely destitute of truth. The outstanding features of classical literature were restraint and sanity, because the whole training of the people was based on these two ideals uncontaminated by those cruder elements of romanticism and sentimentalism which make modern thought so confused and modern education so difficult.[1] Whatever the subject may be, the reader is always convinced that the author has probed into life, has analysed its problems and has sought to present the dominating features of human nature and their influence upon human life. As Greek literature passed further and further from its original inspiring force, and as philosophy, science and education decayed, the elements of sentimentalism and sensationalism began to enter with ever-increasing intensity. The great literature of Greece and Rome was practically unknown to medieval writers, who were able to draw only upon later Greek decadent literature and spurious Latin works which purported to be versions of books older than the earliest writings of Greece. Great literature can arise only from a great inspiring force, and in early periods, before the growth of philosophy and psychology, that force must be based on national sentiment. In modern Europe the writer need not consider national sentiment; in general there will be no national sentiment to consider. Even if he concentrates upon some aspect of human nature or of social life ignored by the community as a whole, there are plenty of readers sufficiently educated to have a critical mind and to assess his work at something like its true value. The medieval author had an audience limited in numbers, limited in education, and entirely lacking in critical ability; he had to please patrons who had definite likes and dislikes, and he had to conform to their tastes or lose their patronage. The opinions of such an audience, though possibly universal, cannot be regarded as true national sentiment—such as

---

[1] The noblest aspects of romanticism and sentimentalism have, of course, been a great inspiring force.

had inspired the earlier heroic poetry. Nations had become too big and too diverse for any one ideal to unite the whole people in the bonds of a common aspiration or endeavour. There was also no great driving force—no national danger or crisis—to stimulate a strong and sincere national sentiment; the Crusades were sufficiently important and aroused sufficient enthusiasm at first to supply such a driving force, but were not sufficiently national, and so, after the first, attracted little interest except spasmodically. Men came to regard them as a routine business of life; they fought in them as a penance for their sins, or to please the Church, or to win fame and glory. The clash with Saracens was not visualised as in defence of France, or even of Europe, and therefore could not arouse a fervent national spirit. The romancer, therefore, had to consider instead the temporary whims and prejudices of an audience that demanded amusement for its leisure hours. Above all else were demanded sensational adventure and sentimental love. And the tastes which arise only from boredom and lack of occupation, then as now, cannot inspire great literature; they can only inspire romance.

In contrast to the Greek unity of sentiment and intensive scholarship, medieval France had a confused diversity of sentiments, a slavish reverence for a hopelessly distorted Latin learning, a complete ignorance of science and philosophy, and a blind superstitious awe, miscalled religion. The few scholars that arose from time to time neither wrote nor encouraged vernacular literature, and so exerted no influence. Even to-day scholarship and sound critical judgment are confined to a comparatively small section of the people, sufficiently large to encourage some good literature, but not large enough to permit the bulk of modern fiction to be of more value than medieval romance. But in the Middle Ages the education of even the most intellectual people was guided by ecclesiastics whose idea of education was merely slavish memorising of past learning, and, while that vicious circle of "the blind leading the blind" remained, an enlightened audience could not be

expected. In religion the supernatural rather than the
ethical and philosophical aspects were most stressed, and
people reverenced the mysterious and the magical more
than wisdom and common sense. There was present
throughout Europe a spirit of longing and yearning, a
desire to escape from the mundane things of Earth, which
roused an ardent faith in miracles and a keen desire for
sensationalism. Of distant countries and periods nothing
was certain, and the most unlikely events could be
expected. Men could not distinguish between the natural
and the supernatural, and so nothing was incredible. The
people could appreciate miracles, which appealed to their
emotions, but not art or wisdom, which required concentration of the mind. Therefore Virgil was revered not
as a poet or as a philosopher, but as a wizard; for every
man who regarded him as a great poet there were thousands who regarded him as a great magician. The one sure
sign of greatness was ability to perform prodigious and, if
possible, magical feats, and romancers fashioned their
stories and portrayed their characters accordingly.

The universal craving for excitement and sensation was
fostered not only because of the emotional strain in religion
and the lack of sound education, but also by the monotony
of castle life. Women who were doomed to spend their
lives in the narrow and gloomy confines of a feudal castle
longed for a literature which would present a vivid contrast—a realm of adventure, of mystery, and of love that
would temporarily transport them from their grim and
dreary prison. The possibilities of realism are almost
infinite, but of sensationalism extremely small; every
author will have his own individual view of life, and so,
without effort, will present a different conception from
that of his fellows, but the romancer seeking novelty in
sensationalism has to rely on invention, and is therefore
compelled to distort life more and more in order to outvie
his predecessors. Invention of entirely new stories was
made difficult because the audience demanded history,
and so romancers were obliged to refashion old stories

already known, adding new elements and new episodes until the original conception was almost entirely lost. The last stage was reached when authors were incapable of revivifying older themes and had to invent fictitious parents and children of already well-known heroes; "Berte aux grands pieds" records the adventures of a fictitious mother of Charlemagne, and "Huon de Bordeaux" was provided with sequel after sequel relating the deeds of the hero's children and even of his grandchildren.

The interest of sensationalism depends upon novelty, and novelty is most easily attained by using sources unfamiliar to the audience. For this reason the most important new feature in romance was the introduction of Eastern influence. Eastern stories had been occasionally introduced before the period of romance and retold not only in Latin, but even in Anglo-Saxon,[1] but from the twelfth century on not only were Eastern stories made the subjects of romance, but Eastern legends and customs became the chief basis of the marvellous and sensational elements in general. The wealth of information brought back by pilgrims and crusaders not only of Eastern legends but also of Eastern luxuries, buildings, and ornaments, was a perfect godsend to romancers. It added a fresh stimulus to their efforts to make the world of romance a fantastic realm of magic and mystery, which in time became so distorted that no link with reality remained either by verisimilitude or through implied contrast. The French romances were filled with long and exaggerated descriptions of men and women, dragons and giants, dress and armour, buildings and gardens, thoroughly imbued with a pseudo-Eastern atmosphere and designed only to excite wonder and admiration.[2] The English versions curtailed many of these descriptions, but frequently exaggerated still further those they retained, in frenzied attempts to impress an audience rapidly becoming *blasé*.

---

[1] As *e.g.* the story of Apollonius of Tyre.
[2] In the "Roman de Troie" 300 lines are devoted to the description of one room.

In "Richard Cœur de Lion" is described a white ship with sails of samite, ropes of white silk, staves of gold and golden-headed nails. The helmet of Sir Ferumbras is studded with pearls, rubies, and sapphires.[1] The bower of Floripas, the Saracen heroine, has windows of jasper and a ceiling of silver and gold.[2] The tent of Launfal's fairy lover has on it crystal pommels, a gold eagle, and a carbuncle.[3] In "Floris and Blauncheflour" Babylon[4] is described as being sixty miles in circumference, with 140 gates and 700 towers. Alexander the Great is attacked by birds which have lambs' fur, men's teeth, and a peacock's cry. He also meets a race of one-legged men who stand on the seashore gazing at the stars[5]—the longshoremen of antiquity. Marvels are always, even to-day, more readily believed if placed in a distant country—whether in romance or in the daily newspaper—and by sending his hero to seek adventures in the East the romancer could give free play to his imagination.

This constant search for novelty also led to the linking up of heroes and localities with famous classical names. The tower of Troyes is stated to have been built by Julius Cæsar;[6] Morgan la fée is described as wife to Julius Cæsar, mother of Oberon the fairy-king, and grandmother of Alexander the Great;[7] Huon of Bordeaux converts the Emperor of the Medes and Persians and enlists him as an ally against the Saracens in Palestine;[7] an ally of the Trojans against the Greeks, called Polydamas, is described as a lover of the Queen of the Amazons;[8] and King Arthur is visited by one Segramore, son of the King of Hungary and grandson of the Emperor of Constantinople.[9]

[1] "The Sowdone of Babylon."
[2] "Sir Ferumbras."
[3] "Sir Launfal."
[4] Here, as usually in medieval romance, the name refers to old Cairo in Egypt, the ruins of which still bear the name Baboul.
[5] "The Life of Alisaunder."
[6] "The Four Sons of Aymon."
[7] "Huon of Bordeaux."
[8] "The Destruction of Troy."
[9] The prose "Merlin."

In spite of all the magic and mystery, the supernaturalism and sensationalism, this unreal realm of romance lacks genuine romantic spirit because portrayed as real and normal. A vivid contrast with real life must be emphasized throughout if romantic glamour is to be attained. In the modern adventure story the scene presented is usually as strange and mysterious to the hero as to the audience; the characters are ordinary mortals living in new and strange surroundings; the spirit of mystery and romance is thus sustained throughout. The realm of medieval romance was simply another realm as normal, often even as dull and conventional to the characters, as ordinary life was to the audience.[1] King Arthur is represented as refusing to begin a meal until he has seen or heard of some strange adventure;[2] but with far less excitement and interest than the modern sport-lover displays when reading the cricket or football news before beginning breakfast. In "Sir Gawain and the Green Knight" the Green Knight enters the Hall, issues his challenge, has his head chopped off, picks it up and walks out, while Arthur impassively looks on. When he has retired Arthur turns to the Queen, remarks that such sport is very suitable to the Christmas season, and states that he is now able to begin his meal. He could hardly have shown less enthusiasm if he had been at a civic banquet listening to a long speech by the Chairman while his soup was going cold. It became almost a point of etiquette that a romancer must not allow his hero to evince any surprise, no matter how great the danger confronting him or the marvels he encountered; Huon of Bordeaux, sent by Charlemagne on an embassy to the East, is instructed to kill the Emir's most powerful lord, kiss his daughter before his face, and bring back his teeth and a handful of his beard, but expresses no astonishment. He certainly considered it a tyrannical act

---

[1] Of course this is not universally true. In the best romances there is some implied contrast with real life, but not in most.

[2] In the prose "Merlin," "Messire Gauvain" and "Sir Gawain and the Green Knight."

on Charlemagne's part, but nevertheless carried out his instructions.

The romancers also, each striving to make his hero out-rival all others, exaggerated physical prowess and skill in arms until all human semblance disappeared. In "Sir Ferumbras," the twelve peers of Charlemagne, when besieged in a castle, frequently make sallies and fight successfully against thousands of their Saracen foes. To represent a champion as attacked by a dozen men where two or three would be sufficient to defeat the average man does enhance his skill and courage, but when a poet represents Gawain as pursued by 10,000,[1] the obvious implication is that the audience had become thoroughly *blasé* and demanded monstrosities; no audience could visualise a distinction between one and ten or a hundred thousand. In the prose "Merlin" the curious statement is made that in those days—when Arthur lived—five hundred was called a thousand. Whether this was in-tended to minimise an exaggeration found in the French original, or whether it implies that the term "thousand" was a conventional term, like the modern "battalion," which varied in strength from time to time, it is impossible to say. But even this explanation cannot remove the inherent absurdity of such exaggerated numbers.

This same desire to exalt their heroes was no doubt partly responsible for the introduction of giants, since mere mortals were too puny to extend fully the powers of famous champions. But even giants became common-place and as insignificant as the Lilliputians were to Gulliver. King Arthur, after killing the giant on Mount St. Michael, casually remarks that he had only once before met so formidable a foe, and that in Araby. In Geoffrey's chronicle this was Mount Aravius, but Araby had a more romantic appeal and was more likely to enhance Arthur's fame; to a medieval audience the monsters of Araby would be more dreadful than those of France, just as to the modern spectator in a picture-theatre adventures in

[1] "Morte Arthure."

Alaska are more impressive than any in England or America. The Roman army sent to oppose Arthur's invasion was strengthened by sixty giants and warlocks but all in vain; Arthur was invincible. In "The Sowdone of Babylon" the peers of Charlemagne had their passage across the bridge at Mantrible barred by a giant with a leopard's head and a boar's tusk, but neither his strength nor hideous visage could avail against such tried warriors. Such dangers could not even damp their boyish spirits, because, when baptising the giant's sons, they named them Roland and Oliver. Sometimes this constant striving for sensationalism endangered the whole fabric of romance; after numberless romancers had painstakingly built up around the knights of Arthur a tradition of indomitable courage, the author of "Sir Percyvelle of Galles" demolished the whole fabric by portraying one and all too cowardly to oppose a Red Knight who insults Arthur in his own hall, while Percival, a young and unknown knight who had never before handled weapon, kills him without the least difficulty. Extreme instances like this are rare, most romancers being content to avoid comparison between their heroes and the popular knights like Lancelot and Gawain.

In this period of cavalry warfare good horses were valuable possessions, and therefore deservedly celebrated in romance. But with horses, as with men, the craving for sensationalism caused romancers to stress marvellous or supernatural features rather than their real value. This no doubt arose from a desire to outrival the famous horses of antiquity, as in "The Four Sons of Aymon," where Bayard, the horse of Renaud, is claimed to be equal to Alexander's Bucephalus in sagacity and strength, and superior in that it could live indefinitely on roots where other horses required oats, and even supply Renaud and his brothers with blood to drink without becoming enfeebled. When it became impossible to magnify still further their strength, fidelity and endurance, romancers attempted to magnify their beauty by all sorts of freakish descriptions: in Chrétien's "Erec" the heroine's palfrey has one white and one black cheek, the two colours being separated by a green line, while "as red as blood" was a universal stock description of horses throughout romance. Iseult's lap-dog, Petit Crû, was of many colours, and a hound in "Lybeaus Disconus" is described as having all the colours that men may see in flowers between May and midsummer. The illiterate mind revels in gay and striking colours, however incongruous to the situation, and it has been thought that horses and dogs may have been artificially coloured. Whether this was so or not, it is quite obvious that the chief object of romancers was to extort admiration and wonder, even though they claimed to be relating historical facts.

Romancers did not, however, rely merely upon exaggerations in description, which were necessarily limited in scope; they made full use of magic and the supernatural, in which no limit need be observed. The long arm of coincidence cannot be stretched indefinitely, but the magician's wand knows no limitations; heroes were so constantly in peril that continual escapes by mere good fortune would have become utterly fantastic even to a medieval audience, but magic talismans and friendly magicians proved never-failing remedies in times of distress. Even in ancient Greece some credit was given to stones which possessed magical properties, though Pliny expressed strong doubt. The advanced state of scholarship in Greece enabled scholars to concentrate upon the medicinal properties of herbs and stones and to ignore the popular belief in their magical ones. The medieval mind was far too credulous to doubt any report of magic, however far-fetched, if it were vouched for by someone reputed to be wise. Even in the seventeenth century Sir Thomas Browne, physician and scientist, shows hardly less credulity in his "Pseudodoxia Epidemica" than any layman of the Middle Ages, and, in spite of the enormous progress made in scientific study, the people of to-day cling to old superstitions and eagerly flock to a charlatan who

professes to foretell the future by gazing into a crystal
or to cure the most serious diseases by a quack remedy.
It is not, therefore, surprising that the medieval people
of Europe attached full credence to the reports that
certain stones, herbs, and springs had magical properties, and that the romances are filled with magic talismans that protect life, foretell danger, yield inexhaustible
supplies of food, and enable the possessor to perform
miraculous feats of every description. These reports and
talismans were gleaned from the pseudo-scientific books
which abounded in this period and which drew their
material from various sources—late Greek and Latin
writings and Eastern legends. The basis of this belief, as
presumably of all reported miracles, was not pure fiction;
herbs, stones, and springs often have medicinal properties
which could not, of course, be comprehended until science
had progressed sufficiently far for an analysis of these
properties to be made. In the most active period of ancient
Greece scientific knowledge was sufficient for men to
understand these medicinal properties. Only scholarship
can keep superstition in check, and as Greek scholarship
decayed superstition again became rampant. The late
Greek writings of Alexandria fostered a belief in these
magical properties, and, in spite of the opposition of the
early Christian fathers, the people of the Middle Ages
gave full credence to their statements. This superstition
was not confined to pseudo-scientific books, romances, and
illiterate people, it permeated the whole nation; in 1232
Hubert de Burgh was solemnly charged with stealing
from the Royal Treasury a gem which would make its
wearer invisible. In "Ywain and Gawain," Ywain is given
a ring which will render him invisible, and in many
romances rings and gems are described as capable of
saving the wearer from fire and drowning.[1] In "Sir
Gawain and the Green Knight" Sir Gawain is given a
girdle which will preserve him from death, and in the

[1] "Huon of Bordeaux," "Richard Cœur de Lion," "Floris and
Blauncheflour."

"Sowdone of Babylon" the heroine, Floripas, is robbed of a girdle which provides an inexhaustible supply of food. These are, of course, examples of complete distortion of the truth, but in many cases the magical properties are but exaggerations of natural ones. The brilliance of precious stones, especially after the riches of the East had been opened up, would naturally lead to exaggeration in the minds of unsophisticated people. So in the "Four Sons of Aymon" Charlemagne's tent is decorated with a carbuncle which acts as a torch, and in "Floris and Blauncheflour" another carbuncle is described as giving sufficient light to illuminate the darkest cellar. The value of any object largely depends upon its rarity, and so the value of carbuncles was enchanced by claiming that they could be found only in serpents' heads.[1] The shields which blind all who look on them—as described in Ariosto's "Orlando Furioso" and Spenser's "Faerie Queene"— may have originated from similar exaggerations, or they may be due to the classical story of the Gorgon's head. The magical origin of swords like Arthur's Excalibur may similarly be attributed to an exaggerated reverence for the medieval knight's most treasured weapon.

The magical properties ascribed to fountains and springs are obviously mere distortions of genuine medicinal properties to be found in many mineral springs. The power of mineral waters to restore health and virility to invalids would not be understood, and would therefore both be attributed to magic and give rise to the widespread tradition of a fountain of youth capable of rejuvenating the old and infirm. Huon of Bordeaux discovers a fountain of youth in the palace of an Emir whom he visits, and Spenser's Red-Cross Knight has his wounds healed in a magical spring during his combat with the dragon.[2]

---

[1] In Gower's "Confessio Amantis" and in "The Romaunt of the Rose," ascribed to Chaucer.

[2] Huon also comes upon a tree which bears apples capable of rejuvenating the old. He is forbidden by an angel to gather more than three, with one of which he rejuvenates the Emperor of the Medes and Persians.

These examples illustrate only exaggeration of genuine properties, but, in accordance with medieval super-stitions, many romancers attributed to springs and foun-tains powers which have no basis in truth. In "Floris and Blauncheflour" the Emir of Babylon has in his garden a well capable of testing the chastity of maidens; the ancient Hebrews had a similar water-test of chastity, which, though utterly fantastic, was based on common sense, because an unchaste woman would be afraid to risk the test. Similar, though less artistically symbolical tests which no doubt originated from a shrewd knowledge of human nature abound in romance—Huon of Bordeaux receives a cup from which only a chaste man may drink, and a popular ballad has for its subject the presentation to each of the ladies at Arthur's Court of a mantle which only a chaste woman may wear; most of them refuse to try it on.[1] Most fantastic and remote from reality of all the magic fountains of romance is that portrayed in "Ywain and Gawain"—when its water was poured upon an emerald stone near-by storms were raised and a knight came forth to combat with the man who had dared to use it.

Of equally great assistance to heroes of romance were advisory wizards like Oberon and Merlin. The former, who placed his magical powers at the disposal of Huon of Bordeaux, could summon warriors from the earth, create mirages of forests and rivers, and raise tempests, all of which were serviceable in checking and harassing Huon's foes. Merlin was magician-in-chief to Arthur, and made warfare against the Saxons the merest child's play. The introduction of supernatural agencies may add to the romantic glamour, but the dependence of the hero's success upon the magical feats of a wizard detracts from his merit, and therefore from the interest of the story.

[1] The most artistic of all chastity tests in literature is that described in the history of Prince Zeyn Alasman in the "Arabian Nights Entertainments"—a mirror which clouds before the face of an unchaste woman.

Don Quixote's statement admirably shows how the introduction of such magicians made the heroes mere puppets. "And had those knights been deprived of those assisting sages and enchanters, who helped them in all emergencies, they would have been strangely disappointed of their mighty expectations."

The romancer never expresses or implies doubt in any feat of magic except for an ulterior purpose, as in "The Destruction of Troy," where the author denies that Medea had caused an eclipse of the sun, as stated in earlier versions, not because he disbelieved her power, but simply because that particular feat brought her into rivalry with Christ. The sun had been eclipsed when Christ was crucified, and to attribute to a mere pagan the power to perform a deed which had been reserved to mark the death of Christ seemed to him sacrilege and blasphemy.

But God was the greatest enchanter of all, because of His unlimited powers. Oberon and Merlin could only aid when near at hand, but God was omnipresent, and ever ready to assist the valorous and the unfortunate, to free them from prison, to kill warders and pursuers, and even to knock down city walls which defied all man's assaults. He sent portents to express His approval or disapproval, changing a council chamber from white to black when treachery had been planned[1] and afflicting France with earthquakes and storms because Roland had been killed through a Frenchman's treachery.[2] Nothing was too great or too trivial to receive His aid, for when a woman masquerading in man's clothing was married to an Emperor's daughter, He changed her sex so that she should be saved from death and the Emperor's daughter from disgrace.[3]

Romancers did not, however, rely entirely on magical and far-fetched episodes to hold their patron's attention, but introduced also devices common in real life. One of the most essential elements in stories of adventure is

[1] "The Four Sons of Aymon."   [2] "Chanson de Roland."
[3] "Huon of Bordeaux."

suspense, and one of the easiest ways of introducing it is by disguising the identity of the characters, since the performance of stirring exploits by apparently mysterious strangers has always exercised a powerful fascination. The use of boys to take the female parts allowed Elizabethan dramatists to disguise their heroines as men, and so add a fresh interest to the plot; Scott's "Ivanhoe," Stevenson's "Treasure Island," and many a modern detective story depend largely for their interest upon similar concealments of identity, and the wearing of visors by knights allowed medieval romancers to introduce the same element in a perfectly natural way. Both in real life and in romance knights fought in tournaments disguised in suits of armour which bore either no heraldic device or an assumed one; the closing of the visor would then prevent all possibility of identification. The Earl of Warwick, when Captain of Calais, appeared at a tournament on three successive days disguised in three different suits of armour, revealing himself only on the third day. In romance knights usually fought on three occasions in suits of white, red, and black armour respectively.[1] Since the wearing of a visor and the omission of family or personal crest from the shield and surcoat effectively prevented recognition even where no deliberate disguise was intended, romancers were also able to make use of a legend common to the traditions of many nations—combat between brothers or between father and son, neither opponent recognising the other. The former is exemplified in "Ywain and Gawain," where the two brothers whose names form the title of the poem fight as champions of two ladies who have rival claims to an estate, and do not recognise each other until exhaustion compels them to rest and to raise their visors. The latter, now most familiar through Matthew Arnold's "Sohrab and Rustum," is exemplified in the prose Merlin, where Gawain fights and unhorses his father, not knowing who he is,

[1] As in "Lancelot of the Lake," "The Life of Ipomydon," "Sir Gowghter," and "Richard Cœur de Lion."

and in "Sir Degore," where a father, fighting against his son, recognises him at length only by his sword, which was a family heirloom.

Other types of disguise were also commonly presented, usually to conceal both the rank and identity of knights, not for the sake of suspense, but as a source of security in their passage through hostile territory. Legend relates that King Alfred spied out the strength and resources of a Danish host and that Blondel searched for his master, King Richard I, both disguised as minstrels. Knights who journeyed to Palestine to expiate their sins usually dressed as palmers, because in those days of constant pilgrimages unknown palmers swarmed all over Europe and Palestine; a palmer, therefore, would arouse no suspicion, where a strange knight would have been closely watched and perhaps taken prisoner by some baron seeking to increase his revenue by the easy method of extorting ransoms. This was therefore the customary disguise of romance when both rank and identity had to be concealed. Under this disguise Richard Cœur de Lion spies out Palestine before his crusade, Huon of Bordeaux regains his captive wife, King Horn visits his betrothed to assure her that rescue is at hand, Bevis of Hamtoun seeks for his beloved in a Saracen city, and Guy of Warwick is sought for by the faithful Heraud. In "The Earl of Toulouse" the hero disguises as a hermit and mingles with the alms-beggars before the German Emperor's palace in order to see the Empress, whose beauty was renowned throughout Europe; he dared not visit her openly because of the Emperor's hostility. When she is later charged with adultery by two knights he becomes her champion, but only after receiving her confession of innocence under the disguise of a monk. If we are to believe the "Arabian Nights Entertainments" and other Eastern stories, the favourite disguise of Eastern princes when wishing to travel incognito was that of a merchant, and so in "Floris and Blauncheflour" which relates an Eastern tale, the hero voyages to Babylon under this disguise.

Q

Another common feature of romance reflecting the custom of the times as well as enhancing the interest of the stories was the use of stock descriptive epithets for knights. In life the epithets usually referred to prominent features of appearance, dress, or character—Harold Long-tooth, William Long-sword, Richard Lion-heart, Louis the Pious, Charles the Bold. In romance the epithets were usually either of a romantic nature or else merely designed for alliterative effect—Morgan la fée, Iseult of the White Hands, Cador the Keen, Bedivere the Bold, Gawain the Good, Lancelot of the Lake.

It will be seen from the foregoing that medieval romance though presented and accepted as history, was designed simply to tell interesting stories. The tradition or legend which provided the base of each romance may have been accepted as literal history by the author and every element incorporated from outside credited as possible, but few if any romancers made any conscientious efforts to give historical instruction. They offered their public what the public wanted, and so present a picturesque and varied panorama of scenes and incidents—knights are loved by fairies and mysterious ladies, carried sleeping in strange barques to unknown lands, where they win the love of beautiful women, presented with magical jewels and girdles which will preserve them from each and every form of death, and with rings which will tarnish when loved ones are in danger; they fight dragons, giants and monstrous Saracens; they receive wounds which may be healed by only one particular lady, or only in a magic fountain; and they are assisted by wizards and enchanters, and above all by God. In this way the stirring narratives of great deeds performed by real men, as portrayed in heroic literature, were replaced by fantastic tales of impossible heroes who move in a shadow-land of unreal adventures and of superhuman love. Intensity can be attained and interest permanently held only by realism, and although people were delighted for a time with the conjuring tricks of romancers, they became quickly tired

of repeated and ever-increasing exaggerations, until the
world of romance crumbled into dust. The worst type of
romance, reiterating the same adventure under different
names and in different localities, was deservedly parodied
by Chaucer in his "Sir Thopas," and may almost be
described in one sentence, "And he went a little further
and came to another place." The most fantastic elements
of romance were also satirised by Cervantes in "Don
Quixote" and by Beaumont and Fletcher in "The Knight
of the Burning Pestle."

But not all romance was worthy of satire, nor despised by
these four authors; not all the sensationalism and the magic
could prevent the most famous heroes and heroines becoming such vivid personalities as to fire the imagination
of Malory and Spenser and many nineteenth-century
poets. Milton, the greatest scholar and supreme classicist
of all our poets, expressed his love of old romance in one
of the most magnificent passages of "Paradise Lost." The
love of romance, of mysterious and strange events, of hairbreadth escapes and daring deeds, remains as strong to-
day as ever it has been, in the most learned as well as in
the simplest minds. Milton and Dr. Johnson loved it as
well as did Tennyson and Morris, as well as does any
school-child of to-day. Nor must we be too scornful of
giants or of dragons. As Mr. Chesterton has pointed out,
the detective story which makes the meek-eyed curate
murderer of the vicar is more thrilling than that which
gives the credit to a band of international anarchists, yet
the former is less probable and almost as remote from real
life as the giant of Mount St. Michael. In good romance
dragons and giants and magic talismans were symbolical,
as the distorted figures of heraldry were symbolical. In
Spenser's "Faerie Queene" the symbolism is obvious and
vivid, but though more obscure in medieval romance,
it was none the less present. Dragons and giants may
symbolise evil as readily as the clergyman's white surplice
symbolises the essence of Christianity, or the Union Jack
British national sentiment. And the dragons and giants

were physical symbols, because the perils of the time were regarded as physical; they embodied the evil powers of nature, and to the medieval mind Satan was far more real than sin.

It matters little, also, that medieval romance abounded in anachronisms. In "Huon of Bordeaux," dealing with the time of Charlemagne, the crusaders' siege of Acre is referred to, in "Roland and Vernagu" Charlemagne is described as ruler of France and Denmark 103 years after Christ's death; Achilles' son is knighted, Alexander summons his barons to pay feudal homage, Athens is ruled by an Emperor, and Demosthenes is a "rich admiral";[1] Alexander, Charlemagne, Arthur and Julius Cæsar are presented as belonging to the same generation. But these crudities detract from the interest and value of romance no more than the introduction of clocks into Shakespeare's "Julius Cæsar." Accurate reflection of past times is rare in fiction of any period, and it is far better to portray the past openly like the present than to cast a false glamour over the past and call it historical truth. Both medieval and modern writers of fiction have pretended to give an accurate picture of the past, but where the average historical romancer of to-day, by trying to make his claim convincing, makes his scenes and characters vague and shadowy, medieval romance, like Elizabethan drama, made its scenes and characters more real by modernising, not more absurd. To the people of the Middle Ages there were two periods of history—the present and the past. The medieval romancer called all periods of the past simply the past, and made them look like the present. The modern romancer recognises that the past includes widely differing periods, but usually amalgamates characteristics from several in a weird and wonderful way, while inducing his audience to regard his sketch as an accurate reflection of one period. Both methods, no doubt, have their advantages, but though both are useless as an aid to history, anachronism does, as Mr. Chesterton has said, represent eternity.

[1] =Emir, Eastern term for ruler.

The essence of old romance, in spite of its medley and incongruity of elements, was simplicity, although a bizarre simplicity; arising from child-like minds, not from deep study, conscious art and severe restraint, as in a Milton or a Wordsworth. It presents the direct and straight-forward simplicity of the child who becomes an Indian Chief without a costume and visualises the paved back-yard of his home as the limitless prairies of the West. His imagination supplies him with all the trappings of romance, which are only incidental to his constant goal— to kill other alien redskins. The gorgeous pageantry of romance, the magic, the supernatural, the varied foes to be encountered, and the kaleidoscopic scenes to be traversed are similarly but trappings, which do not detract from its simplicity; the heroes pursue their quests un-swervingly, never vexed with psychological complexes or insoluble problems, but seeing a definite goal ahead which they aim at steadfastly and achieve.

CHAPTER XIII

THE LOVE ELEMENT

THE DISTINGUISHING FEATURE OF RO-
mance in every period of history has been love.
Love is not essential—though just what is essential to bring any work into the category of romance it would be difficult to define—but the average
reader and the average audience would consider any
romance that lacked it sadly imperfect. The love of
romance is a literary love, the result of long-continued
tradition and convention, that idealised love which we
all, unless devoid of imagination, have conjured up in
our day-dreams as a result of reading love romances.
It is not mere sexuality, nor is it mere devoted service;
it is rather a complex web of strands containing the
essence of both inextricably combined. It must be clearly
recognised that the love of literature is an artificial convention, and that this long-continued *literary* tradition
has permeated us all through and through, so that it is
not easy to discover just where the love element of any
story departs from what is natural in human life. The love
element in medieval romance varied in kind at different
periods, in different countries, and under the hands of
different authors, but it is an artificial literary love, and
as such will be discussed and analysed.

Love between the sexes arose, of course, from mere
sexuality, the instinct to satisfy sexual desires, but this is
neither the whole of love between man and woman in
civilised races nor is it a fitting subject for romance. To it
must be added the element of esteem and respect roused
by the personal characteristics of the loved one and the
desire to serve. This—which may be called spiritual love
—can fully develop only when strong individuality has
developed. As long as men and women are mere pawns
in a tribal group the highest conception of love is impossible, and it will play little or no part in literature.

Furthermore, when warfare and national or feudal duties are the supreme interest, it will play little part in literature even if it has become an accepted feature of life. For these two reasons love plays little part in heroic literature, whether in ancient epic or more modern chansons de gestes, because it can have little or no place in the lives of men who have consecrated themselves to national or religious service.

Of the works which come within the scope of this book "La Chanson de Roland" alone is of the heroic type, and has but one brief episode of love—on Charlemagne's return from Spain Oliver's sister, Aude, asks news of Roland, her betrothed, and hearing of his death dies of a broken heart. That one short passage intensifies the tragedy of Roland's death and stamps vividly upon our minds the domestic misery which arose from continual fighting, but Roland and Aude are nowhere brought face to face; no passages of tender emotion deflect the attention from the one essential theme—warfare against the infidel and a hero's death through treason. The later Charlemagne romances, lacking the stimulus which inspired this poem, present only fantastic adventures devoid of any dominating objective; they therefore drew inspiration from various sources, including the Arthurian romances, and contain attempts at love stories which are little better than sexual adventures rendered decorous on most occasions by a marriage contract and by a wholesome absence of any attempt to pander to the salacious tastes of readers.

The usual love-theme of these romances was the infatuation of a Saracen maid for a Christian knight, presented as it would be in life, a vigorous and lusty passion inspired by physical desire. The Saracen maid, like Floripas in "The Sowdone of Babylon" and "Sir Ferumbras," is a strong-minded, stubborn damsel resolved to gratify her desires no matter what the cost. Floripas, having fallen in love with one of Charlemagne's peers, rescues two others, Roland and Oliver, from prison, killing both her governess and the jailer without scruple or hesitation. She sides with them against her father, is frankly pleased at her father's death, regards the burning alive of another Saracen prince as a mere jest, offers her maidens to the peers as concubines and strips herself before the whole French host to be baptised, completely unashamed. She is not evil or immoral, but merely primitive woman, governed solely by desire and animal passions. Beves of Hamtoun loves a Saracen maid called Josian, who, in his absence, is forcibly married to a villainous knight called Miles. The wedding guests of Miles attempt to make her drunk in order to provide some exciting sport, and Josian is left devoid of friends and linked to a husband she detests. But she too is the primitive woman, capable of deserting family and faith to follow Beves, but also too strong-minded to subjugate herself to a detestable mate; instead of bewailing her misfortunes, she strangles her husband in the bedchamber before the marriage is consummated. In "King Horn," the heroine, Rimenhild, falls in love with Horn at first sight, sends a messenger to bring him to her room, and frankly declares her love. This type of theme represents normal life purged of the veneer of social etiquette—sexual desire, quickly roused and frankly shown, but not immoral or obscene. It is not libertinism, but downright primitive love, the woman choosing her mate and quite prepared to be faithful once his love is won. Where marriage was possible they married, and this was the usual culmination in romance; where it was forbidden they indulged in illicit love, presented not as noble, but simply as natural, and often even as unfortunate.

Similar to this type of love is that, particularly common in English romance, of a woman's love aroused by admiration for a man's strength and courage. The urging force is largely sexual impulse, but imbued with a little more idealism and reasonably under restraint. "Beves of Hamtoun" and "Guy of Warwick" offer good examples. Josian, in the first, is a strong and vigorous maid, willing to make any sacrifice for love, but setting great value on her chastity; she loves Beves, as thousands of women have loved men, for his strength and valour. The courage with which Guy of Warwick meets all opponents and his continual victories bring him offers of love from so many ladies that the author of the romance confuses their names in his narrative.

These types of love, arising from instincts in human nature and devoid of those idealistic features which are the chief cause of the universal interest of love stories, require no lengthy treatment. The love of romance, as the modern reader understands the term, first appears in the middle of the twelfth century, incorporated by poets into classical stories and Arthurian legends. This type of love—whether the formal conventional love of Lancelot for Guenivere, the passionate love of Marie de France's heroines, or the idealised childlike love of Floris and Blauncheflour—is the fountain head of modern literary love, and has its own sources in literature. These sources are many and varied—Biblical stories, late Greek romances, the poems of Ovid, and the songs of the Troubadours. To the Biblical influence—particularly of the "Song of Songs," the greatest example in all literature of beautiful, sensuous, and unchecked passion—was later added that of the emotional elements in Church teaching.

It may sound paradoxical to say that a Church, which regarded celibacy and asceticism as the greatest of all virtues, was also a primary source of influence in the love themes of romance. But the ideals of the Church were perfectly consistent, even though they clashed so frequently in life. From Christ's statement, "My Kingdom is not of this world," was built up a theory of life based on absolute unworldliness, in which all pleasure, natural or unnatural, was to be regarded as a blemish on man's purity. Sexual impulse in itself is a pure and natural instinct, but indulgence of this instinct is in so many and such varied circumstances base and unmanly, that in all periods many people have come to regard the mere possession of that instinct as unnatural or wrong. No legal ceremony can make any instinct pure, nor the absence of such ceremony render it impure; marriage can only serve to regulate sexual intercourse so that disruptive consequences will not ensue. Women had been regarded by men as a means of gratifying their desires, and so came to be regarded by the Church as a snare and a pitfall to men; even marriage was considered a blemish, though less sinful than unlegalised intercourse. Side by side with this doctrine of asceticism the Church fostered intense emotionalism, which had its origin in the new teaching of Christ and the later adoration of the Virgin Mary, who became in men's eyes a sort of goddess of beauty and of love. The good Christian was expected to imbue his worship with fervent enthusiasm, and regard the love of Christ and of Mary His mother as something real and vivid. The Church, however, failed to realise that emotionalism cannot be turned on or off at will, and that man will more naturally invest his human relationships with this enthusiasm than relationships with powers unseen and but dimly understood. In modern times men are confronted with a similar problem. The youth of both sexes live continually in an emotional atmosphere by reading love-stories and seeing unchecked passion presented as an ideal in drama and on the film, and must be strongly influenced thereby. But many men, short-sighted even as was the medieval Church, still argue as though emotionalism can be kept in water-tight compartments and the atmosphere fostered by fiction be rigidly excluded from life. The result has been, both in medieval and modern times, the investment of sex relationships in life with an emotionalism designed for an ulterior purpose.

The medieval intensity of emotionalism was reflected in many types of work—in the Latin hymns used in Church services, in the religious lyrics which employed the terms coined for secular love to describe the relationships of men with Christ and the Virgin Mary, in sculpture, painting, mosaic work, and Gothic architecture. It must have served to foster the gentler emotions which were in danger of

becoming stultified by the sterile dogmas of the Church;
it also must have fostered sentimentalism and over-pitched
passion in sexual love and encouraged writers to incorporate into romance the love-themes which were to be
found in earlier alien literatures.

The introduction of love as a theme into romance seems
to have begun no earlier than the middle of the twelfth
century,[1] but long before this time the troubadours of
Provence had been composing love-songs and had built
up a convention that every knight must have a mistress
and every married woman a cavalier, the relationship
being similar to that between a vassal and his feudal overlord. Thus during the twelfth century arose a woman
worship as exaggerated as, but more artificial and fantastic than the prevalent adoration of the Virgin Mary;
from Provence it passed into Northern and Central French
romance, became even more exaggerated in French
romance of the seventeenth century, and has influenced
to some extent even modern French fiction. The love
poetry of the troubadours was killed by the Albigensian
Crusade of 1208, in which so many of the leading families
of Provence were massacred because of heresy that their
literature never revived. But the essence of their work—
the courtly devotion paid by men to women—had already
permeated Northern French romance, and remained an
irresistible and lasting source of fascination to the French,
though only rarely to the English race.

The introduction of this courtly love from the Southern
love-songs into Northern romance was due to the influence of a group of noble ladies who, during the twelfth
century, became the chief patrons of literature—Aliénor
of Guyenne,[2] Marie of Champagne, Marguérite of Flan-
ders, Ermenjart of Narbonne, and Yolande, daughter of
Count Baldwin of Hainault. Aliénor had large domains

---

[1] The earliest *written* romances, apart from "La Chanson de Roland"
and perhaps the romances of the First Crusade, are of this time, but
it is impossible to say how much earlier *oral* romance had flourished.
[2] Or Aquitaine. Both titles are commonly used.

in the South of France and there became interested in the poetry of the troubadours. After her marriage to Henry of Anjou she influenced ladies in Northern France to take an interest in courtly love, and her own daughter, Marie of Champagne, became the most famous of all these patronesses, because she not only had been inspired by her mother, but had under her patronage the most famous of all French romancers—Chrétien de Troyes. He it was who made Arthurian stories popular, and under Marie's influence transformed them into tales of courtly love, thus starting a vogue which for long remained supreme. It would be rash to attribute to either Marie or Chrétien the general form of all Arthurian romance and untrue to state that Chrétien was the first to write a love-story—earlier romances had contained love episodes—but it seems certain that Marie, using Chrétien as her agent, caused Lancelot to become the most famous knight and his love for Guenivere the most popular theme in all romance. At intermittent intervals love has been the supreme element of many literatures,[1] but these patronesses, and chiefly Marie of Champagne, caused love to become the supreme topic of French romance and courtly conventional love the chief type. French romance is saturated with this element, but a passage in the English "Sir Gawain and the Green Knight" will serve sufficiently to illustrate the supremacy of courtly love; the lady of the castle who offers her love to Gawain reproves him because he has no mistress, and says to him, "Of all chivalry the chief part is love, the literature of arms; it is the title and text of their works, how men for their loved ones have endangered their lives, endured great hardships, avenged them with valour, removed their sorrow, and brought bliss into the bower."

The absolute domination wielded by this new element in romance is exemplified by its incorporation into classical themes, in which love had originally played no part. Æneas is prostrated with illness because of his love for Lavinia, and in "The Destruction of Troy" Achilles not

[1] Cf. Biblical—Song of Songs; and late Greek romance.

only falls in love with Priam's daughter, Polyxena, but promises to raise the siege if she will marry him. A female craze for tales of love thus became responsible for a complete distortion of Homer's "Iliad." The keynote of Homer's story is the "Wrath of Achilles," his refusal to fight because he has been deprived of a captive maid to please Agamemnon. The disruption of an army because of dissension between leaders is a tragic theme, but all tragic, all heroic spirit is destroyed when one great leader is portrayed as willing to desert and deceive his allies in order to win a woman's love. But this distortion reflects the essence of courtly love; it was an art rather than an emotion, a philosophy of love designed to make woman supreme; its essence was neither passion nor even esteem arising from character, but simply service, the devotion of a man to a woman as his mistress.[1] The lover must devote himself to the service of his lady, willing to suffer any hardships to satisfy her most trivial desires. Therefore in theory love could never be too exaggerated. Hence, though Achilles would be a traitor if he deserted his allies for any other reason than love, he would be still more a traitor if he allowed his mere duty as a soldier and a Greek to interfere with the greatest of all duties—fidelity in love.

Courtly love had as its chief basis the love poetry of Ovid, and particularly his "Ars Amatoria," in which the whole art of love was classified in a simple, logical, and systematic style, eminently suited to French tastes. The analytical mind of the French race was strongly attracted by a book which, in place of the romantic ecstasies and sweet nothings so common in love poetry, formulated definites rules for the guidance of lovers and analysed the sentiments of sexual love. A common type of modern love-story—especially in English—presents the tragedy or pathos which arises from the concealment of love, both

[1] The same term is still used for the woman in an illicit love relationship, and therefore liable to be misunderstood. It first arose because the lover—in this theory of courtly love—regarded his lady as a superior to be implicitly obeyed.

youth and maiden pining away, like Shakespeare's Viola, because too shy and too modest to reveal their affection. Ovid's precept was that love should never be concealed— that neither sex should risk unhappiness by concealing affection, whether from real or false modesty; and this precept became the gospel of French romance. Marie de France in her lay of "Guigemar" refers to Ovid's statement that if a man represses his love, his fever will only be increased, and adds on her own behalf, "Love is a wound in the body; he who does not show his hurt cannot hope for any cure."

Although most of the troubadours and romancers would be quite capable of reading Ovid for themselves, translations and adaptations of his "Ars Amatoria" were made from an early date. A translation was made by Chrétien de Troyes, and the most famous treatise based upon Ovid's poem was a Latin work of André le Chapelain—"The Three Books of Love"—written about the year 1200. This is a kind of scientific or philosophical treatise on the whole subject of love—its origin and nature, the duties and obligations of lovers, and the rules which must guide their conduct. The subject is classified in five categories: (1) what love is; (2) what is the effect of love; (3) between whom love may be; (4) how love is acquired; (5) how the one lover must act if the other fails in his or her duty The most significant of his many regulations are: (1) marriage is not a legitimate excuse for refusing love to another; (2) love must never be divulged to others; (3) no one may have two lovers; (4) it is unfitting to love any lady whom one would be ashamed to marry; (5) merit alone renders man worthy of love; (6) love may refuse nothing. These rules are sufficient to show the essence of courtly love, and to show that love was to be a law unto itself, respecting no social conventions, but based on honour; that honour might clash with duty, the duty of wife to husband, but was equally opposed to libertinism. As long as it was rigidly maintained that no man should accept the love of any lady whom he would not willingly marry if he could, any real moral perversion was impossible.

André states that the Countess of Champagne had declared that true love was possible only between un-married couples, because husband and wife are legally bound to loyalty, and real love can only arise from per-sonal faith subject to no legal compulsion. He also states that this judgment was given in a "Court of Love," and both he and other writers give examples of such courts presided over by influential ladies who passed judgment on codes of love and infringements of them by lovers. It is now strongly doubted whether such courts ever existed, but there is no reason against believing that ladies of rank met from time to time and discussed problems put before them by people of lesser rank. In any period when etiquette reigns supreme, conduct is regarded very seri-ously, and severely judged by all members of society. Furthermore, the opinions expressed on matters of conduct by influential ladies are highly reverenced, because their patronage is the only passport to society. It is therefore probable that ladies like the Countess of Champagne did hold and express rigid opinions on the proper conduct of lovers and had their opinions accepted as seriously as legal judgments. During the thirteenth and fourteenth cen-turies a poem called "La Roman de la Rose" was written, the first part by Guillaume de Lorris, and completed by Jean de Meun, which fashioned this medieval "art of love" into a story; the lover has to obey all the conventional codes before he may pluck the Rose which symbolises the fruition of his desire. An English translation of part of the poem still exists and has been ascribed to Chaucer.

Chrétien de Troyes, though not the first, was certainly the most influential poet who made this courtly love the basis of his work, and even he made only one attempt to follow the spirit of the troubadours exactly. "Lancelot" alone, the worst constructed and least interesting of all his poems, presents love between a bachelor and a married woman, but the influence of female patrons caused this and the similar story of Tristram and Iseult to become the most enduring and most popular of all love themes. His other poems deal with married love, but love imbued with the essence of troubadour love poetry, its courtliness and sentimentalism, which he so clearly crystallised that other poets took him as their model. The chief feature is "sensibility," the analysis of love's emotions, which reached its most fantastic heights in seventeenth-century romance —as in the works of Mde. de la Scudéry and Mme. de la Fayette. Logical analysis of sentiment is suited to French racial character, and Chrétien was a master of this art. He portrays not deep nor passionate love, but a superficial love of the senses, voluptuous, delicious, and exhaling the atmosphere of the hot-house. It is the natural product of a refined and courtly atmosphere where courtesy and gallantry reign supreme, and where the chief recreation is hearing tales of love. This type of love cannot be deep or lasting, because arising not from the lover's character, but from a confined and sheltered life of leisure. The heroine falls in love rather with the idea of love than with a man whose merit would be likely to attract enduring esteem. And the interest of such stories lies not in the depth or strength of the emotions portrayed, but in the accurate reflection of life and the minute analysis of the lovers' sentiments. Love between a knight and a married woman would be too artificial to remain long in vogue, and love which eventually resulted in marriage would not only have the advantage of preserving decorum, but would also be thoroughly romantic, because so divorced from reality in an age when marriage was purely a business contract. Except for this difference the spirit of Chrétien's work is that of the earlier troubadours, all of the above-mentioned rules being faithfully observed.

To the courtly essence of troubadour love-poetry Chrétien and French romancers in general added elements from Greek romance of the early Christian era. This was thoroughly imbued with a pathetic and emotional spirit and, although representative only of Greek decadence, was more appreciated, and therefore more widely known, in the later Middle Ages than earlier classical literature. The most charming feature of Chrétien's work—the presentation of ideal pairs of lovers such as Eric and Enid, Cliges and Fenice—constituted the essence of Greek love romance.[1] Some of his most romantic episodes were also borrowed from Greek romance, as in "Cliges," where the heroine, Fenice, saves herself from an undesirable marriage and so preserves her troth-plight to the hero by drinking a potion which makes her appear as dead.[2] But, even though the lovers in Chrétien's, and most romances, marry, the emphasis is not upon sexual passion, but upon service, devotion, loyalty; and that is the essence of courtly love.

A transplanted theme never exercises as powerful an influence as an indigenous one. Therefore courtly love never gripped Northern French writers so strongly as it did the troubadours. The general spirit remained because writers were accustomed to borrow from others rather than to seek originality; but there was a continual tendency to stress the emotional aspect of love, to regard it as more than a service; and this is seen most clearly in the lays of Marie de France and in romances independent of the Arthurian legend such as "Fleure et Blanche-fleure" and "Aucassin et Nicolette." Although most of Marie's lays present love between a bachelor and a married woman, there is less artificiality and conventionality than *e.g.* in Chrétien's "Lancelot"—more stress is laid upon passion, and the love is therefore more idealised. In the two other romances named the love agrees closely with that of modern love romances, both in essence and in the inevitable conclusion—marriage.

The love element in medieval romance is seen, therefore, to have passed through three general stages—the frankly

---

[1] Cf. "Theagines and Chariclea" of Heliodorus, "Cleitophon and Leucippe" of Achilles Tatius, and "Daphnis and Chloe," usually ascribed to Longus.
[2] From the "Habrocomas and Anthia" of Xenophon. Cf. the similar episode in "Romeo and Juliet."

R

sensual love of the chansons de gestes, the artificial courtly
love of the troubadours, and the idealised and more
passionate love of Marie de France and other writers.
This last stage has close affinities with the love element of
modern fiction, and the predominance of the love interest
in romance of chivalry has made it the direct ancestor of
the modern romantic novel.

The love element of medieval romance is, broadly speaking, anti-social. It is usually either adulterous love between a bachelor and a married woman or love between a
knight and maiden in defiance of parental wishes—sometimes secret, sometimes open defiance, and whether con-
cluding in marriage or not, absolutely opposed to law or
custom. To understand the reason for both the pre-
eminence of love in romance and the frequency of these
illicit types it is necessary to understand the social conditions of the Middle Ages. In the first place, love will
naturally be the dominant theme of literature designed for
women in almost any age and any country; as long as
women remain in any way dependent upon men they will
remain more interested in men than in their own sex, and
this interest naturally finds expression in tales of love; if
women ever attain the independence of men they may
come to be as little interested in love-stories as men. In
the Middle Ages women were more dependent and also
less free to satisfy their love. Throughout the knightly
class marriage was purely a business contract; the sexual
aspect rarely entered, for women were married to men
either to link estates together or to provide them with
the protection that only a husband could afford. Love
matches may occasionally have occurred, but in the
overwhelming majority of marriages love existed on neither
side. A loveless marriage, especially when ordained by
external authority, usually thwarts those natural instincts
which cannot with safety be repressed, and a marriage
which is merely a business partnership is liable to become
galling because dissolution is impossible without disgrace
to one or both parties. The restrictions upon personal

freedom which marriage always entails may be more than counteracted by advantages when love or esteem exists upon both sides, but under medieval conditions became extremely irksome to both husband and wife. Chrétien's "Erec" was largely designed to illustrate how marriage hindered a knight from following the only profession which could bring him fame and respect,[1] and Malory makes Lancelot say, " But to be a wedded man I think never to be, for if I were, then I should be bound to tarry with my wife and leave arms and tournaments, battles and adventures."

But the restrictions on man's freedom were nothing as compared with those on the woman's. By marrying she simply exchanged the jurisdiction of a father for that of a husband, her freedom being still more restricted by the confined castle life of the period. The woman, therefore, from an early age was doomed to a life in close confinement with a husband who had never been attractive and who must have often become actually distasteful, because there was no hope of eventual freedom. The romances, though entirely without set purpose, clearly illustrate the confined life which women were compelled to live. Huon of Bordeaux on one occasion leaves his daughter in the care of an abbot when he has to leave home on business. On his return the abbot gives an account of his stewardship, proudly relating that the girl has been kept out of the sun and is therefore as beautiful as before. To be tanned by the sun was considered a disfigurement, and "white as whale's bone" or "white as foam" was a stock description of romance heroines. Each isolated castle formed a separate community, so that the diversions of modern city life were impossible and visits from other families would be infrequent. An inactive life of dull routine will always make both men and women long for excitement, even if attended by grave perils. The women had no wholesome occupation beyond a few household duties, and even tournaments, hunting, and hawking were not sufficient to occupy

[1] The story is told in Tennyson's "Eric and Enid."

men fully in times of peace. The knights and ladies were therefore thrown together in a confined and inactive life, and naturally sought diversion in love-making. Flaubert's "Madame Bovary" vividly portrays how the dullness of country life may drive a woman to seek for novelty and excitement in illicit love; Madame Bovary was not vicious nor even passionate, she simply was unoccupied and bored. Medieval castle life was similarly dull, but much more so. than country life of a century ago. The bachelor knight had no prospect of married love, and therefore sought temporary solace in flirtation. Unmarried girls were more closely watched and more fearful of unfortunate consequences than married women, who, in addition, had more reason to dread the prospect of a loveless life. Illicit love was therefore usually with a married woman. But in either case love to both sexes was impossible unless illicit, and romance in presenting illicit love merely reflects life as it was, while in presenting lovers who may and do marry it presents a story equally romantic, but far more remote from life.

The courtly love of the troubadours, which implied a married woman, was therefore a reflection of actual life, and was naturally incorporated into romance, the chief examples being the stories of Lancelot and Tristram. Many romancers wished to preserve decorum by presenting lovers who could and did marry, but, in accordance with contemporary conditions, had to portray their love as illicit, culminating in marriage only as a result of unusual and fortuitous circumstances. King Horn cannot at first marry Rimenhild because he is her father's vassal and also destitute of wealth; he is therefore her illicit lover, but eventually becomes powerful enough to compel her father to consent to their marriage. "Aucassin et Nicolette" excellently illustrates both medieval conditions and romantic love. Aucassin wishes to marry a captive maiden, Nicolette. His father insists that he marry a lady of his own rank, and imprisons the lovers to bring them to reason. They eventually escape and, after many vicissitudes, marry and return home. In the similar story of "Floris and Blauncheflour" the father sells the captive maid to foreign merchants, but has to yield to his son because he attempts to commit suicide. In real life elopement with the daughter of a powerful baron was impossible, since none would dare to give them shelter and few sons would dare to marry a girl of inferior rank in defiance of their father's will. Only the romancer's magic wand could make either possible, and so it is not surprising that illicit love, whether resulting in marriage or not, was the usual theme of romance.

Since women had less freedom and more leisure than men, the romances which present women as the most active agents in love will undoubtedly reflect contemporary conditions. It must also be remembered that superficial emotionalism was fostered by the continual reading of romances which filled girls' heads with visions of ideal lovers. This last affliction has continued down to modern times, and will probably remain for ever. In many romances women make the first advances—as in "King Horn" and some of Marie's lays—and sometimes become so infuriated when their love is refused as to seek a terrible revenge. A knight who refused the love of a lady in a higher station than his own ran even greater risks than by refusing to accept in marriage the daughter of his superior, because, although in both cases pride is offended, in the first is added unchecked passion, which blinds the woman to all justice and reason. "La Châtelaine de Vergi" and Marie's lay of "Lanval" both present married ladies whose love is refused by knights of lesser rank and who seek vengeance as did the wife of Potiphar by openly accusing them of attempted insult.[1] The readiness with which ladies burdened with dull or distasteful husbands offered their love to handsome or famous strangers is reflected in many romances, and especially in Marie's lays. In the lay of "Guigemar" the hero throughout his travels is overwhelmed with offers of love from both maidens and

[1] In "Lanval" it is Queen Guenivere.

married women, and when eventually he has been carried sleeping to a strange land he falls in love with the ruler's wife, who yields herself immediately. In "Eliduc" a young girl becomes infatuated with a strange knight on first beholding him, and in "Milon" another maid falls in love with a stranger only on hearing of his reputation. These three lays of Marie illustrate the fundamental basis of the theme. Marie de France and other poets framed their stories so as to symbolise true love, yet in reality it is not love at all, but mere infatuation. The love arises only from novelty; a woman, doomed to live a narrow and confined life, hears of a handsome or illustrious knight, gives full play to her imagination, forms romantic visions of him, and so falls headlong into love at their first meeting. Stendhal, in his treatise on love called "De L'Amour," illustrates this infatuation roused by novelty by means of a very significant anecdote. A young girl, living the confined life customary in his time, and longing for freedom, stands frequently at her window looking at the passers-by; daily she sees the same young man pass her window, and, weaving romantic visions round him, becomes thoroughly infatuated. The parents, wishing to cure her of this infatuation, invite the young man to their home and arrange that the young couple shall be constantly together, with the result that the girl's infatuation is quickly cured; she comes to realise that he is but an ordinary unromantic mortal, not a fairy prince. That of course is *life;* the romancer must portray such infatuation as *love*, and will necessarily influence his female readers to regard it as true love and possible in everyday life. But apart from sheer novelty, the bachelor knight would be more attractive to a married woman because more attentive, more willing to offer those little courtesies which a woman dearly loves. He could afford to, because not doomed to spend his whole life with her. Frequently also the husband would be considerably older than the wife, and for that reason alone less attractive. In most stories of triangular love—husband, wife, and lover—the husband is portrayed as old and jealous. Marie de France invariably makes the husband older, and offers as a general excuse for all such stories the axiom "that all old men are jealous." By emphasising the jealousy and harshness of the husband, in the case of married women, or the tyranny of parents, in the case of unmarried girls, the romancer could present illicit love in an idealised instead of in an obscene light.

The love themes of romance, whatever their type may be, have all the same design—to show love triumphing over all barriers, whether of national or conjugal duty, filial affection, or caste distinction. Feudal custom made duty to an overlord paramount, but the theory of courtly love, under woman's influence, insisted that the lover's duty to his mistress was superior even to that. In "Ywain and Gawain,"[1] Ywain, though a Knight of the Round Table, expresses his willingness to fight against King Arthur to win the love of a lady whom he has seen but once. Not even his feudal oath was regarded as more sacred than devotion to his beloved. The poet was not, however, illustrating a theory, so conflict with Arthur never comes to pass; he was merely accepting a tradition —the tradition that love was supreme. The same romance also illustrates another rigid principle of love—the necessity of maintaining absolute and perfect faith; Ywain suffers misery upon misery because he forgets to return from Arthur's Court to his wife on the exact day promised. The Crusader's Song of Conon de Bethune expresses a Crusader's grief because his duty to God conflicts with his love. Marie's lay of "Eliduc" offers the greatest illustration in all romance of the supremacy of love in presenting a wife who is willing to forfeit all her rights in obedience to the law of love. Eliduc, during an absence from his wife, comes to be loved by a maiden who insists upon accompanying him home, and when his wife learns of their love she enters a convent in order to leave her husband free to accept it. She does not leave him in dis-

[1] Adapted from Chrétien's "Yvain."

gust or because she feels insulted; she merely refuses to
be a hindrance to their love, and so gives happiness to
two others at the expense of her own. And so with all the
love themes of romance; Achilles ready to deceive his
allies for Polyxena;[1] Lancelot willing to degrade his knighthood for Guenivere;[2] Fenice drugging her husband so that
he will not know she has surrendered her virginity to a
lover;[3] Iseult deceiving King Mark at every turn; Aucassin
deserting his father in order to marry an infidel slave[4]—
all have but one object, to show that love is above all law
and can never be impure so long as it is true to itself.

The actual practice in real life need not be considered
in this respect; the ideal stressed by romancers was service
and devotion not sexual desire. Many of the troubadours
wrote songs in praise of spiritual and chaste love, as *e.g.*
Bernard of Ventadour:

> "God keep my lady fair from grief and woe,
>   I'm close to her, however far I go;
> If God will be her shelter and her shield,
> Then all my heart's desire is fulfilled."[5]

Guirot Riquier:

> "For chaste and pure my love has always been,
> From my 'sweet bliss' I've never asked a boon;
> If I may humbly serve her night and noon,
> My life be her inalienable lien."[5]

Sordello:

> "Thus, lady, I commend to thee
> My fate and life, thy faithful squire;
> I'd rather die in misery
> Than have thee stoop to my desire." [5]

The love of chivalric romance, though rarely of this ideal
type, was no mere gratification of sexual impulse, but a
compound of emotion and desire to reward a lover for
his devotion. Illicit love is portrayed as noble and pure
not from any wish to make vice seem pleasant or to appeal

---

[1] "The Destruction of Troy."   [2] Chrétien's "Lancelot."
[3] Chrétien's "Cliges."   [4] "Aucassin et Nicolette."
[5] All three passages are taken from Emil Lucka's "Evolution of
Love."

to salacious tastes, but simply because in life true love could only be illicit. Rarely is life made pleasant for the lovers; their love implied self-sacrifice, particularly on the woman's part. Even though the pleasures of love are often alluringly portrayed, the hardships and misery which it usually entailed are fully emphasised. The love of neither Iseult nor of the heroines of Marie's lays was an incentive to women of weak character; their sufferings were too great and their humiliation was too profound to foster any eagerness for unlawful love in women who desired only excitement and were not prepared to accept the risks involved. In actual life the great exemplar was Heloise, who gave her love to Abelard, but refused to marry him because marriage would ruin his career. He could only marry by leaving the Church, thus abandoning his profession and all hopes of fame. His later reputation as a scholar and teacher shows how much France owed to her self-sacrifice.

Even if the most common result of love romances was to fill the heads of women with romantic ideas and to foster emotions better restrained, they must have exercised a beneficial influence upon many of the knights. Continual fighting tends to brutalise men, who at the best of times are in constant need of woman's refining influence. The soldier in all periods and countries has numberless opportunities to satisfy his sexual desires, and the readiness of women to accept his love usually breeds contempt for their sex in general. In life the knight would see little of the sacrifices made and the misery suffered by women whose admiration for courage made them surrender without reserve. But the romances constantly riveted his attention on this sacrifice and suffering, and must have increased his respect for and made him realise the inherent nobility of women who were willing to reward courage and devotion at any cost, however great. Walther von der Vogelweide, the greatest minnesinger[1] of Germany, said "he who carries hidden sorrow—let him think upon a

[1] Composer of love songs.

good woman—he is freed,"[1] and Guirot Riquier wrote
in one of his songs:

> "Thus love transfigures every deed we do,
> And love gives everything a deeper sense.
> Love is the teaching of all genuine worth.
> So base is no man's heart on this wide earth
> Love could not guide it to great excellence."[1]

And just as other elements in romance fostered in knights
a sense of duty, loyalty, and devotion to the service of God
and their overlord, so the love element must have given
great impetus to the spirit of chivalry, which made men
regard as the greatest of all services the protection of the
feeble and oppressed, above all, of women.

In medieval English romance—such as was adapted from
and not mere literal translation of French romance—love
plays a relatively small part. The lower classes who
formed the audience of English romance lived under
different conditions from the knightly classes who formed
the audience of French romance. Love and marriage were
quite compatible—indeed most marriages must have been
love matches; therefore illicit love would have little attraction and would appear actually immoral. Lancelot
and Tristram—symbolising adulterous love—apparently
aroused little enthusiasm, while Gawain—symbolising
abstinence from adultery and sometimes from all forms of
love—was apparently very popular. The ordinary type
of love-story—presenting secret illicit love rendered necessary by parental tyranny, but culminating in marriage—
would be free from all suspicion of immorality, and would
please by reason of its romantic nature. Furthermore,
the audience was not composed of highly cultured women
of leisure, but of working men and women who prized
strength and courage more than fine sentiments and
revelled more in sensational incident than in tender love
scenes. They liked to have a love theme running through
a romance, but not as the supreme topic, and the average
English romancer catered for their tastes. Even the higher

[1] Taken from Emil Lucka's "Evolution of Love."

classes in England had probably never been greatly attracted by the conventional courtly love fostered by the troubadours, and the lower classes would appreciate only a love which arose from physical prowess.

Modern English conditions render it so easy to prejudice the reader against the love themes of French romance and make him regard it as a deliberate pandering to vicious tastes that it is necessary to emphasise the conditions which gave it birth. Unmarried intercourse at any time may have disastrous consequences, and it is certainly anti-social, but not necessarily impure; marriage legalises sexual relations and so safeguards the women and children, but it cannot make those relations pure or noble. The preservation of society depends on the elimination of unmarried intercourse, but if social conditions make legalised love impossible, then unlawful love will flourish, because law, whether social or judicial, cannot with impunity ignore natural impulses and desires. In the Middle Ages feudal custom made it almost impossible for men and women to marry from love or esteem, just as Church Law forbade priests to marry. The result was that, in spite of Church teaching and Church edicts, men and women indulged in illicit love, just as priests kept illicit mistresses. In modern times love and marriage are compatible, although women still must suffer to some extent, as they have less choice than men—at least openly. In the Middle Ages love and marriage were incompatible, and so the urge to illicit love, which still remains so strong, was far stronger then than now.

Finally it must be borne in mind that there is a vast difference between unlawful love and free love, just as there is between a belief in Prohibition and a belief that to drink alcoholic liquor is wrong. Free love means philandering, the seduction of women under the pretence of love, or the indulgence by either sex in varied sexual intercourse solely as a means of pleasure; the immortal exemplar of this type is Don Juan. Unlawful love simply means cohabitation not legalised by Church or State authority. Marie de France, though portraying unlawful love in nearly all her lays, has nothing but the severest condemnation for free love. "The courtly villain who takes his pleasure everywhere and boasts of his success—that is not love, but folly, wickedness, and lechery." In "Lanval" she censures Guenivere for offering her love to Lanval not because immoral, but because she already had a lover—Lancelot. Chaucer's "Troilus and Criseyde," though celebrating unlegalised love, is nevertheless one of the world's greatest love-stories, because of the characters portrayed and because it emphasises the need for loyalty in love. The exponents of courtly love insisted that unlegalised love was more binding than married love, because in marriage man was compelled by law to support and remain loyal to his wife; in an unlawful relationship loyalty was commanded only by his sense of honour, and was therefore more sacred. Sordello, one of the greatest troubadours, emphasises this in a song:

> ✳ "Only one love a woman can
> Prefer. So let her choose her man
> With care. To him she must be true,
> For choosing once she ne'er may rue,
> More binding than the wedding-tie
> Is love."[1]

The stories of Tristram and Iseult and of the Nut Brown Maid were so fashioned as to show that the supreme virtue was faith and constancy, and Spenser in his "Faerie Queene" remarks:

> "For unto knight there is no greater shame
> Than lightness and inconstancy in love."

The hopeless confusion that reigns in people's minds over the meaning of the word immoral has led to endless confusion in judging character. Immoral originally meant "opposed to the prevailing custom"; therefore in a state where marriage ceremonies were established sexual relationship not sanctioned by marriage was immoral. The term then came to mean "opposed to some imaginary

[1] From Emil Lucka, "The Evolution of Love."

ideal code of conduct," but opinions as to what was immoral did not change. Therefore it is necessary to realise clearly that a certain course of conduct may not be impure, may even be actuated by high ideals, and yet lead to disastrous results, because conflicting with those laws by which men are bound together in social unity. Lancelot is held up as an ideal lover, actuated by devotion and loyalty, but at the same time as the chief cause of the dissolution of the Round Table, because his love caused strife and dissension amongst Arthur's knights. So did Christianity assist disruption within the Roman Empire, but in neither case had the result anything to do with the purity or impurity of the actual incidents which produced those results. But the inherent prudery of the English race has caused the bulk of the people to make no distinction between unlawful and free love, with the result that the themes and characters of medieval love-stories have often been misjudged.

CHAPTER XIV

CONCLUSION

MEDIEVAL ROMANCE FLOURISHED from the eleventh to the fifteenth century, and naturally did not retain the same form and spirit throughout; it underwent a process of evolution, reflecting contemporary manners and ideals and changing as those manners and ideals also changed. The chronicles of Geoffrey of Monmouth, Wace, and Layamon represent the earliest stage—when legends of bygone heroes were both presented and accepted strictly as history. The poets who based their work partly on such chronicles and partly on popular traditions unrecorded in writing claimed also to be historians, but made their primary aim the entertainment of their patrons. The fictitious element in chronicles largely arose from the inability of the authors to discriminate true from false records, whether in earlier writings or in oral legends; that in romance proper chiefly arose from the authors' desire to entertain and their habit of incorporating romantic elements from every available source. As time went on the historical element became smaller and smaller, the fictitious greater and greater, until romance became a mere imaginative entertainment, entirely devoid of its original purpose.

Medieval romance was the literature of feudalism, reflecting all its phases, military and social. Feudalism was the practical basis of chivalry, and medieval romance is romance of chivalry. When feudalism died, the real spirit of chivalry died also, and medieval romance, deprived of its chief stimulus and support, ceased also to exist. But even if feudalism had remained, the older form of romance could not have flourished after the Renaissance had begun; the invention of printing, the habit of private reading, extended and improved education were all alien to a literature intended only to reflect the general sentiments of the knightly class and designed at first for oral recitation. An educated audience demanded books which gave the author's individual thoughts, which would appeal to solitary meditation, and which therefore would have to probe more into the real problems of life and character instead of offering sensational tales devoid of reality and presenting rigid ideals of conduct and morality.

The fifteenth and sixteenth centuries saw the rise of pastoral romance, followed by the French heroic romance of the seventeenth century. Both were thoroughly artificial revivals of medieval romance, but more artistic, more literary, and also frequently allegorical, contemporary personages being presented under the guise of historical names. In the eighteenth century Richardson's "Sir Charles Grandson" is but a modernised variant of the hero of seventeenth-century, and even to some extent medieval, romance; he is the perfect hero, and therefore as characterless as perfection always is. Sensationalism and emotionalism reached their most fantastic heights in the Tales of Terror and Wonder of the late eighteenth and early nineteenth centuries, and with these the old form of romance may be said to have concluded. These mark the climax of a series of revivals, each more fantastic, more exaggerated, and more distorted than the last, and later writers had to infuse a new spirit before romance again became of vital interest to an educated public. But readers are not always craving for romance; they do not expect that literature shall always transport them from the realm of reality to the dream-world of illusion, and the eighteenth century also saw the rise of realistic fiction in Defoe, Fielding, and Smollett. Finally, Sir Walter Scott paved the way for a combination of the best features of both types which historical novelists in particular have usually attempted to adopt.

The modern versions by our well-known poets of themes of old romance, the "Faerie Queene," the "Idylls of the King," and many others, are so imbued with the spirit of romance, as we now conceive the term, that the very name

"Medieval Romance" has become suffused with a romantic glamour. But medieval romance is almost completely lacking in romantic glamour. The spirit of romance cannot be defined, it can only be felt. It has been described as the "magic of distance," a magic which gives a sense of far-off things and persons, removed from human scope and lifted above the material world in which we live. The essence may be seen in "Christabel," "The Ancient Mariner," "Kubla Khan," and "The Lady of Shalott." But at its best it still implies reality; it does more than merely lift us from the real world into a realm of illusion; it reflects through that mist of illusion the realities of earth and life and human nature. And the most genuine romance is often to be found in works which aim professedly at something very different—in Shakespeare's plays, in Milton's and Homer's epics, and in Dante's "Divine Comedy." The form and spirit of medieval romance were capable of more than was performed, as may be seen in one of our greatest modern stories, Bunyan's "Pilgrim's Progress." That has the essence of true romance—a simple story of adventures, a quest pursued with steadfast faith, as were the quests of Gawain, Galahad, and Percival, but infused with the realities of life and based on the noblest ethical ideals. In some of the old romances may be found this romantic glamour—in the lays of Marie, in "Aucassin et Nicolette," in "Floris and Blauncheflour," in "Sir Gawain and the Green Knight," and in the German poems of "Tristan" and of "Parzifal"; but in most it is almost entirely lacking. The original legends were no doubt thoroughly romantic, but the French adapters replaced the spirit of romance by mere mechanism. They realised the fascination of their originals, and culled romantic episodes from every source to please their patrons, but their logical minds analysed and classified until the spirit was entirely lost. By omitting to state or imply any contrast with reality they offer an unreal world which has no point of contact with the actual, and present that unreal world as normal. They arrange their stock conventions of magic feats and talismans, impossible adventures and superhuman heroes, as though they were commonplace episodes of everyday life. This defect comes not from any lack of ability in the writers, but from their conscientious efforts to claim historical authenticity for their work. Furthermore, the central theme of most French romance was a philosophy of love so artificial and conventional as to stifle the romantic spirit which would have naturally arisen from the adventures undergone. There is a more genuine romantic glamour in "La Chanson de Roland," even in the clumsiest English versions of French love romance, simply because this stifling philosophy of courtly love is absent and the spirit of adventure has more play. The love of French romance, whether in medieval or in modern times, is a love of the drawing-room and the boudoir, because the French race is a race with great social aptitudes and seeks its romance in social surroundings. The English race in comparison is unsociable, isolative, and individualistic; it seeks its romance in far-off scenes and incidents, and even its love is an outdoor love; the more isolated the scene of a declaration of love, the more the English reader is pleased—a garden rather than a parlour, a forest or mountain-top rather than a garden, beneath the light of the moon rather than in the glare of an electric chandelier.

Panegyric by men of books they edit or review has reached in modern times such great extremes that the would-be critic must be careful not to err in this direction. But in spite of its lack of true romantic spirit, medieval romance is still worthy of some praise. It is so easy to discern the exaggeration and distortion, to notice only the absurdities and miss the merits that the value of romance to the people for whom it was composed may easily be ignored. We may assume that it fulfilled its primary object—to please and to entertain; and how many of our modern readers still demand more of fiction? Its influence upon character may be over-estimated, but may more easily be under-estimated. The social life of the

s

tenth and eleventh centuries was sadly deficient in courtesy and refinement. Feudalism was a practical system, not an ideal, and was, no doubt, as materialistic as modern industrial life. There was a "romance" of feudalism, as there now is a "romance" of commerce, but neither could or can be developed except by men of imagination. The romantic spirit of feudalism was chivalry, with its ideals of loyalty, courtesy, and protection of the weak and helpless. And the romances, by constantly stressing these ideals, must have brought into disrepute all brutality, coarseness, and contempt of women, and fostered refinement, courtesy, and respect for women in their place. The patronage of women enabled romancers to strengthen that refining influence of women which is always so urgently needed, and never more than in times of warfare.

In spite of excessive sensationalism, the romancers also emphasised moral worth; the Arthurian and other heroes may seem mere puppets to the modern reader, but they were concrete symbols to the medieval audience. They harmonised with Church teaching, where nothing was real, but all symbolical. In this respect their design was as serious and impressive as that of the best modern novelists. There were none of the quibbles of modern minor fiction, no nominal punishments for evil or for sin with a sort of evangelical conversion to angelic character; if they erred at all it was on the side of severity. Fidelity to pledge was regarded so seriously that Ywain[1] suffered intense misery, because he broke faith with his wife, even though only through forgetfulness, and Gawain[2] considered it a grievous sin to have retained the girdle given him by his host's wife instead of returning it to his host, even though he believed his life depended on retaining it. The moral ideals of romance were stereotyped ideals, it is true, but very definite; the undeveloped mind can thrive upon clear-cut dogmatic regulations where the complications of real ethics would but bewilder and retard.

[1] In "Ywain and Gawain."
[2] In "Sir Gawain and the Green Knight."

Finally, although the phrase "In the name of honour" came to mean so little in the seventeenth and eighteenth centuries, in the Middle Ages it was practically synonymous with "In Christ's name"; in this modern commercial age men are content to leave their honour in the keeping of law courts and solicitors, while an army of barristers is maintained to keep that honour flexible and elastic.

Perhaps it was this strong ethical flavour that ensured the popularity of medieval romance until fairly recent times. Translations of French, Spanish, and Italian romances remained popular until the reign of Charles I, and many of the well-known stories exercised a great fascination even over the most judicial and unromantic minds of the eighteenth century—Dr. Johnson was inordinately fond of old romance, just as Milton had been. It was only in the nineteenth century that this interest began to wane. The eighteenth century did not make romance the subject of its literature, but reprinted the older versions for the people; the nineteenth-century poets incorporated it into their work, which was read only by a select few, while the mass of the people were provided with few or no popular versions. The result has been that romances well known to the school-boy of the eighteenth century—"Beves of Hamtoun," "Guy of Warwick"—are not even known by name to the people of to-day, and where men like Dr. Johnson, so often accused of being hostile to romance and imaginative literature, revelled in these stories, the average adult, priding himself on his great imaginative gifts, does not read them at all. In recent years, however, there has been a great revival of medieval romance in versions suitable for children. The combined simplicity of design and fantastic nature of the incidents appeal to modern children as they appealed to the child-like minds of our ancestors. The child mind is not attracted by the ordinary and commonplace, but is impressed in proportion to the exaggeration employed as long as it is logical. Courage and heroism seem proportionately greater when the combat

*

is with a giant or dragon than when with a mere man, and so with the other virtues.

It is very necessary to regard romance as much as possible in the same way as our medieval ancestors regarded it. There is too great a tendency to regard past literature too exclusively from the archæological point of view, and to forget that through earlier literature we may visualise the lives and thoughts and aspirations of our forefathers, and understand their attitude towards the moral and social aspects of life with which they were confronted. By sympathetic study of such literature, not as linguistic texts or antiquarian studies, but as a reflection of life, we may be able to visualise and comprehend our own problems more clearly and with greater tolerance.

SELECT BIBLIOGRAPHY

The following works, which have been extensively used in the compilation of this book, are recommended to readers who wish to make a deeper study of the subject:

J. Bédier: "Les Légendes Epiques."
J. D. Bruce: "The Evolution of Arthurian Romance."
Gaston Paris: "Histoire Poétique de Charlemagne."
    "La Poésie du Moyen Age."
L. Gautier: "Les Epopées Françaises."
W. P. Ker: "English Literature, Medieval."
    "Essays in Medieval Literature."
    "Epic and Romance."
J. Loth: "Contributions à l'Etude des Romans de la Table Ronde."
Paulin Paris: "Romans de la Table Ronde."
A. Nutt: "Celtic and Medieval Romance."
J. Rhys: "Celtic Folk-lore."
    "Studies in the Arthurian Legend."

"A Manual of Middle English Writings," by J. E. Wells, provides a complete list of English romances (as well as of all types of medieval English works) with a short account of each, the manuscripts in which they are written, and the published editions.

INDEX